'Dr Scott offers a unique and refreshing perspectiv
trauma, particularly when they don't neatly fit into
come to be defined by their experiences. Taking a c
and at turns thought-provoking and light-hearted, ...
clinical pearls with a robust critique of the modern realities of service delivery. He presents
the first practical guide to implementing event centrality theory into a personalised,
restorative CBT therapy with idiosyncratic formulation at its heart. Full of rich clinical
examples and dialogue that brings the reader into his therapy room, he takes you step-by-
step through his clinical decision making and interventions. He demonstrates how to
combine rigorous diagnostic practice with a humane, respectful and personalised
therapeutic style, helping people rebuild, restore and redefine themselves outside of their
traumatic experiences, and in so doing reclaim their future selves from their past. An
immensely useful guide for working with traumatised patients, you will find ideas,
metaphors, stories, techniques, materials, and resources that you will return to time and
again. Highly recommended!'

Sharif El-Leithy, *Principal Clinical Psychologist,*
Traumatic Stress Service

'In *Personalising Trauma Treatment: Reframing and Reimagining* Dr Scott delivers an
approach to treatment grounded in pragmatism and real-world functioning. After
considering the pitfalls of poor assessment he guides the reader through the process of
detailed and accurate diagnosis questioning whether treatments work for the supposed
reasons they give. He then introduces a range of evidence-based techniques that allow the
client's sense of self identity to remain central to the therapy process. Dr Scott especially
considers the role of IAPT and the limitations IAPT protocols impose on the effective care
of clients which goes to the heart of treatment effectiveness and in doing so presents a
rational for Restorative CBT in returning the client back to being themselves again. This
book is a must for all IAPT & CBT therapists, counsellors and clinical psychologists
involved in the care of individuals suffering with trauma.'

Sundeep Sembi, *Consultant Clinical Neuropsychologist,*
Psychology Chambers Ltd

'Motherhood, apple pie, ... improving access to psychological therapies? Whereas IAPT
satisfies an NHS England mental health policy aspiration, it fails traumatised individuals
in its organisational objective. Improving Access too often denied by administrative
barrier, simplistic assessment, and lengthy delay. Psychological Therapies too frequently
limited off-the-shelf, performed inadequately and/or incompletely, and with markedly
differing outcome objectives for individual and service. Michael Scott identifies the
paradox, coolly critiques the evidence, and illustrates and emphasises the collaborative
and crucial role of the creative, empathic, and restorative therapist in enabling the client's
natural resilience and preferences for today and tomorrow, without pathologizing
normality, imposing supposed processing, and unconstrained by complacent diktat.'

Greg Wilkinson, *formerly: Editor,* The British Journal of Psychiatry *and*
Professor of Liaison Psychiatry, The University of Liverpool; currently:
Consultant Psychiatrist, Liverpool University Dental Hospital and
Liverpool University Hospitals NHS Foundation Trust

Personalising Trauma Treatment

Personalising Trauma Treatment is about helping trauma victims back to their old selves and focuses on altering the perception of the centrality of the trauma.

In this book, clients are taught to rediscover their sense of self by reframing the trauma. Within this new framework the focus is on the client's mental time travel from the trauma to today and reimagining their future. The therapeutic targets are the thoughts and images (cognitions) that interfere with day-to-day functioning. It does not assume that arrested information processing lies at the heart of the development of PTSD, with a consequent need for the client to re-live the trauma. For those clients who were abused in childhood, their experiences are viewed through a particular central window, but other 'windows' may make for more appropriate engagement with their personal world and a reimagining of their view of themselves. Treatment delivery options from telephone consultation, group work and videoconferencing are discussed. With illustrative examples, the author highlights the pathway to recovery for a wide range of clients with the comorbidity often found in real-world settings.

The book will be essential reading for therapists and other mental health professionals working with trauma survivors.

Michael J. Scott is a Consultant Psychologist, and author of 13 books, including an edited 4 volume work on 'Traumatic Stress' and a self-help book *Moving on After Trauma*. He divides his time between treating clients, medico-legal work and writing.

Personalising Trauma Treatment

Reframing and Reimagining

Michael J. Scott

Routledge
Taylor & Francis Group

LONDON AND NEW YORK

Cover image: © Getty Images

First published 2022
by Routledge
2 Park Square, Milton Park, Abingdon, Oxon OX14 4RN

and by Routledge
605 Third Avenue, New York, NY 10158

Routledge is an imprint of the Taylor & Francis Group, an informa business

British Library Cataloguing-in-Publication Data
A catalogue record for this book is available from the British Library

Library of Congress Cataloging-in-Publication Data
A catalogue record has been requested for this book

ISBN: 978-1-032-01313-8 (hbk)
ISBN: 978-1-032-01312-1 (pbk)
ISBN: 978-1-003-17813-2 (ebk)

DOI: 10.4324/9781003178132

Typeset in Times New Roman
by MPS Limited, Dehradun

To Martha

'........dance wherever you may be'

Contents

Part I

Distilling a New Direction

Introduction

Evidence-supported treatments (EST) for post-traumatic stress disorder (PTSD) have been around for over a decade, but though they are effective, only about half of sufferers fully recover. This makes the development of new treatments essential. There is a paradox that different treatments produce a similar impact on negative appraisals of the trauma and its consequences. McNally and Woud (2019) ask 'What is it about pro-longed exposure therapy that persuades traumatized crime victims that not everyone in the world is untrustworthy?'. Thus, the precise mechanisms by which ESTs achieve their results are not wholly transparent. The suggestion is that it is negative appraisals about self, others and the personal world that leads to PTSD. These cognitions have been incorporated into the diagnostic criteria for PTSD in the DSM-5 (American Psychiatric Association, 2013). McNally and Woud (2019) also review a study that suggests that it may be the centrality accorded to the trauma that may be pivotal to the development of PTSD.

In Part 1 of this volume, the author challenges the evidence that it is incomplete processing of the trauma that leads to PTSD and thereby the necessity of somewhat toxic trauma-focussed interventions. It is suggested that the hallmark of PTSD is a state of 'terrified surprise' and this distinguishes the condition from other trauma-related disorders that may develop such as a specific phobia or depression. The author underlines the finding that there are a wide range of possible responses to trauma, each deserving of appropriate treatment. He cautions that PTSD should not be assumed on the basis of an extreme trauma and intrusions. Consequently, there is a need for reliable diagnosis, particularly as comorbidity is the rule rather than the exception. He adds that centrality can also be an issue in disorders beyond PTSD.

DOI: 10.4324/9781003178132-1

References

American Psychiatric Association. (2013). *Diagnostic and statistical manual of mental disorders* (5th ed.). Washington, D.C.: APA.

McNally, R. J., & Woud, M. L. (2019). Innovations in the study of appraisals and PTSD: A commentary. *Cognitive Therapy and Research, 43*, 295–302. 10.1007/s1 0608-018-09995-2.

Chapter 1

Client's Complaints Post-trauma

Trauma victims may experience a myriad of issues. For some victims, financial and/or occupational problems may result in lowered mood which can become a ready therapeutic target. For other victims, a sense of shame or guilt is not something that they would readily volunteer but is nevertheless debilitating. More generally, trauma is a painful memory and not something most people would wish to detail. Thus, a client's vocalised presenting problem may be a small part of a bigger story. Nevertheless, there can be such graphic descriptions of physical, social and occupational impairment post-trauma, that the therapist can feel easily overwhelmed and both may short circuit the discussion. It is tempting for the clinician to use speedy 'rules of thumb' (heuristics) to propel the client into a particular treatment. For example, a reflex referral to a bereavement or pain management group for a client injured in a fatality. Such a rule of thumb may reduce the demands on the therapist's empathy but circumvent detailed consideration of the different factors involved in the client's distress. Heuristics include stopping at the first complaint identified, using the graphic detail of a particular horror or symptom as evidence of a particular debility, offering anything that the clinician is familiar with, focussing primarily on an organisational target and minimising discussion of matters outside their area of expertise or of pre-existing problems. Matters may be complicated further when a client's concern is about a traumatised child or adolescent, and they may or may not have been involved in the same trauma themselves. In such circumstances, the clinician may feel torn that on the one hand they cannot provide the 'one stop' shop the adult would wish but on the other hand, there are no readily accessible credible alternative pathways.

'What brought you here today?'

This is often a therapist's opening gambit in encountering a client for the first time. In response, the client is likely to cite a crisis event such as a car accident, a relationship breakdown or loss of a job. The commonality amongst crises is that the client has experienced one or more as destabilising and is seeking restitution, but the proximal crisis may mask an earlier,

DOI: 10.4324/9781003178132-2

perhaps more significant distal crisis. Not only might there be a series of crises to consider but also the client will likely present all of their problems. This should come as no surprise, as the client experiences the totality of their difficulties and may not separate them into the therapist's preferred demarcations of 'psychological', 'physical', 'social' and 'spiritual'. Frustratingly giving the therapist 'mental indigestion' by repeatedly jumping from one domain to another. At that point, the therapist might fantasise longingly about the possibility of the 'fire alarm' going off.

Under Duress?

Some clients may have effectively been brought by others to the therapist. This is fairly obvious when children and adolescents present, but oftentimes, they have the good grace to signal this to the therapist by being mute or giving monosyllabic answers. However, adults with less than obvious learning difficulties can sometimes present as a consequence of family members post-trauma concerns. In such instances, it can be questionable as to who has chosen treatment. More generally, adult clients often need space to make admissions such as 'I am a private person' or 'you should sort your problems out yourself'. It may be inferred from such utterances that the hand of others may be operative in the client's presence. Alternatively, it can be that the clients' increased irritability since the crisis has so soured their relationship with their significant other and that the attendance at therapy may be a way of placating their partner. This might particularly be the case if substance abuse/dependence has become an issue since the crisis, but they may be highly ambivalent about addressing this. Teasing out a client's capacity to benefit from treatment and the limits of their autonomy can be a challenge.

What Is a Trauma?

Stressors have been variously termed, hassles, negative life events and extreme traumas, indicating stressors of different severity. The underlying model of Zubin and Spring (1977) is that the more severe the stressor the more likely it is that a person would decompensate, with relatively few people decompensating at lower stressor levels and many more at extreme levels. Not everyone succumbs to the ill effects of even an extreme trauma suggests that response may be cognitively mediated. This mediational role of cognition (thoughts and images) is very apparent in our varying responses to everyday difficulties, such as being late or not meeting a deadline. Traumas are commonly thought of as occupying the high end of the stressor spectrum, but there are no clear demarcations, e.g. a person may be bullied at work, go off sick and experience flashbacks of the bullying episodes, this would probably be best placed at the border between negative life events and extreme trauma.

Hassles (Nezu et al. 1989) and negative life events (Brown & Harris, 1978) have been implicated in the aetiology of depression whilst extreme traumas have been linked to post-traumatic stress disorder (PTSD). However, what determines that a life event should be regarded as negative and a possible causal agent for poor mental health? Spence et al. (2019) have suggested that the negativity can be addressed with regards to the following four considerations:

- *Attachment* – events that involve negative changes in close relationships often involving loss or rejection.
- *Achievement* – events that prevent or hinder reaching the desired goal.
- *Security* – events that jeopardise physical or mental safety and uncertainty of possession, routine or physical existence.
- *Identity* – events that compromise how we and others view the self, involving stigma, belonging or physical deterioration.

The DSM is the diagnostic 'bible' of the American Psychiatric Association and in its current iteration, DSM-5 lists the type of traumas (criterion A) that may lead to PTSD (DSM-5 p274; American Psychiatric Association, 2013) and include, but are not limited to, exposure to war, threatened or actual physical or sexual assault, being kidnapped, being taken hostage, terrorist attack, incarceration as a prisoner of war, natural or man-made disasters, severe motor vehicle accidents and anaphylactic shock. Such traumas are the necessary gateway to PTSD and are commonplace. The estimated lifetime prevalence of exposure to potentially traumatic events according to DSM-IV criterion A was 43.8% (Knipscheer et al., 2020). Further, the lifetime prevalence of exposure to potentially traumatic and other life events was 71.1%.

The Subjective Response to a Trauma

In contrast to its predecessor DSM-IV, there is no specification in DSM-5 American Psychiatric Association (2013) of a necessary emotional reaction at the time of the trauma. This change does not sit easily with the claims of trauma-focussed therapy theoreticians (Ehlers & Clark, 2000; Ehlers & Wild, 2020) that the trauma memory is disjointed (Beierl et al., 2020). If indeed there were problems at the laying down of the traumatic memory (encoding) one would presumably expect some effective signature, such as 'intense fear helplessness or horror' as stipulated in DSM-IV-TR (American Psychiatric Association, 2000). The DSM is avowedly atheoretical but having ventured into aetiology by specifying the necessary type of trauma for the development of PTSD, it has strayed into the arena of causation. In so doing it has, however unwittingly, raised a question mark about one of the fundamental tenets of trauma-focussed therapy theoreticians.

The DSM-5 Criteria for PTSD

In the DSM-5 (American Psychiatric Association, 2013), PTSD symptoms are categorised under four headings (see Table 1.1). However, the DSM and Table 1.1 are not checklists, to protect against such misuse, symptoms have to be simultaneously present i.e. the time frame for each symptom has to be clarified, whether it is present in the last month or up to a particular point in time. The symptoms must be evaluated with regards to the same traumatic event/s. For a symptom to be endorsed as present, it must represent a worsening of negative alterations in cognition and mood (clusters D) and hyperarousal (cluster E), whilst the intrusion (cluster B) and avoidance (cluster C) symptoms must originate with the trauma. Importantly, a symptom is only endorsed if it is at a level that it has functionally impaired the person e.g. not only nightmares of the trauma but also ones that woke the person up and they had difficulty getting back to sleep. It is necessary to elicit from the client-specific examples of the manifestation of a symptom, monosyllabic 'yes', 'no' responses to a therapist's question about a symptom are insufficient, if necessary the therapist should ask clarifying supplementary questions. The interviewer should elicit enough information to gauge the frequency, intensity and time course of each symptom.

If one of the Trauma questions is answered in the affirmative, the clinician can ask 'just to put me in the picture, what happened exactly?', leaving the client to tell as much or as little as they wish. Clients may well have different responses to the Symptom questions at different points in time since the trauma, so the clinician has to be clear about the time frame e.g. 'in the last month', and it will often be necessary to reiterate during the assessment time frame that is the focus. It is quite common for clients to drift into describing a symptom at their worst point in time, whilst the therapist is often focussed on their current state and the two can be at cross purposes. Fulfilling the diagnostic criteria is only possible if there is the simultaneous presence of sufficient symptoms in each of the four clusters. The clinician should not be satisfied with a monosyllabic positive response to a Symptom question, rather they should ask how frequently the symptom occurs and how distressed they are by their occurrence. Without eliciting examples of how the symptom is interfering with functioning e.g. 'woke from a nightmare of it last night, couldn't get back to sleep for an hour', there is insufficient information for endorsement of the presence of the symptom. It should be remembered that memory of an extreme trauma and discomfort at this memory is normal and that what is being assessed is the degree of functional impairment arising from it i.e. symptoms have to clear a threshold to be considered as present.

Table 1.1 DSM-5 Criteria for PTSD – Trauma and Symptom Prompts

A. TRAUMA
    a. Have you been in a situation in which you thought you were going to die as a result of what happened?
    b. Have you been in a situation in which you thought others were going to die as a result of what happened?
    c. Have you been in a situation in which you thought yourself or others were going to have a serious injury as a result of what happened?
    d. Have you been in a situation in which you were or thought that you were going to be sexually violated?

A positive response to at least one of the above is required

B. INTRUSIONS
    1. Do memories of a traumatic incident play on your mind?
    2. Do you get upset by them?
    3. Do you have distressing dreams of the traumatic incident?
    4. Do you lose awareness of your surroundings when you get pictures/ thoughts of the traumatic incident coming into your mind?
    5. When something reminds you of the traumatic incident, do you get distressed?
    6. Do you get any particularly strong bodily reactions when you come across reminders of the traumatic incident?

A positive response to at least one of the above is required

C. AVOIDANCE
    1. Do you block out thoughts or pictures of the incident(s) that pop into your mind?
    2. Do you avoid conversations or people or places that bring back memories of the incident(s)?

A positive response to at least one of the above is required

D. NEGATIVE ALTERATIONS IN COGNITION AND EMOTION
    1. Is there an important gap in your memory of the incident?
    2. Since the incident(s) do you feel very negative about yourself, others or the world, or more negative than you used to?
    3. Do you blame yourself or others for the incident(s) more than you really need to?
    4. Since the incident(s) do you feel negative emotions such as fear, anger, horror, guilt or shame most of the time?
    5. Since the incident(s) have you stopped doing activities that used to be important to you or lost interest in them?
    6. Since the incident(s) do you feel cut off from others?
    7. Since the incident(s) are you almost always unable to feel good?

A positive response to at least two of the above is required

E. HYPERAROUSAL
    1. Since the incident(s) are you more snappy or having more outbursts of anger?
    2. Since the incident(s) do you do dangerous or destructive things?
    3. Since the incident (s) are you on guard, checking things?
    4. Since the incident (s) do you jump at unexpected noises or sudden movements?
    5. Since the incident (s) have you had problems with concentration?
    6. Since the incident (s) do you have problems either getting to sleep or staying asleep?

A positive response to at least two of the above is required

Table 1.1 indicates that there are a possible 20 symptoms in the DSM-5 classification of PTSD. At least one symptom is required from each of the intrusion and avoidance clusters, whilst at least two symptoms are required from each of the negative alterations in cognition and hyperarousal clusters. This means there are 636,120 ways to have PTSD according to Galatzer-Levy and Bryant (2013). It is therefore unlikely that any one treatment will be appropriate for all these manifestations of PTSD.

PTSD in DSM-5 may be specified as with dissociative symptoms either depersonalisation (persistent or recurrent experiences of feeling detached from and as if one were an outside observer of one's mental processes or body) or derealization persistent or recurrent experiences of the unreality of surroundings or with delayed expression if the full diagnostic criteria are not met until at least six months after the event. If it is possible to have PTSD with delayed expression this casts doubt on trauma-focussed therapy theoreticians who have contended that PTSD arises from a disjointed traumatic memory laid down at the time of the trauma (Beierl et al., 2020).

The ICD-11 (World Health Organisation, 2018) takes a different view of PTSD to DSM-5, whilst recognising PTSD it also recognises complex PTSD (CPTSD) as a distinct diagnostic category. CPTSD has been hypothesised as arising from chronic and severe interpersonal trauma that can lead to pervasive emotional and interpersonal difficulties (Cloitre et al., 2012). It is claimed that in addition to having PTSD those with CPTSD have great difficulties managing their emotions, interpersonal problems, problems with dissociation and suicidality. However, it is not at all clear that the symptoms unique to CPTSD could not be most parsimoniously explained by more severe presentations of the PTSD symptoms in Table 1.1. There is a danger that the term 'complex' may be taken to mean that CPTSD is intractable. However, the ICD-11 has highlighted that oftentimes non-fear-based emotions such as shame are part of the response to enduring chronic trauma. Further related emotions, such as shame can be an important feature of a person's response to enduring chronic trauma, reflected in adulthood in significant interpersonal problems. Unfortunately, focussing on the ICD-11 highlighted matters has not been part of traditional cognitive behaviour therapy approaches to PTSD. Nevertheless, it is possible to expand the horizons of CBT without resorting to the notion of a separate diagnostic category of CPTSD.

DSM-5 recognises that children may manifest PTSD differently from adults and offers specific criteria for children aged 1–6. The gateway stressor criteria for young children includes not only directly experiencing/witnessing the traumatic event but also learning that the traumatic event/s occurred to a parent or caregiving figure. The intrusion symptoms are slightly reframed from those for adults in Table 1.1, in that spontaneous and intrusive memories may not necessarily appear distressing and may be expressed as play reenactment. As with adults at least one intrusion symptom and at least one avoidance symptom is required. The negative alterations in cognition cluster C are significantly different in young children and require at least two of substantially increased frequency of negative emotional states, loss of participation in significant activities (including constriction in play), socially withdrawn behaviour and persistent reduction in positive emotions. For young children, cluster D is termed 'alterations in arousal and reactivity associated with the traumatic event/s', and developmentally appropriate expression of increased irritability is spelt out thus 'irritable behaviour and angry outbursts with little or no provocation typically expressed as verbal or physical aggression towards people objects (including extreme temper tantrums)'. As with adults, two symptoms are required in cluster D.

Beyond PTSD

PTSD is but one disorder in a category of 'Trauma and Stressor-Related Disorders' defined in DSM-5 (American Psychiatric Association, 2013). It is noted in the DSM-5 (p265; American Psychiatric Association, 2013) that some responses to traumatic or stressful events can be best understood within an anxiety or fear-based context but for others the most common clinical characteristics are loss of pleasure response (anhedonia), dysphoria, anger or dissociative symptoms. Thus, PTSD would be thought of as more fear-related but an adjustment disorder may involve some PTSD symptoms. While social neglect, the absence of caregiving during childhood, is a diagnostic requirement of both reactive attachment disorder and disinhibited social engagement disorder. The trauma and stressor-related disorders are distinguished by different emotional responses but in any one individual there can be an admixture of symptoms. However, one would anticipate some broad differences in neurobiology across the trauma and stressor-related disorders. Scott and Stradling (1994) observed a number of clients with the symptoms of PTSD but the stressors were chronic and not as intense as those usually thought necessary to meet the gateway stressor criteria, e.g. bullying at work, caring for a relative with a progressive illness and termed it prolonged duress stress disorder (PDSD). This suggests that there will always be gaps in any classificatory system. Interestingly Marsh (2003) examined the patho-physiology of PTSD and PDSD, finding that the latter had a less severe response than the former, but there was not a difference in kind. DSM-5 criteria interview questions for the disorders most commonly associated with trauma are contained in Appendix.

Psychological and Biological Explanations

In the Zubin and Spring (1977) stressor-vulnerability model, it is not a biological vulnerability per se that leads to mental ill-health but only when there is an interaction of vulnerability with psychosocial stressors that include, life crises, substance abuse, interpersonal and occupational stressors. It is as if the vulnerability is a fault line in a glass-tumbler, but it requires a particular event, e.g. catching the tumbler on the tap for it to become unusable (decompensation).

If different disorders have different biological correlates, considering which mechanism the particular stressor has the potential to activate highlights the candidate disorders. However, this is not to say that biology determines the psychological expression of difficulties as this will also be affected by factors such as perceived social support, prior psychiatric history and the ongoing appraisal of self and personal world.

There are no biological tests for any of the psychiatric disorders. This has made some sceptical of the very notion of psychological disorders, e.g. Dalgleish et al. (2020), call for a radical 'hard' transdiagnostic approach. This has not led to a specification of what new treatment for trauma victims would be better than existing treatments or is it clear what transdiagnostic process, e.g. intolerance of uncertainty, may be operative across disorders such as PTSD, depression and panic disorder yet not present across other disorders. However, Dalgleish et al. (2020) refer to a 'soft' transdiagnostic approach, which preserves the underlying diagnostic classification while seeking to elucidate processes or develop interventions that have relevance to one or more of the diagnoses as traditionally formulated. This 'soft' diagnostic transdiagnostic approach recognises that there are no sharp boundaries between disorders, and it is often arguable to say whether a particular individual's difficulties are best described as depression rather than generalised anxiety disorders. Nevertheless, the distinctions between the disorders are not unreasonable as they may be distinguished by a different cognitive content and cognitive profile – Beck's (1976) cognitive content specificity hypothesis. For example, loss and negative views of self, world, and future were believed to characterise depression, whereas threat and danger cognitions characterised anxiety. With regards to PTSD, the distinctive cognitive content is summarised in the post-traumatic cognitions inventory (Wells et al., 2019). In a similar way, the anxiety disorder appears typified by the involvement of the amygdala (the brain's alarm), which can become less responsive by the operation of the prefrontal cortex whilst the locus coeruleus drives up amygdala activation (Brehl et al., 2020). The amygdala also receives information about the outside world from the thalamus and hippocampus. Amygdala hypersensitivity may be a vulnerability factor for debility post-trauma. Neuroimaging studies show that clients with PTSD have greater amygdala activation than controls (Liberzon & Sripada, 2007).

Role Impairment

Clients are propelled into seeking professional assistance by the role impairment that may be the consequence of a trauma. For example, a building site worker may be injured at work, see his GP who signs the victim off sick, until say his back pain has resolved. It is unlikely in such circumstances that there will be much focus on his/her psychological symptoms beyond perhaps the prescription of a hypnotic for sleep problems. However, when a return to work is canvassed the psychological effects of the trauma can become a public issue, the client is perhaps too afraid to return to the context of his/her injury. In a similar way, the uncharacteristic irritability of a trauma victim will likely be tolerated initially by family but when it becomes apparent that this has become coupled with a disconnection from all significant others, the injunction can become 'you need to see someone'. Thus, there is often a time lag between the trauma and sufficient role impairment that the victim seeks professional help.

If a particular role has been central to a person's identity, then the forced removal from it by trauma or stressful event can have a particularly deleterious consequence reflected in depression and/or PTSD. For example, a parent may perceive that because of post-trauma they are no longer physically able to play with their young children as they did before, that they are a failure as a parent. This may be exacerbated further if they have become unemployed post-trauma no longer able to perform a valued role as 'breadwinner'.

Dignity and Indignity

One of the important changes from DSM-IV-TR (2000) to DSM-5 (2013) is the inclusion of a negative view of self, others and the world as a possible symptom of PTSD. At first glance, this looks just like highlighting the negative cognitive triad that Alford and Beck (1997) suggested lies at the heart of depression. There is some truth in this in that about 50% of PTSD clients are also suffering from depression. In depression, each element of this triad can be thought of as an axis along which can be marked the severity of their negativity in one of the three domains, and the severity scores will likely differ. However, in PTSD, the severity scores on each axis tend to be extreme and the client is located at a point that is best characterised by a sense of a loss of dignity. PTSD sufferers often have a profound sense of loss of dignity, which is rarely articulated by the sufferer. Oftentimes, it is accompanied with a pervasive sense of indignity at the sources of the loss of dignity, e.g. the drunken driver given a light sentence or at any others that are perceived as mirroring them, e.g. an assessor at the Department of Works and Pensions. The indignation can serve to distract from efforts to restore dignity by very gradually increasing risk-taking. It is reflected in another of the PTSD symptoms uncharacteristic irritability which in turn increases the disconnect with others (another of the PTSD symptoms). The loss of dignity persists because of a near-total aversion to risk-taking, this is reflected in the avoidance symptoms in the DSM-5, American Psychiatric Association (2013).

An exaggerated fear or perception of risk related to a potential threat may be heightened by significant others or the media. Post-trauma the person may develop a loss aversion not wanting to lose what 'little' they have now, so that the present moment becomes an overvalued reference point and 'war' may be inappropriately waged to defend it. Restoration involves constructive risk-taking, to ensure that caution does not remain excessive.

Time as a Healer

A systematic review by Morina et al. (2014) reported that on average 44% of clients had PTSD remission, without treatment, after a mean of 40 months of follow-up from baseline. However, as those with PTSD of shorter duration PTSD are more likely to remit, a 'no treatment' choice might be more reasonable for those clients with a recent onset of PTSD.

In asking about the likelihood of recovery clients likely have in mind their experience of physical injury, e.g. if you break your leg and are normally in good health, you might anticipate six weeks in a cast and gradual improvement over the next six months. This protype is often then applied to mental health problems such as bereavement or a miscarriage with the adage 'time is a great healer'. However, in the mental health domain, it is not so simple. It is the case that if a trauma is so extreme as to lead to PTSD only a significant minority will still have the condition 12 months later. The proportion succumbing to PTSD will be greater if the trauma is interpersonal, e.g. an assault rather than impersonal, e.g. a serious road traffic accident. Further, the chances of natural recovery are less if the person has previously had mental health problems. Matters are complicated further by whether the victim perceives that they have social support. Nevertheless, there is a period of probably about three months post-trauma when a 'monitor and watch' approach is probably indicated, provided that there are not very serious acute problems such as suicidal behaviour or substance dependence. Some destabilisation after an extreme trauma is to be expected but human beings appear to have natural means of adapting long before the advent of therapists. Adverse reactions to extreme trauma have been noted from antiquity, Samuel Pepys wrote in his diary on 2 September 1666 of the beginning of the Great Fire of London and five months later, on 28 February 1667, he wrote 'it is strange to think how to this very day I cannot sleep a night without great terrors of fire; and this very night I could not sleep until almost 2 in the morning through thoughts of fire' (Pepys, 2003). Disrupting the natural mechanism of recovery can have deleterious consequences, despite not knowing with certainty what that mechanism is, Bisson et al. (1997) assigned burn victims to either a psychological debriefing (PD) group or no intervention and 13 months later 26% of the PD group had PTSD compared to only 9% of the control group.

As I write, 8 December 2020, I have just heard a BBC News item on the Archbishop of Canterbury, Justin Welby and the Chief Rabbi, Ephraim Mirvis. Both lost their eldest child, the Archbishop's 7-month-old daughter died following a car crash and the Chief Rabbi's 30-year-old daughter died of cancer. The latter recounted his daily thoughts about his daughter and his irritation at being told I understand what you are going through. The Archbishop talked about most days being predictable and then something happening that reminds you of the loss and it becomes more of a struggle. Theirs is a beautiful illustration of how it is not as simple as time being a great healer, no doubt they bring their own spiritual framework to bear on their tragedies.

References

Alford, B. A., & Beck A. T. (1997). *The integrative power of cognitive therapy.* New York: Guilford Press.

American Psychiatric Association. (2000). *Diagnostic and statistical manual of mental disorders.* (4th ed., Text Revision). Washington, D.C.: APA.

American Psychiatric Association. (2013). *Diagnostic and statistical manual of mental disorders* (5th ed.). Washington, D.C.: APA.

Beck, A. T. (1976). *Cognitive therapy and the emotional disorders.* New York: New American Library.

Beierl, E., Böllinghaus, I., Clark, D., Glucksman, E., & Ehlers, A. (2020). Cognitive paths from trauma to posttraumatic stress disorder: A prospective study of Ehlers and Clark's model in survivors of assaults or road traffic collisions. *Psychological Medicine, 50*(13), 2172–2181. 10.1017/S0033291719002253

Bisson, J. I., Jenkins, P. L., Alexander, J., & Bannister, C. (1997). Randomised controlled trial of psychological debriefing for victims of acute burn trauma. *The British Journal of Psychiatry: The Journal of Mental Science, 171*, 78–81. 10.1192/bjp.171.1.78

Brehl, A. K., Kohn, N., Schene, A. H., & Fernández, G. (2020). A mechanistic model for individualised treatment of anxiety disorders based on predictive neural biomarkers. *Psychological Medicine, 50*, 727–736. 10.1017/S0033291720000410

Brown, G. W., & Harris, T. (1978). *Social origins of depression: A study of psychiatric disorder in women.* London: Tavistock Publications

Bufka, L. F., Wright, C. V., & Halfond, R. W. (Eds.). (2020). *Casebook to the APA Clinical Practice Guideline for the treatment of PTSD* (pp. 91–121). American Psychological Association. 10.1037/0000196-005

Cloitre, M., Courtois, C. A., Ford, J. D., et al (2012). *The ISTSS expert consensus treatment guidelines for complex PTSD in adults.* ISTSS. https://www. istss.org/ISTSS_Main/media/Documents/ISTSS-Expert-Concesnsus-Guidelines-for-Complex-PTSD-Updated-060315.pdf.

Dalgleish, T., Black, M., Johnston, D., & Bevan, A. (2020). Transdiagnostic approaches to mental health problems: Current status and future directions. *Journal of Consulting and Clinical Psychology, 88*(3), 179–195. 10.1037/ccp0000482. PMID: 32068421; PMCID: PMC7027356.

Ehlers, A., & Clark, D. M. (2000). A cognitive model of posttraumatic stress disorder. *Behaviour Research and Therapy, 38*(4), 319–345. 10.1016/s0005-7967(99)00123-0

Ehlers, A., & Wild, J. (2020). Cognitive therapy for PTSD. In L. F. Bufka, C. V. Wright, & R. W. Halfond (Eds.), *Casebook to the APA Clinical Practice Guideline for the treatment of PTSD* (pp. 91–121). American Psychological Association. 10.1037/0000196-005

Galatzer-Levy, I. R., & Bryant, R. A. (2013). 636,120 ways to have posttraumatic stress disorder. *Perspectives on Psychological Science, 8,* 651–662.

Knipscheer, J., Sleijpen, M., Frank, L., de Graaf, R., Kleber, R., Ten Have, M., & Dückers, M. (2020). Prevalence of potentially traumatic events, other life events and subsequent reactions indicative for posttraumatic stress disorder in the Netherlands: A general population study based on the trauma screening questionnaire. *International Journal of Environmental Research and Public Health, 17*(5), 1725. 10.3390/ijerph17051725

Liberzon, I., & Sripada, C. S. (2007). The functional neuroanatomy of PTSD: A critical review. *Progress in Brain Research, 167,* 151–169.

Marsh, C. (2003). A psycho-physiological comparison of post-traumatic and prolonged duress stress disorders. *Behavioural and Cognitive Psychotherapy, 31*(1), 109–112. 10.1017/S1352465803001115

Morina, N., Wicherts, J. M., Lobbrecht, J., & Priebe, S. (2014). Remission from post-traumatic stress disorder in adults: A systematic review and meta-analysis of long term outcome studies. *Clinical Psychology Review, 34*(3), 249–255. 10.1016/j.cpr.2014.03.002

Nezu, A. M., Nezu, C. M., & Perri, M. G. (1989). *Problem - solving therapy for depression: Theory research and clinical guidelines.* New York: John Wiley & Son

Pepys, S. (2003). *The diaries of Samuel Pepys – A selection.* Harmondsworth: Penguin Books.

Scott, M. J., & Stradling, S. G. (1994). Post-traumatic stress disorder without the trauma. *British Journal of Clinical Psychology, 33,* 71–74.

Spence, R., Kagan, L. & Bifulco, A. (2019). *Why are life events troubling/the psychologist.* June.

Wells, S. Y., Morland, L. A., Torres, E. M., Kloezeman, K., Mackintosh, M.-A., & Aarons, G. A. (2019). The development of a brief version of the Posttraumatic Cognitions Inventory (PTCI-9). *Assessment, 26,* 193–208. 10.1177/1073191116685401

World Health Organization. (2018). *ICD-11 for mortality and morbidity statistics (ICD-11 MMS) version.* https://icd.who.int/browse11/l-m/en.

Zubin, J., & Spring B. (1977). Vulnerability: A new view of schizophrenia. *Journal of Abnormal Psychology, 86,* 103–126.

Chapter 2

Making Sense of the Client's Response

Any assessment of the client's difficulties must begin with an open-ended interview in which the client has the opportunity to tell their story of the trauma. But the client's trauma and their response do not exist in a vacuum, the client also needs the space to put this material in the context of their pre-trauma functioning. Of particular importance is any change in their view of themselves, their ability to connect with others and discharge valued roles such as parent, partner and employee. Thus, the distilling of a wide range of information is a necessary condition for a thorough assessment of the client. However, in itself, this is not a sufficient indicator of treatment need. The clinician has to clearly delineate which symptoms occurred when, whereas the client's concern may simply be to tell how awful life has been since the trauma. In addition, the clinician is trying to apply a threshold as to whether a particular symptom is or has been present at a level of discomfort, i.e. below the threshold or above the threshold of impaired functioning. Importantly, the clinician's role is not to pathologise normality and signpost unnecessary treatment. This is a pressing concern in the current COVID-19 pandemic; when is the threshold crossed between 'normal' concerns about safety and safety behaviours (adaptive coping) to an 'excessive' concern (maladaptive coping), is this new pathology or perhaps an exacerbation of a pre-existing health anxiety?

Formulation stresses the uniqueness of the individual and in the case of post-trauma debility, the idiosyncratic nature of the response. Nevertheless, there are some common themes in responses. The client's treatment history is also important, they may e.g. have been previously offered psychological help but declined it. Understanding precisely why treatment was not taken up is a first step to prevent premature disengagement. Similarly, if the client dropped out of previous treatment, it is essential to know why, so that potential saboteurs can be navigated. When children or adolescents are the focus, the clinician has to be aware of the developmentally appropriate manifestations of a trauma response. The clinician will also need the skill set of generally working with both simultaneously, even though parent/child may not always be simultaneously present in the consulting room.

DOI: 10.4324/9781003178132-3

The Definition of the Situation

The therapist is often the last of a series of professionals that have seen the client. At least some may have communicated their perspective on the client's functioning to paper, but it is common for psychological therapists to operate with at most limited documentation, much less than is available in the GP records. The more extensive the range of data available the more likely it is that inferences are reliable. However, weighing up extensive data is time-consuming and it is very tempting to short circuit the process by the use of a heuristic, consciously or non-consciously employing a credibility hierarchy, with say consultant psychiatrists at the top, followed by clinical psychologists, other medics, next high intensity (Improving Access to Psychological Therapies) therapists with psychological wellbeing practitioners at the bottom. Does this beg the question as to what evidence is there that the summations of one professional group are better than others? It may be customary to prefer one professional group's account over another's is not evidence of a more reliable description. Taking into account the perspective of other clinicians in assessing the client is important but should never be definitive. Often a particular label has been attached to a client by a professional high up in the hierarchy and it has been taken for granted by those lower down, the descriptor used has become 'sticky'. To add to the difficulty, different professionals within the same professional groupings may offer very different summations of the client's difficulties.

The client themselves may take serious issues with a diagnostic label such as 'emotionally unstable personality disorder'. This should be a clarion call for the therapist to critically examine the context in which such a diagnosis was arrived at, and whether it is legitimate according to published criteria, i.e. the reliability of labels applied, should be a matter for constant scrutiny.

Simply describing the client as a 'case of....' will likely be a grave injustice to the client, firstly, most commonly if the client is found to be suffering from one diagnosable psychological condition, he/she most likely suffers from at least one other. Secondly, the treatment of any one condition is likely to be deleteriously affected by the other. However, it is always tempting for clinicians to stop at the first disorder identified and exclusively focus on this – 'not wanting to open a can of worms'. Further, the patient's physical state will likely limit the range of actions they can engage in to elevate mood, whilst there is likely to be a reciprocal interaction between pain and emotion. The social context of the client may be very germane to the appropriateness of psychological therapy, e.g. unless the client is safe from harm and has somewhere to live therapeutic efforts are likely to come to naught. The basic human needs in Maslow's hierarchy of needs have to be met before the higher ones are addressed.

The true story of a client is likely to form a very rich tapestry. Although this is often the case, this itself must not be allowed to become a heuristic e.g.

insisting that an adult client's anxiety must be related to their historic sexual abuse, when they are insistent it is not.

Formulation

It is taken as axiomatic by therapists of all persuasions that making a formulation of the client's difficulties is a necessary first step towards therapeutic intervention. Further, that this formulation will be unique to the individual i.e. it is personalised, but this leaves unanswered the question of what range of information is pertinent for what intervention? The data available on any one individual's functioning are virtually limitless. Whilst it is tempting to focus on the client's most important presenting problem, this can vary from consultation to consultation. At one appointment, the client might focus on their low mood and the therapist might conclude that depression is the main problem and at another, the client's focus might be on their flashbacks and nightmares and the therapist might think that post-traumatic stress disorder is the problem. Thus, the presenting problem per se is not an indicator of treatment direction. A view can be taken that the term 'treatment' is inappropriate and that it represents a medicalisation of a psychological therapist's craft, but this leads to a treatment that is idiosyncratic and does not represent fidelity to an evidence-based treatment protocol. Worryingly, these difficulties are given expression in the Improving Access to Psychological Therapies (IAPT), description of 'A Good Assessment', (see Table 5.1.1 of the IAPT Manual (2019) National Collaborating Centre for Mental Health) in which an 'appropriate problem descriptor' is used to select a diagnostic code. The IAPT manual (2019) states that its therapists do not make diagnoses. Giving a client a diagnostic code only makes sense if a reliable diagnosis has been made. At best the IAPT (IAPT, 2019) assessment approximates to the open-ended Overview section of standardised semi-structured interviews such as the SCID (First et al. 2016). The Overview asks for biographical detail, including employment, history of current illness, treatment history, medical problems, suicidal ideation and behaviour, suicide attempts and about problems with mood and drugs. The intent of the Overview is to suggest a range of possible diagnoses (a differential diagnosis). The danger of relying entirely on an open-ended interview is that information gleaned early in the interview is given a greater weighting (the primacy effect heuristic) and once a preliminary diagnosis is made further information is sought that would only confirm the conclusion, information that might disconfirm it is not sought (confirmatory bias) (Lilienfeld & Lynn, 2015). Standardised semi-structured interviews confer some protection against taking shortcuts (employing heuristics) in the making of reliable diagnoses. Following the open-ended interview, the standardised interviews become semi-structured in that questions are asked about each symptom that composes a diagnostic set (i.e.

information variance is controlled for) and published thresholds are used for determining whether a symptom is present at a clinically significant level (i.e. that criterion variance is controlled for). It is not a checklist in which clients are asked to choose 'yes', 'no' responses to questions, rather the assessor has to elicit detailed examples of material pertinent to the particular symptom enquiry and is provided with supplementary questions to help tease this out. Whilst a clinical judgement is necessary to determine whether a particular symptom can be considered present there are boundaries for this judgement. Beck et al. (1962) observed that the traditional open-ended psychiatric interview was too unreliable with levels of agreement no greater than 54%, because of a failure to control for information and criterion variance. This led to the development of standardised semi-structured interviews. Open-ended interviews are an important springboard for the main body of standardised semi-structured diagnostic interviews such as the SCID (First et al., 1997), but they were never intended to stand alone. In effect, IAPT has resurrected a myth that open-ended interviews by themselves are reliable. The penchant of its psychological therapists for formulation should be replaced by an insistence on 'case formulation', i.e. which disorder/s does the client meet diagnostic criteria for. Scepticism about the diagnostic labels applied to a client by others is necessary until it is established that the diagnosis was made reliably.

Missing PTSD by Focussing on the Client's Chief Complaint

Formulation-based intervention strategies assume that the client's presenting problem/s are of primary importance. But whilst they are of importance they do not merit this exalted status. Most clients with PTSD actually present for treatment of a mood disorder (Kiefer et al., 2020), only one-fifth of the patients with PTSD received it as their principal diagnosis. The principal diagnosis referred to the disorder that the client indicated was the main reason for seeking treatment. Whilst it is the case that following a public extreme trauma such as a bombing, clients may report red flag symptoms of PTSD such as intrusive memories, avoidance and hypervigilance as their primary concern this is much less likely in routine mental health services, where complaints related to depression and anxiety are likely to be the focus. Further, when people have experienced sexual assault and abuse they are less likely to vocalise this because of feelings of shame and guilt, instead focussing on associated mood disorder. Kiefer et al. (2020) found that PTSD was most common in clients with major depressive disorder (24.5%), bipolar disorder (30–38%), panic disorder (27–35%) and borderline personality disorder (40.3%). However, the prevalence of PTSD was greater than 19% in each of the categories social phobia, specific phobia, generalised anxiety disorder, obsessive-compulsive disorder, alcohol/drug abuse/dependence, binge eating disorder, hypochondriasis, undifferentiated somatoform disorder, body dysmorphic disorder and intermittent explosive disorder.

Premature Therapeutic Intervention

The time pressures in routine practice make it very tempting to stop enquiry once the Chief Complaint is established. Then, to provide a therapeutic intervention for the identified problem, but without a full picture of how the client has become destabilised (or is no longer operating at their best level of functioning), the intervention may amount to no more than putting a sticking plaster on a wound. The client may be grateful for any help and concern preferred, but this may make no difference to their functioning. A client's gratitude is not a sufficient indicator that an intervention has made a real-world difference.

Nevertheless, therapists are mindful of the organisational constraints within which they operate, e.g. a limited number of sessions, a need to provide a diagnostic code for the client's chief complaint and to operate as their supervisor deems fit. In such circumstances, detailed enquiry about a possible range of disorders may be viewed as 'opening a can of worms'. Rather the pressure may be to be seen to do something that can be 'sold' as an evidence-based intervention, even though its fit has not been determined. The therapist proceeds pragmatically, changing the intervention if it does not bear fruit or alternatively casting doubt on the client's motivation and deeming the case 'complex', without a clear specification of the criteria for the latter.

Focussing on the Chief Complaint Is Like Driving Looking Only Straight Ahead

Most typically, clients are suffering from more than one disorder. This is especially true of clients with PTSD, the DSM-5 (p280) (American Psychiatric Association, 2013) notes that 'Individuals with PTSD are 80% more likely than those without PTSD to have symptoms that meet diagnostic criteria for at least one other mental disorder'. Thus, a focus on the Chief Complaint post-trauma will likely miss the boat. To do so is to operate a heuristic that has speed and simplicity at the expense of accuracy. The therapist may well conclude that it is his/her lack of skill at treating the Chief Complaint that is the problem. Perhaps, referring on for a 'more skilled therapist' dealing with aforesaid Chief Complaint. Simply having goals with regards to the Chief Complaint or having the client express how they would like things to be different will not resolve the problem of too narrow a focus. Unfortunately, this narrow focus may serve the interests of the Organisation, which can shift the focus to a number of clients through the system and short waiting lists to attract and maintain funding.

Zimmerman and Mattia (1999) compared the incidence of disorders in 500 clients undergoing a routine psychiatric interview with a further cohort of 500 clients assessed using the SCID interview (First et al., 1997) and found that two-thirds (64.8%) of the latter had two disorders compared with a third (36.6%) of the former. With 36.0% of the SCID sample having three or more diagnoses compared to 7.6% in routine assessment. Thus, comorbidity is the rule rather than the exception. Further clients wish for treatment of all their difficulties not just their Chief Complaint, overall 86% of clients with depression wanted their treatment to address a comorbid anxiety disorder (Zimmerman & Mattia, 2000).

It is possible to argue that rather than try to differentiate disorders post-trauma, it would be better to operate transdiagnostically, with a single traumatic stress construct. Notwithstanding that no treatments have been evaluated with this transdiagnostic target, there is evidence from the study by O'Donnell et al. (2004) that different diagnoses post-trauma follow different trajectories. In a study of 363 people admitted to hospital for more than a day following injury, 74% of whom had a motor vehicle accident, 15% met full criteria for PTSD, depression or both at three months. While a majority of those with PTSD, or PTSD and depression at 3 months continued to have a disorder at 12 months, 92% of those with depression alone at 3 months had no diagnosis at 12 months.

Spotting PTSD

In a study by Kiefer et al. (2020) of 3800 clients, 17.4% had PTSD a further 6.5% had PTSD in partial remission. This is important as they cite studies that have shown a lack of differences in impairment (i.e. social, and occupational functioning and a number of suicide attempts) between those with full PTSD and PTSD in partial remission. Historically, using DSM-IV-TR criteria (American Psychiatric Association, 2000) sub-syndromal PTSD has been used to describe clients who had disturbing intrusions of the trauma and either insufficient or hyperarousal symptoms. Those with sub-syndromal PTSD were found to be only slightly less functionally impaired than those with full PTSD (Stein et al., 1997). Using DSM-IV nomenclature sub-syndromal clients were those having at least one intrusion symptom and meeting criteria for either the avoidance or hyperarousal cluster. In DSM-5, it may be best to define sub-syndromal as experiencing one or more intrusion and avoidance symptoms and meeting the required symptom criteria for either negative alterations in cognition and mood or for hyperarousal. Thus, from a clinical perspective, it would make sense to treat a client with sub-syndromal PTSD as one would treat a client with full PTSD. But clients in partial remission do not necessarily meet the criteria for sub-syndromal PTSD.

Interestingly in the Kiefer et al. (2020) study, only 4.1% of clients were diagnosed with an adjustment disorder but examination of routine medical records reveals that this diagnosis is commonplace. In a study of 145 non-psychotic clients attending community clinics, Shear et al. (2000) found that 58 had been diagnosed as having an adjustment disorder using a routine open-ended psychiatric interview. By contrast, when the gold-standard SCID (First et al., 1997) interview was used, only five met the criteria for an adjustment disorder. in addition, the SCID identified 22 sufferers from PTSD whilst the routine interview identified only one.

A Typology of the Trajectory of PTSD Symptoms

There is no inevitability about the progression of PTSD symptoms, rather as Bryant (2021) has highlighted a traumatised individual may belong to any one of four classes: (a) a resilient class with consistently few symptoms, (b) a recovery class with initial distress then gradual remission, (c) a delayed re-action class with initial low symptom levels but increased symptoms over time and (d) a chronic distress class with consistently high PTSD levels. It is thus probably more efficient to reserve psychological treatment for trajectories (c) and (b) but this does require ongoing assessments. The existence of the category (c) class suggests, that it is unlikely that it is damage occurring at the laying down of the traumatic memory, encoding, that is of prime importance in the development of PTSD in general. A study by Bryant et al. (2015) illustrates the fluidity of diagnostic status, of those with PTSD or sub-syndromal PTSD, when assessed at 3, 12 and 24 months post-trauma, half had shifted their diagnostic status by the next assessment.

Poor Agreement Between Routine Interviews and Semi-structured Diagnostic Interviews

Rettew et al. (2009) aggregated 38 studies reporting the agreement between clinician-generated diagnoses and those from structured diagnostic inter-views and reported categorical agreement, kappa, of only 0.27 across all disorders. The kappa would be 0.5 by chance if 50% of a particular popu-lation had depression, and thus the results are scarcely better than randomly choosing the diagnosis. The poor agreement between routine open-ended interviews (i.e. those routinely used by clinicians) and semi-structured in-terviews is not only confined to emotional disorders but also applies to the recognition of personality disorders. Samuels (2015) reviewed the literature on the concordance between clinician's judgements of personality disorder and that established by a semi-structured interview and found a poor median level of agreement, kappa 0.26. Accurate identification of a per-sonality disorder is important as it portends a poor prognosis for coexisting disorders, e.g. depression (Newton-Howes et al., 2006). Ramirez Basco et al. (2000) found that combining semi-structured interviewing with a review of the medical record appears to produce more accurate primary diagnoses and to identify more secondary diagnoses than routine clinical methods. However, neither standardised semi-structured interviews nor review of records are included in IAPT's 'good assessment', as detailed in the IAPT Manual (2019).

The Time Necessary for a Reliable Assessment

The DSM criteria have been the most widely used portal for the diagnosis of PTSD in randomised controlled trials. However, these criteria are rarely applied in routine practice, in part because they are judged too time-consuming. Conducting a standardised semi-structured diagnostic interview such as the SCID in routine practice typically takes 75–90 minutes. The first 30 minutes are likely to be devoted to an open-ended interview in which the therapist elicits the diagnostic possibilities and makes enquiries about any traumas. This latter is usually made more challenging because of the client's distress at recounting an extreme trauma. If PTSD is a possibility then the enquiry is made about whether the client has distressing intrusions related to the trauma (cluster B) and is significantly avoiding either cognitively and/or behaviourally reminders of the trauma (cluster C). This is likely to take a further 20 minutes. It is thus almost an hour into the interview and there are still 13 (clusters D and E) symptoms to enquire about. In addition, there is a need to enquire about the symptoms of the disorder/s that are most co-morbid with PTSD. The therapist also has to be mindful of the appropriate threshold used to determine whether a symptom is present at a clinically significant level. Whilst carefully establishing the time course of any symptom, because a diagnosis requires the simultaneous presence of symptoms. Given such time demands and the stresses, clients are under it is however perfectly possible to spread the assessment over two sessions.

Without the use of a standardised semi-structured interview, the danger is that assessors stop enquiry at the first identified problem. For example, a client may report being troubled by panic attacks, this becomes the therapeutic target and the client is discharged when they were no longer having attacks. But it may be that the client is having no panic attacks because they are avoiding feared situations and still live in fear of having panic attacks. In such a circumstance, the client would be judged as suffering from the panic disorder which has gone unrecognised and untreated. Superficially, a formulation/solution-focussed approach is a time saver but leaves the clients maladaptive functioning unaddressed.

In practice, a reliable assessment is usually jettisoned. But evidence-supported treatments (ESTs) are based on reliable assessments. How then do practitioners and agencies square this circle? By using various rules of thumb (heuristics), inflating the significance of the trauma e.g. the trauma was so extreme that it is just the sort of thing to cause PTSD, elevating certain symptoms, most commonly nightmares and avoidance, using questionnaires in lieu of a diagnostic interview. Usage of such heuristics may be underpinned by an organisation's focus on the number of cases seen and the length of waiting lists which are easily understandable targets for their paymasters e.g. Clinical Commissioning Groups.

The Marketing of Psychological Wares

The UK Government has a chain of command with regards to the provision of psychological therapy services, with NHS England the first link. In turn, NHS England advises, monitors and funds Clinical Commissioning Groups (CCGs), who manage service providers. However, it is not unusual to find NHS England staff also employed by the Improving Access to Psychological Therapies (IAPT) service, presenting a clear conflict of interest. CCGs are largely comprised of General Practitioners who have had limited training in mental health as undergraduates and will have experience of treating patients in General Practice. However, they would not be regarded as experts in this field, in that they would not enter the medico-legal arena claiming to be a mental health Expert Witness. They are therefore likely to feel at something of a disadvantage dealing with Charities or bodies whose sole purpose is to provide psychological treatment. However, as medics they will be very familiar with the concept of evidence-based practice and experience relief when the service providers talk the same language. Thus, when agencies claim to implement NICE Guidance for evidence-based treatments they look no further.

Service providers such as IAPT espouse evidence-based practice (Kellett et al., 2021; Wakefield et al., 2021), but there can be conflicts of interest (Scott, 2021). In evaluating the Government's IAPT service, it should be borne in mind that (a) there is no evidence of fidelity to an evidence-based protocol within IAPT, (b) no independent assessment of the service has been conducted using a standardised semi-structured diagnostic interview and (c) the limited evidence available suggests that only the tip of the iceberg of clients recover (Scott, 2017). This is not at all the message service providers would like to communicate to CCGs and they do not do so. Rather they assuage any concerns of politicians and the media about mental by claiming a 50% recovery rate (IAPT Manual, 2019; National Collaborating Centre for Mental Health) and assure them that they can be on the side of the virtuous by increased funding for mental health. Claims of a 50% recovery rate are based on a misuse of psychometric tests (Scott, 2017).

The combination of CCG's lack of expertise in mental health and the clever marketing by service providers has been the catalyst for the funding and expansion of services but without any evidence of making a real-world difference to client's lives. Unfortunately, bodies such as the British Psychological Society (BPS) have endorsed IAPT's modus operandi, by validating IAPT's low-intensity training and the British Association for

Behavioural and Cognitive Therapies (BABCP), publication *CBT Today*, is replete with the missives of IAPT staff.

The Use of Psychometric Tests

Psychometric tests can furnish important information about the cognitive content of a particular disorder. For example the Posttraumatic Cognitions Inventory (PTCI-9) (Wells et al., 2019) is a nine-item measure in which the client is asked about the extent to which they agree (on a scale 1–7 where 1 is totally disagree and 7 is totally agree), with statements in three domains: 1. 'negative cognitions about the self' e.g. 'I feel like I don't have any future', 2. 'negative cognitions about the world' e.g. 'people can't be trusted' and 3. 'self-blame' e.g. 'somebody else would not have gotten into this situation'. It fleshes out the negative alterations in cognition in cluster D of the DSM-5 criteria in Table 1.1. The cluster D symptoms were not included in the previous version of the DSM, DSM-IV-TR, or are they included in the most recent version of the ICD criteria for PTSD, ICD-11. The DSM working group for DSM-5 was prompted to include cluster D symptoms because of evidence that negative posttraumatic cognitions lead to the development and maintenance of PTSD symptoms. Thus, the PTCI-9 furnishes important therapeutic targets. The PTCI-9 total score was significantly correlated (r = 0.48) with the severity of PTSD as assessed by a standardised semi-structured diagnostic interview the CAPS (Blake et al., 1995) but this still left the major part of PTSD severity unexplained by cognitive factors. This lead Wells et al. (2019) to conclude that posttraumatic cognitions are an aspect of PTSD but they are not representative of the entire PTSD diagnosis and are only one of several determinants including startle response and disrupted extinction learning. Interestingly, the correlation between the PTCI-9 total score and depression (r = 0.67) was even higher than with the severity of PTSD. This highlights that the two conditions are often co-morbid and that addressing PTCI-9 cognitions may also impact depression.

The Abuse of Psychometric Tests

It has become common practice in the UK Government's IAPT service to use two psychometric tests to identify 'cases' of depression (using the PHQ9 Kroenke et al. (2001), necessitating a score of 10 or more) and 'cases' of anxiety (using the GAD7 Spitzer et al. (2006) a score of 8 or more). Further changes in these scores are then used to chart therapeutic progress. The tests are administered in the context of an open-ended interview and together inform the treatment pathway that clients then follow. In IAPT, psycho-metric tests have become a portal rather than the 'gold standard', standar-dised semi-structured interviews that were used as the portal to protocols in randomised controlled trials. However, these two tests are screening instruments that are not intended to make a diagnosis. They are not stand-alone, but intended to be a precursor for a 'gold standard' semi-structured diagnostic interview. Screening instruments necessarily generate many false positives, as it is important not to miss any possible case. When used as stand-alone instruments the danger is that many people will be needlessly treated for depression and anxiety. There is a wide range of anxiety and trauma-related disorders including PTSD and panic disorder, but the GAD7 only taps generalised anxiety disorder. Further, there are many disorders beyond depression and GAD, body dysmorphic disorder, binge eating disorder, etc. The prior selection of these two tests is likely to encourage the assessor to stop enquiries when there is a felt sense of sufficient information to confirm a positive 'case' (above a 'cut-off' score) on either measure. Thereby, pushing the assessor into operating a confirmatory bias, only looking for information that confirms the initial impression and not seeking information that might disconfirm it. This may be aided and abetted by the organisation's insistence that assessments should usually take place by phone and last no more than 30–45 minutes.

There can be no certainty that the measure of depression used, the PHQ9 (Kroenke et al., 2001) is actually measuring depression. Imagine the PHQ9 completed by a person with long-term COVID, he/she would likely score highly on at least seven of the nine items: low mood, loss of interest, loss of appetite, insomnia (because of breathing difficulties), fatigue (a key feature of COVID), feeling worthless and impaired concentration (the COVID brain fog). In a similar way, the long-term COVID client completing the GAD7 (Spitzer et al., 2006) might indicate worrying a great deal about their health, their job, their finances and difficulties in performing a family role but this does not mean that they are suffering from generalised anxiety disorder. The psychometric tests without the frame of reference of a standardised semi-structured interview are meaningless and can lead to the pathologising of normality. It can be objected that these two tests are used in IAPT in the context of an open-ended interview, the latter might highlight that a test for another disorder such as PTSD might be useful and in some instances is so administered. However, such tests were originally conceived in a context in which a high proportion of patients would have PTSD as determined by a 'gold standard', and they were used as a measure of outcome. This is quite a different context to routine practice where the prevalence of PTSD is likely to be much lower and no 'gold standard' is used at all.

Psychometric tests can be used to screen for a disorder or as a measure of the severity of a disorder. A screen will necessarily err on the side of a large number of false positives (high sensitivity) because it is important not to miss anyone who might have the disorder. But following a screen, the further assessment has to make sure that no one is declared well who actually has the disorder (high specificity).

The discharge of a client without a determination of whether the client has returned to their pre-trauma functioning or has returned to their best functioning will inevitably lead to entrapment in a revolving door. Unfortunately, the IAPT service has no procedure in place to counter this. IAPT will inform any referring source of the differences between PHQ9/GAD7 scores at the beginning of treatment and the last treatment session, together with a commentary by the therapist on what these changes mean. But such commentaries take no account that (a) the tests are likely of doubtful relevance because primary and additional diagnoses have not been reliably determined, (b) the tests were administered at each session, so the client could remember what they scored last time and may want to feel that they have not been wasting their time and score themselves lower on this account, (c) the client has a concern for the feelings of the therapist, so that in completing the tests in his/her presence, may indicate a more positive response to therapy than is the case. The situation is akin to one's response to a waitress asking did you enjoy your meal as you leave a restaurant – the situation has demand characteristics and (d) the therapist (and the organisation) has a vested interest in believing that, at the very least the client has made a significant improvement and changes in test score are readily seized on as indicative of progress. But neither therapist nor IAPT recognises that the 'observed' changes may be no more than regression to the mean, in that clients inevitably present at their worse but with the passage of time matters do improve (e) psychometric tests such as the PHQ9 and GAD7 refer to functioning in the previous two weeks, given that anxiety and depression symptoms wax and wane, it is perfectly possible to appear well on these measures but it is little more than a flash in the pan. Enduring change has been operationalised as at least eight consecutive weeks free of a disorder, see Bruce et al. (2005) and these authors found that the natural history of those suffering from anxiety disorders was that in total they were only suffering from the disorders 80% of the time.

In administering say the PHQ-9 (Kroenke et al., 2001), the IAPT worker does not know whether this is pertinent to whatever the client is suffering from e.g. OCD or PTSD (as there is no reliable standardised diagnostic interview). Further, the client is not informed of the purpose to which the test result will be put, e.g. it will be used by IAPT in such a way that any positive change on it greater than six will be publicised as indicating the difference the organisation makes.

Psychometric tests indicate only probable case of a disorder and should be followed up with an evaluation (Spitzer et al., 2006). Usually, the diagnostic accuracy of a test is assessed with reference to a 'gold standard', thus Spitzer et al. (2006) assessed the GAD7 against the SCID, First et al. (1997) [with an 89% sensitivity and 82% specificity]. However, the PHQ9 (Kroenke et al., 2001) was assessed against the PRIME MD, which is not an acknowledged 'gold standard' – questions from the latter were extracted for the former.

The diagnostic accuracy of a screening test can be assessed using QUADAS-2, Quality Assessment of Diagnostic Accuracy Studies 2nd Edition, Whiting et al. (2011) and these authors insist that the reference standard contains more accurate information than the index test. But this seems unlikely in the case of the PHQ9 evaluation. This doubt about the usage of the PHQ9 is compounded by Zimmerman's (2019) observation that the severity scores in the PHQ9 were not empirically derived, a pragmatic decision was made to designate certain intervals with particular severity tags. He adds that the PHQ9 (Kroenke et al., 2001) overdiagnoses depression severity and treatment decisions should be based on a clinical interview and not the score. Caution is needed in the use of the GAD7 (Spitzer et al., 2006) in using it to make a DSM diagnosis as the former refers to functioning in the past two weeks whilst the latter refers to functioning most of the time over the past six months.

References

American Psychiatric Association. (2000). *Diagnostic and statistical manual of mental disorders*. (4th ed. Text Revision). Washington, D.C.: APA.

American Psychiatric Association. (2013). *Diagnostic and statistical manual of mental disorders* (5th ed.). Washington, DC: APA.

Beck, A. T., Ward, C. H., Mendelson, M., Mock J. E., & Erbaugh J. K. (1962). Reliability of psychiatric diagnosis. 2. A study of consistency of clinical judgments and ratings. *American Journal of Psychiatry, 119*, 351–357.

Blake, D. D., Weathers, F. W., Nagy, L. M., Kaloupek, D. G., Gusman, F. D., Charney, D. S., & Keane, T. M. (1995). The development of a Clinician-Administered PTSD Scale. *Journal of Traumatic Stress, 8*, 75–90. 10.1002/jts.24 90080106

Bryant, R. A., Nickerson, A., Creamer, M., O'Donnell, M., Forbes, D., Galatzer-Levy, I., … Silove, D. (2015). Trajectory of post-traumatic stress following traumatic injury: 6-year follow-up. *British Journal of Psychiatry, 206*(5), 417–423. 10.1192/bjp.bp.114.145516.

Bryant, R. A. (2021). A critical review of mechanisms of adaptation to trauma: Implications for early interventions for posttraumatic stress disorder.*Clinical Psychology Review*, https://www.sciencedirect.com/science/article/pii/S0272735821 000246

Bruce, S. E., Yonkers, K. A., Otto, M. W., Eisen, J. L., Weisberg, R. B., Pagano, M., Shea, M. T., & Keller, M. B. (2005). Influence of psychiatric comorbidity on recovery and recurrence in generalized anxiety disorder, social phobia, and panic disorder: A 12-year prospective study. *American Journal of Psychiatry, 62*, 1179–1187. 10.1176/appi.ajp.162.6.1179. PMID: 15930067; PMCID: PMC3272761.

First, M. B., Spitzer, R. L., Gibbon, M., & Williams, J. B. W. (1997). *Structured clinical interview for DSM-IV axis I disorders-clinician version (SCID-CV)*. New York: State Psychiatric Institute, Biometrics Research.

First, M. B., Williams, J. B. W., Karg, R. S., & Spitzer, R. L. (2016). *Structured clinical interview for DSM-5 disorders – Clinician version (SCID-5-CV)*. Arlington, VA: American Psychiatric Association.

IAPT Manual (2019). *The improving access to psychological therapies manual*. National Collaborating Centre for Mental Health.

Kellett, S., Wakefield, S., Simmonds-Buckley, M., & Delgadillo, J. (2021). The costs and benefits of practice-based evidence: Correcting some misunderstandings about the 10-year meta-analysis of IAPT studies. *British Journal of Clinical Psychology*, *60*, 42–47. 10.1111/bjc.12268

Kiefer, R., Chelminski, I., Dalrymple, K., & Zimmerman, M. (2020) Principal diagnoses in psychiatric outpatients with posttraumatic stress disorder: Implications for screening recommendations. *Journal of Nervous and Mental Disorders, 208*, 283–287. 10.1097/NMD.0000000000001131. PMID: 32221181.

Kroenke, K., Spitzer, R. L., & Williams, J. B. (2001). The PHQ-9: Validity of a brief depression severity measure. *Journal of General Internal Medicine, 16*(9), 606–613. 10.1046/j.1525-1497.2001.016009606.x

Lilienfeld, S. O., & Lynn, S. J. (2015) Errors/biases in clinical decision making. In R. L. Caitin & S. O. Lilienfeld (Eds.), *The encyclopaedia of clinical psychology First edition*. New York: John Wiley & Sons Ltd. 10.1002/9781118625392.wbecp567.

Newton-Howes, G., Tyrer, P., & Johnson, T. (2006). Personality disorder and the outcome of depression: Metaanalysis of published studies. *British Journal of Psychiatry, 188*, 13–20.

O'Donnell, M. L., Creamer, M., Pattison, P., & Atkin, C. (2004). Psychiatric morbidity following injury. *The American Journal of Psychiatry, 161*(3), 507–514. 10.1176/appi.ajp.161.3.507

Ramirez Basco, M., Bostic, J. Q., Davies, D., Rush, A. J., Witte, B., Hendrickse., W., & Barnett, V. (2000). Methods to improve diagnostic accuracy in a community mental health setting. *American Journal of Psychiatry, 157*(10), 1599–1605. 10.1176/appi.ajp.157.10.1599. PMID: 11007713.

Rettew, D. C., Lynch, A. D., Achenbach, T. M., Dumenci, L., & Ivanova, M. Y. (2009). Meta-analyses of agreement between diagnoses made from clinical evaluations and standardized diagnostic interviews. *International Journal of Methods Psychiatric Research, 18*, 169–184. 10.1002/mpr.289. PMID: 19701924; PMCID: PMC6878243.

Samuels, D. B. (2015). A review of the agreement between clinicians' personality disorder diagnoses and those from other methods and sources. *Clinical Psychology Science and Practice, 22*, 1–19.

Scott, M. J. (2021). Ensuring that the Improving Access to Psychological Therapies (IAPT) programme does what it says on the tin. *British Journal of Clinical Psychology, 60*, 38–41. 10.1111/bjc.12264

Scott, M. J. (2017). *Towards a mental health system that works: A professional guide to getting psychological help (p. 168)*. Taylor and Francis. Kindle Edition.

Shear, M. K., Greeno, C., Kang, J., Ludewig, D., Frank, E., Swartz, H. A., Hanekamp., M. (2000). Diagnosis of nonpsychotic patients in community clinics. *American Journal of Psychiatry, 157*, 581–587. 10.1176/appi.ajp.157.4.581. PMID: 10739417.

Spitzer, R. L., Kroenke, K., Williams, J. B., & Löwe, B. (2006). A brief measure for assessing generalized anxiety disorder: The GAD-7. *Archives of Internal Medicine, 166*(10), 1092–1097. 10.1001/archinte.166.10.1092

Stein, M. B., Walker, J. R., Hazen, A. L. , & Forde, D. R. (1997). Full and partial posttraumatic stress disorder: A community survey. *American Journal of Psychiatry, 154*, 1114–1119.

Wakefield, S., Kellett, S., Simmonds-Buckley, M., Stockton, D., Bradbury, A., & Delgadillo, J. (2021). Improving Access to Psychological Therapies (IAPT) in United Kingdom: A systematic review and meta-analysis of 10-years of practice-based evidence. *British Journal of Clinical Psychology, 60*, 1–37. e12259. 10.1111/bjc.12259

Wells, S. Y., Morland, L. A., Torres, E. M., Kloezeman, K., Mackintosh, M. A., & Aarons, G. A. (2019). The development of a brief version of the posttraumatic cognitions inventory (PTCI-9). *Assessment, 26*(2), 193–208. https://doi.org/10.1177/1073191116685401

Whiting, P. F., Rutjes, A. W., Westwood, M. E., Mallett, S., Deeks, J. J., Reitsma, J. B., Leeflang, M. M., Sterne, J. A., Bossuyt, P. M., & QUADAS-2 Group (2011). QUADAS-2: A revised tool for the quality assessment of diagnostic accuracy studies. *Annals of Internal Medicine, 155*(8), 529–536. 10.7326/0003-4819-155-8-201110180-00009

Zimmerman, M., & Mattia, J. I. (1999). Psychiatric diagnosis in clinical practice: Is comorbidity being missed? *Comprehensive Psychiatry, 40*, 182–191.

Zimmerman, M., & Mattia, J. I. (2000). Principal and additional DSM-IV disorders for which outpatients seek treatment. *Psychiatric Services, 51*, 1299–1304.

Zimmerman, M. (2019). Using the 9-item patient health questionnaire to screen for and monitor depression. *JAMA*, 10.1001/jama.2019.15883. Advance online publication.

Chapter 3

What Works for Whom in Routine Practice?

Randomised controlled trials (RCTs) have been the cornerstone for evaluating the efficacy of psychological and pharmacological interventions. They provide a possible benchmark for evaluating the effectiveness of psychological therapy in routine practice, but without an understanding of the context of the RCTs, they can be mistranslated for application in everyday practice. For example, 'recovery' and 'diagnosis' mean something quite different in RCTs compared to usage in common parlance. The RCTs tell the clinician not to expect that more than one-half of clients will return to their pre-trauma level of functioning even if they faithfully reproduce the National Institute for Health and Care Excellence (2005, 2018) recommended protocols. Treatments can capitalise on a natural waxing and waning of symptoms so that the duration of time that the person is back to their old self is of critical importance. Making single-point assessments of doubtful value. Augmenting one TFCBT with another TFCBT appears not to work. Assessing whether it is possible to generalise from a particular RCT to the presenting client requires clarity about the important hallmarks of the latter. Some designations such as a 'complex' case may serve to muddy the waters. But can it be assumed that TFCBT will be effective when PTSD occurs in the context of co-existing pain and/or loss of valued role or in the presence of other disorders such as panic disorder or substance abuse? When disorders beyond PTSD are traumatic and occur independently what is the evidence that standard CBT works? Interventions that are less costly are clearly at a premium, but there are doubts about the extent to which they clear the heightened methodological bars for evidence-based treatments of the past decade. There is a need across the spectrum of trauma responses for more effective studies.

NICE Guidance and Beyond

In the United Kingdom, the National Institute for Health and Care Excellence (2005, 2018) has issued guidance (clinical Guidelines CG26 and NG116) on assessing and treating PTSD. They recommend p7 'When assessing for PTSD, ask people specific questions about re-experiencing,

DOI: 10.4324/9781003178132-4

avoidance, hyperarousal, dissociation, negative alterations in mood and thinking, and associated functional impairment'. Importantly, NICE does not recommend psychological de-briefing after a trauma, suggesting that it can make matters worse. Trauma-focussed CBT (TFCBT) and eye movement desensitisation processing (EMDR) are recommended first-line treatments, for those with PTSD or with p49 'clinically important symptoms of PTSD… who are assessed as having PTSD on a validated scale, as indicated by baseline scores above the clinical threshold, but who do not necessarily have a diagnosis of PTSD'. NICE also recommends usually treating the PTSD first 'because the depression will often improve with successful treatment'. NICE also recommends that consideration be given to the use of psychometric tests for PTSD to be administered a month or more post-trauma and with refugees and asylum seekers. NICE accepts, without question, the validity of the 'complex PTSD' diagnosis and the need for treatment different to the standard PTSD protocol. The NICE recommendations represent the consensus view of a Committee, they are not based on a review of studies, as such, they are not definitive and open to challenge. Thus, e.g. NICE changed its endorsement of graded exercise therapy for chronic fatigue syndrome. Mr. Chrisp, the Director of the Centre for Guidelines at NICE stated on 10th November 2020 'The recommendations…have been developed by an independent committee that was guided not just by the clinical evidence, but also by the experience and testimony of people with ME/CFS'. Thus, taking into account the 'experience/testimony' of sufferers from trauma-related disorders may be as important as clinical evidence in relation to PTSD treatment, i.e. the acceptability of a treatment may be a key determinant of its provision.

With regards to the treatment of PTSD, the International Society of Traumatic Stress Studies (2019) has followed NICE's lead, echoing similar recommendations in the Australian Centre for Posttraumatic Mental Health (2007) and American Psychological Association (2017). Whilst there is an international consensus on what is the 'best' treatment, this does not mean that the treatments are always effective or that they are being delivered optimally in routine care.

The Applicability of the NICE Guidance

The recommendations of NICE are based on RCTs of treatments for PTSD. The RCTs have focussed largely on populations where PTSD is the primary presenting problem but have admitted some clients with additional comorbidities, e.g. depression, substance abuse and panic attacks. However, clients with additional diagnoses of substance dependence, personality disorder, bipolar disorder and schizophrenia have typically been excluded. Thus, care has to be taken in generalising from the RCTs to clients encountered in routine practice.

Over three-quarters of those with PTSD have another disorder (Kessler et al., 1995). The National Comorbidity Survey data (Kessler et al., 1995) suggests that of those with PTSD, 16% have one coexisting psychiatric disorder, 17% have two coexisting psychiatric disorders and 50% have three or more coexisting psychiatric disorders.

Depression is commonplace, affecting 48% of males with PTSD and 12% of females. Approximately 20% of people with PTSD have reported the use of alcohol or other substances to reduce tension. A large United States sample found that 24% of patients with PTSD had a diagnosis of borderline personality disorder (BPD). Compared with people who had PTSD alone or BPD alone, those with comorbid PTSD and BPD had more comorbidity, increased likelihood of suicide attempts, and high levels of traumatic events in childhood (Scheiderer et al., 2015).

Clients Wish for all Their Disorders to Be Treated

The work of Zimmerman and Mattia (2000) suggests that clients do not want a narrow focus on one disorder but wish for treatment for all their disorders. They experience their problems as a whole and want this totality addressed. The danger for organisations set up with a particular rationale, e.g. eating disorders, alcohol treatment unit, trauma centre, pain clinics is that they do not provide a comprehensive enough service. There is a tradition of advocating a focus on one disorder, e.g. National Institute for Health and Care Excellence (2018) that PTSD would usually be treated first before any associated depression, and a hope that any comorbid disorder will resolve before any necessary further treatment. However, a PTSD client with a substance dependence problem is, in practice, unlikely to return to a therapist after referral to specialist alcohol services. Clients fall down the steps of a stepped care approach. There is no empirical evidence that clients cannot be treated simultaneously for their psychological disorders.

Comorbidity Impinges on Outcome

Prolonged exposure therapy is one of the National Institute for Health and Care Excellence (2018) recommended treatments for PTSD, but in a study by Markowitz et al. (2015) half of clients with comorbid depression dropped out of treatment. Clients with comorbid depression were nine times more likely to drop out of prolonged exposure than non-depressed exposure patients. Whilst it is always possible that treating one disorder successfully will lead to the resolution of an accompanying disorder this can be by no means guaranteed. In treating clients simultaneously for disorders, it is important to ensure that clients receive an adequate dose of treatment for each disorder. There is a danger when clients are treated simultaneously for their disorders that the therapist simply 'strays' from the disorder of primary focus and offers 'morsels' to the comorbid disorders.

Screening Clients

Clients often do not improve, not because of a lack of therapeutic skill, but because of something else going on that they never thought to ask about (Scott & Sembi, 2006). Screening clients for all common disorders is a protection against missing an important therapeutic target and its importance has been highlighted in the *IAPT Manual*, p25 National Collaborating Centre for Mental Health (2019).

Table 3.1 provides starter questions for the most common disorders. The PTSD questions are based on the Primary Care Screen (Prins et al., 2016) and it is assumed that the therapist has first identified an unusually or especially frightening, horrible or traumatic event, that the symptoms are based around. The GDIQ in Table 3.1 can be used to structure a conversation with the client. It is important that if the client has not quite grasped the meaning of a question, e.g. the client might talk about nightmares as they are trying to get to sleep, and there will be a need for the therapist to clarify the question. It is intended that if the therapist distils sufficient evidence that the client clears the screen for a particular disorder, questions are then asked about each of the remaining DSM symptoms of that disorder. The GDIQ should not be used as a checklist, rather it is necessary to elicit examples of the manifestation of a symptom and determine whether a particular symptom reflects significant impairment. The GDIQ can be usefully supplemented by asking whether the client wants help for the identified disorder. In this way, anticipating the expression of ambivalence to treatment e.g. a client may indicate drink problems, be unsure whether he/she wants help for it, further discussion with the client may reveal the source of the ambivalence e.g. 'the drinking helps me get to sleep'.

With regards to PTSD (item 3), using a score of 3 or more identifies 95% of those who have the disorder and 85% of those who do not have the disorder. In a study by Prins et al. (2016), comparing this screen with a diagnostic interview (MINI, Sheehan et al., 1998), the screen identified approximately twice as many cases (26.4%) as the 'gold standard' (14.3%). Thus, relying on the screen alone, for every PTSD case treated appropriately another person would be treated unnecessarily. Further, the population studied in the Prins et al. (2016) work were male veterans in their 60s, it is unknown whether the same cut off would apply to other populations.

The borderline personality disorder, BPD screen (item 11) is based on a paper by Zimmerman et al. (2017). Of those with BPD over 90% endorsed the affective instability question, but only 38% of those with affective instability had BPD i.e. most of those with affective instability do not have BPD. This illustrates that screening questions are only ever a starting point, if you don't ask further clarifying questions in terms of the full DSM-5

Table 3.1 Gateway Diagnostic Interview Questions (GDIQ)

1. Depression (*evidence that at least one of the answers to the following questions is in the affirmative*)

   1. During the past month, have you often been bothered by feeling, depressed or hopeless?
   2. During the past month, have you often been bothered by little interest or pleasure in doing things?

2. Panic Disorder (*a positive response to at least the first question is required*)

   1. Do you have unexpected panic attacks, a sudden rush of intense fear or anxiety?
   2. Do you avoid situations in which the panic attacks might occur?

3. Post-traumatic Stress Disorder

   In your life, have you ever had any experience that was so frightening, horrible or upsetting that, in the past month, you
   1. Have had nightmares about it or thought about it when you did not want to?
   2. Tried hard not to think about it or went out of your way to avoid situations that reminded you of it?
   3. Were they constantly on guard, watchful, or easily startled?
   4. Felt numb or detached from others, activities, or your surroundings?
   5. Felt guilty or unable to stop blaming yourself or others for the event(s) or any problems the events may have caused?

   Evidence that at least three of the answers to the symptom questions above are in the affirmative

4. Generalised Anxiety Disorder (*a positive response to all three questions is required*)

   1. Are you a worrier?
   2. Do you worry about everything?
   3. Has the worrying been excessive (more days than not) or uncontrollable in the past six months?

5. Social Anxiety Disorder (*a positive response to at least the first question is required*)

   1. When you are or might be in the spotlight say in a group of people or eating/writing in front of others do you immediately get anxious or nervous?
   2. Do you avoid social situations out of a fear of embarrassing or humiliating yourself?

6. Obsessive-Compulsive Disorder (*a positive response to at least three questions is required*)

   1. Do you wash or clean a lot?
   2. Do you check things a lot?
   3. Is there any thought that keeps bothering you that you would like to get rid of but can't?
   4. Do your daily activities take a long time to finish?
   5. Are you concerned about orderliness or symmetry?

(*Continued*)

Table 3.1 (Continued)

---

7. Binge Eating Disorder *(a positive response to at least the first question is required)*

   1. Do you go on binges where you eat very large amounts of food in a short period?
   2. Do you do anything special, such as vomiting, go on a strict diet to prevent gaining weight from the binge?

8. Alcohol Dependence *(evidence is that the response to at least three of the following questions is in the affirmative)*

   1. Have you felt you should cut down on your alcohol/drug?
   2. Have people got annoyed with you about your drinking/drug taking?
   3. Have you felt guilty about your drinking/drug use?
   4. Do you drink/use drugs before midday?

9. Psychosis *(a positive response to at least two questions is required)*

   1. Do you ever hear things other people don't hear, or see things they don't see?
   2. Do you ever feel like someone is spying on you or plotting to hurt you?
   3. Do you have any ideas that you don't like to talk about because you are afraid other people will think you are crazy?

10. Bipolar Disorder *(a positive response to at least the first question is required)*

   1. Have there been times, lasting at least a few days when you were unusually high, talking a lot, sleeping little?
   2. Did others notice that there was something different about you?

   What, if anything, did they

11. Borderline Personality Disorder *(a positive response to both questions is required)*

   1. Do you have a lot of sudden changes of mood, usually lasting for no more than a few hours?
   2. Do you often have temper outbursts or get so angry you lose control?

---

criteria they can be very misleading. (Adding the anger item, see item 11 to the BPD screen meant that 97% of those with BPD answered 'yes' two both symptom questions according to Zimmerman et al. (2017).) The questions on alcohol drug use, item 8 (Malet et al., 2005) in Table 3.1, using the first three items yields a sensitivity of 70% (i.e. missing about a third of those who are dependent) and a specificity of 94% (i.e. correctly identifying the vast majority of those who are not dependent). It remains to be seen how much the question about wanting help adds to diagnostic accuracy across all the disorders. However, it is known that it does so for the depression screen, item 1, Arroll et al. (2005) with a sensitivity of 96% and a specificity of 89% (up from 78% using the two depression symptom questions alone).

Screening as Part of a Conversation

National Institute for Health and Care Excellence (2018) recommends that in determining a PTSD diagnosis the clinician asks questions about each of the symptom clusters: intrusions, avoidance, negative alterations in cognition and emotion and hyperarousal. Thus, it is assumed that the use of any screen would take place in the context of a conversation. Importantly, the assessment is not reduced to eliciting dichotomous 'yes', 'no' answers to probes from the screen. How then should the conversation be structured?

A conversation is different to an interrogation, it is not like a Barrister's cross-examination with intimidating 'please answer "yes" or "no"', instructions. In a conversation, both parties need the space to express themselves. For a first encounter, it is doubtful that this can be achieved in under 75 minutes unless there is a sole disorder with impairment in one domain e.g. car driving.

The conversation begins with an enquiry by the therapist as to the start of any difficulties and any associated events. The client is encouraged to tell their story of their difficulties, including what led them to seek help now. This open-ended interview generates a set of diagnostic possibilities, each of which is enquired about further to make a diagnosis.

The Clinician-Administered PTSD Scale for DSM-5 – A Gold Standard

The CAPS-5 (Weathers et al., 2015) is a gold standard for assessing the presence of PTSD and is available free online or from the National Centre for PTSD. Systematic enquiry is made about each of the 20 DSM-5 symptoms of the disorder and there is a delineation of the frequency and severity of each symptom. For example, to determine cognitive and behavioural avoidance, item 6 of the CAPS reads (Table 3.2).

The avoidance of thoughts was the most common (90%) PTSD symptom initially endorsed in samples of PTSD clients undergoing cognitive processing therapy (CPT) or prolonged exposure (PE) (Larsen et al., 2019) For a symptom to be regarded as clinically significant it would have to score at least a '2' on the above rating. In conformity with DSM-5, the symptom criteria would only be met if there was at least one symptom in both the intrusion and avoidance clusters, at least two symptoms in the negative alterations in cognition and mood cluster and at least two symptoms in the hyperarousal cluster. The CAPS-5 also yields a total score so that the severity of the client's PTSD before, during and after treatment can be gauged.

Table 3.2 Example of CAPS Item – Cognitive and Behavioural Avoidance

Item 6 (CI): Avoidance of or efforts to avoid distressing memories, thoughts, or feelings about or closely associated with the traumatic event(s).
In the [past month/worst month], have you tried to avoid thoughts or feelings about (EVENT)?
What kinds of thoughts or feelings do you avoid?
How hard do you try to avoid these thoughts or feelings? (What kinds of things do you do?)
[If not clear:] (**Overall, how much of a problem is this for you? How would things be different if you didn't have to avoid these thoughts or feelings?**)
Circle: Avoidance = Minimal Clearly Present Pronounced Extreme
How often in the [past month / worst month]? Number of times _____
   0. Absent
   1. Mild/subthreshold
   2. Moderate/threshold
   3. Severe/markedly elevated
   4. Extreme/incapacitating
Past Month _____ Worst Month _____
Key rating dimensions = frequency / intensity of avoidance
Moderate = at least 2 x month/avoidance clearly present
Severe = at least 2 x week/pronounced avoidance

Covering all Bases and Avoiding Pathologising Normality

A therapist has to be aware of operating a confirmatory bias, only looking for what he/she expects to find. For example, if the therapist knows that that the client was in a serious road traffic accident only enquiring about PTSD. Alternatively, if the therapist is working in a generalist agency they may not enquire routinely of clients whether they were abused in childhood. Not only can other disorders be associated with PTSD but also it is equally possible that they occur minus the latter. Appendix contains DSM-5 interview questions for the disorders that are commonly triggered or exacerbated by trauma: depression, PTSD, alcohol/substance dependence, panic disorder with agoraphobia, specific phobia, obsessive-compulsive disorder and generalised anxiety disorder. Alternatively, a generic standardised interview such as the DIAMOND (Tolin et al., 2018) can be administered but it is lengthy, albeit that it can be viewed on-screen at the same time as interviewing a client remotely via Facetime or WhatsApp.

However, there can be organisational constraints on a therapist taking the time to use a standardised semi-structured interview but it may be feasible to utilise Table 1.1, Chapter 1, ensuring that all the pertinent information regarding a PTSD diagnosis is covered. But making the interview CAPS informed: ensuring that the client is referring to current functioning for each symptom and the therapist does not endorse a symptom as present when from the client's account it simply occurred for a period after the trauma. For a reliable diagnosis based on the DSM criteria, it is necessary to ask about all the symptoms in a diagnostic set and not 'cherry pick' an individual symptom e.g. nightmares, that the therapist idiosyncratically considers the hallmark of the disorder. Technically this controls for information variance i.e. that all assessors are considering the same range of information. (This information is not restricted to what the client verbalises but may be furnished also by records or friends/family members of the client.) Assessors also need to agree on the threshold level of impairment that has to be cleared for a symptom to be regarded as present i.e. criterion variance has also to be controlled for. Like the CAPS-5 the SCID (Osorio et al., 2019) interview details the requisite thresholds, e.g. a client may report nightmares of their trauma, and this symptom would be endorsed if it woke them and they had difficulty getting back to sleep but not if they simply remember them the next day. There is thus a need to ask about the frequency of each symptom, e.g. 'how often do you have these nightmares?' and their intensity (how much, if at all, they bother the person). This can only be gauged by asking for specific examples of the experiencing of such a symptom and the therapist judges whether there has been minimal impairment of functioning e.g. momentary/very brief destabilisation/discomfort or something more. The concern is not to pathologise normality e.g. discomfort on the anniversary of a trauma. The DSM operates with a symptom count for clusters in the diagnosis of PTSD, and symptom counts are also used for other disorders. By contrast, the ICD-11 (World Health Organisation, 2018) only operates with a symptom count for depression and is governed largely by whether on the basis of the symptoms elicited (symptoms are specified for each disorder) the therapist gauges the client to be an exemplar of a particular disorder.

Certain prompt questions in assessing PTSD symptoms, lead very naturally to enquiry about other possible diagnoses. Thus, asking question 5 in the intrusions cluster of Table 1.1, Chapter 1, can lead very naturally to a panic disorder enquiry, 'do you ever get these physical symptoms out of the blue, without any reminder?' In a similar way asking question 1 in the avoidance cluster, facilitates asking 'do you do anything special to get the memories out of your mind, such as drinking alcohol more than you used to?' If the client reports a negative view of themselves or loss of interest, in response to cluster D questions 2–6, this can act as a conduit for enquiry about the presence of depression. Whilst these 'detours' are very conducive to the flow of the conversation with the client, care has to be taken that it is not at the expense of coverage of all the particular symptoms of possible disorders over the course of an assessment. It is very easy to end an assessment and discover that you were distracted from covering all the information required for a particular diagnostic set. DSM-5 questions in relation to the common disorders associated with trauma are detailed in Appendix.

Avoiding a Pandemic of Disorders

On 13th January 2021, the BBC TV News announced a new disorder 'Intensive Care PTSD'. This heralded a study by Greenberg et al. (2021) who six months earlier had asked Intensive Care Unit (ICU) Staff to complete the PHQ-9 (Kroenke et al., 2001), GAD-7 (Spitzer et al., 2006), Post-traumatic Stress Disorder Checklist (PCL-6) (Lang & Stein, 2005) and the AUDIT-C (Bush et al., 1998) checklist for problem drinking. Their results indicated 40% with probable PTSD, 6% with severe depression, 11% with severe anxiety and 7% with problem drinking. But what was not mentioned by the media was that only about half of those available for the study completed the questionnaires. Further, Greenberg et al. (2021) cautioned 'this study used self-report measures of mental illness rather than gold-standard diagnostic interviews'. This study is a salutary reminder that questionnaire-based assessments of mental health problems following trauma, taken at face value, would suggest the need for much more widespread psychological interventions than are needed. Unfortunately, service providers sometimes seem unaware of the limitations of self-report measures. It is easier to attract funds for a claimed pandemic of psychological disorders. As a consequence, it is not therefore in the interest of service providers to critically appraise studies, rather to emphasise the humanitarian case for offering more support.

Identifying Disorders

The framework of the GDIQ, Table 1.1 can be truncated by just asking questions about the most common comorbidities of PTSD, depression, panic disorder and alcohol dependence. This would not be unreasonable for example in assessing the response of medical staff to the pandemic. With follow-up, detailed questions about all the DSM-5 symptoms that comprise those disorders. But the questions should be part of a conversation with the client, such that detailed examples of the expression of any one symptom are elicited. It is inappropriate to use diagnostic criteria as a symptom checklist requiring 'yes', 'no' responses from the client.

An interview allows the assessor to consider the context in which trauma-related symptoms are being expressed. For example, if a medic is continuing to work in ICU and reports PTSD symptoms this is likely to be quite a different matter to a staff member who has retired or off on long-term sick reporting the same symptoms. The former may be best termed a Prolonged Duress Stress Disorder (Scott & Stradling, 1994) whilst the latter might more likely be a candidate for PTSD. These would carry different treatment implications, with a watchful waiting and extra resources necessitated for PDSD. Whilst examination and reappraisal of the meaning of the ICU experience with regards to the present may be more appropriate for PTSD.

Reliance entirely on self-report measures does not allow a teasing out of these differences.

The GDIQ, Table 3.1 is intended to be useful rather than comprehensive. For example whilst some disorders such as a specific phobia and body dysmorphic disorder (BDD) are not directly included, in the GDIQ, Table 3.1 in the process of questioning clients about possible PTSD symptoms, the more circumscribed problem of a specific phobia often emerges, with avoidance driven as much by embarrassment about scarring (possible body dysmorphic disorder) as by avoidance of reminders of the traumatic event. Thus, focussing on a likely small subset of disorders in Table 1.1 oftentimes leads to the identification of unanticipated disorders. The process is not unlike an archaeological dig revealing unexpected finds needing a dating and a context.

Those with co-morbid PTSD and psychosis have more severe delusions and hallucinations (Shaw et al., 2002). In the past decade, there has been an increased emphasis on Trauma-Informed Care (TIC) (Buswell et al., 2021) which involves services recognising that the experience of psychosis can be traumatic, screening patients for PTSD and offering evidence-based treatments. Buswell et al. (2021) suggest that PTSD can arise directly from the experience of psychosis itself or from features of treatment: involuntary hospitalisation, coercive restraint, forced medication, length of admission and number of traumatic hospital events. Buswell et al. (2021) cite a study (Abdelghaffar et al., 2018) using the CAPS (Blake et al., 1995) which found 23.1% suffering from PTSD in relation to the symptoms of psychosis and 19.2% suffering from it in relation to treatment characteristics. But they also suggest coercive practices appear to be increasing in the UK for people with psychosis. However, they also note that in the DSM-5 experiencing psychotic symptoms would not be regarded as meeting the gateway stressor criteria for the condition. But the ICD-11 criteria (World Health Organization, 2018) for PTSD, would accept that a subjective experience could be a gateway into PTSD. It may be difficult for clinicians to implement TIC, if their employer insists on a narrow focus on psychosis, which has been the historical focus in Secondary and Tertiary Care in the UK. Whether this improves with the UK Government's promised (Department of Health and Social Care Published March 27, 2021) increased access to psychological therapies for those with psychosis remains to be seen.

Supplanting Conversation with Psychometric Testing

A psychometric test should never be used to short circuit a conversation with a client. Whilst there is some utility in having a client arrive 20 minutes early for their initial assessment to complete a psychometric test this should not be done at the expense of building up an alliance with the client.

There is a need to proceed cautiously in the use of psychometric tests. The Post-traumatic Stress Disorder Checklist (PCL) is advocated as a screen for PTSD, IAPT Manual update 2019 with a recommended cut-off of 32 (established in two studies of veterans). But in a study of veterans (Yeager et al., 2007) for every two correctly identified PTSD sufferers one person would be incorrectly classed as a case. This led McDonald and Calhoun (2010) to caution 'even the most accurate screening test will have no practical utility if there is no structure in place to provide adequate second-level assessment'. Further, these authors observe that without knowing the prevalence of PTSD in a particular population, it is not possible to gauge the appropriate cut-off. Given that there has been no reliable estimate (determined by a 'gold standard' diagnostic interview) of the prevalence of PTSD in client's availing themselves of the UK Government's IAPT service, the use of any cut-off is hazardous.

These concerns over diagnostic accuracy also call into question the advice of National Institute for Health and Care Excellence (2018) to identify and treat 'Clinically important symptoms of PTSD' on the basis of a score on a psychometric test alone. Whilst there is evidence from randomised controlled trials as to the efficacy of treatments for PTSD there is no such body of evidence for the NICE category of 'Clinically important symptoms of PTSD'. NICE is unwittingly encouraging diagnostic creep, without reference to an evidence base and is likely to increase the treatment burden.

Sub-syndromal PTSD

Clients with a sub-syndromal level of PTSD, have sometimes been included in studies of PTSD, usually with a stipulation that at least 70% of the study population had full PTSD. However, such studies have not been based on DSM-5 criteria and the definition of 'sub-syndromal' has had a range of meanings from (a) one symptom in each of the intrusion, avoidance and hyperarousal clusters, of DSM-IV (Stein et al., 1997), (b) the number of symptom criteria being met for two clusters, one of which had to be intrusions (Blanchard et al., 1996) and (c) both a and b being required (Gillock et al., 2005). The term 'sub-syndromal' has not been defined with regards to the four symptom clusters in DSM-5. Whilst clinically there is some merit in treating those who just fail to meet DSM-5 criteria for PTSD with a PTSD protocol if this becomes as loose as 'Clinically important symptoms of PTSD' it will likely result in unnecessarily complex treatment.

Those who meet the criteria for sub-syndromal PTSD may well meet full diagnostic criteria for another disorder. Treatment of the additional disorder may be less onerous/toxic than utilising a trauma-focussed intervention and may be the first step in the treatment of these trauma victims. With re-assessment at the end of treatment to determine whether PTSD symptoms are causing significant functional impairment.

There is always the possibility that a person with 'sub-syndromal' PTSD, however defined, may go on to develop full PTSD and for this reason, extra monitoring following treatment for any comorbid disorder is warranted. A study of 3,360 recovery workers who attended the World Trade Centre following the 11 September 2001 attack (Cukor et al., 2010) found (using the Blanchard et al. (1996) definition of sub-syndromal PTSD), that at initial assessment 9.7% met these criteria, a year later 29% of the initial sample met criteria for sub-syndromal or full PTSD and a year further on the proportion was 24.5%. Thus, although there is a great deal of naturally occurring recovery in the sub-syndromal group, treatment for the co-existing disorder and monitoring is called for. Indeed in the Cukor et al. (2010) study, depression was a predictor of the course of the sub-syndromal PTSD.

Evidence-based Practice (EBP)

What is evidence-based practice post-trauma? NHS England C De Brun (2013) defines EBP as the 'integration of best research evidence with clinical expertise and patient values'. In their document 'Finding the Evidence' (2013), they provide guidance on finding 'the best research evidence'. But they are mute on the delineation and weighting of clinical expertise and patient values. They recommend the use of the mnemonic PICO, the P refers to the patient/problem/population studied, I the intervention/exposure of interest, C the comparison condition and O for the outcome. At first glance, an appropriate search strategy for the literature with regards to a probable client with PTSD might be (Table 3.3):

Table 3.3 PICO Search Strategy for PTSD

Patient/Problem/Population	Intervention/Exposure	Comparison	Outcome
PTSD	Cognitive Behaviour Therapy	Waiting list	Loss of diagnostic status

but the search strategy can greatly influence what studies are considered pertinent. For example, it can be argued that waiting lists are a poor comparison group as patients on a waiting list do not expect to get better, rather comparison should be made with a credible alternative therapy. Using this 'C', Carpenter et al. (2018) identified 14 studies of CBT for PTSD. But loss of diagnostic status the 'O' can only be gleaned for some of the 14 studies as in many of the studies recovery is reported in terms of improvement of symptoms. PICO has been expanded to become PICOT where the T represents time frame, to help answer the question of how enduring gains made with the treatment/s were. For example, it may be that by the end of treatment many people are no longer suffering from say, PTSD but that may matter little if the recovery does not last. PICOT has been expanded further to become PICOTS (Tolin et al., 2015) where the S refers to the setting of treatment. This latter helps to assess the generalisability of research findings to routine practice, e.g. a study conducted in a prestigous research centre with a highly educated population may not translate well when delivered in a deprived inner-city area. Later in this chapter, the results of these 14 studies are critically examined. But a different search strategy may be justified for example extending the 'I' to CBT and EMDR (Eye Movement Desenstisation Reprocessing). Some search strategies, e.g. clients with a specific phobia following a trauma may constitute the 'P', the 'I' may be CBT but no credible active comparisons, i.e. the C can not be found. In such instances, reliance has to be placed on the clinician's expertise and client preference.

As opposed to what constitutes 'best research evidence', in the literature the term 'clinician expertise' is not elaborated or is 'client preference'. Clinician expertise can involve an audit, e.g. Scott and Stradling (1997) assessed PTSD patient's compliance with exposure to an audio tape of their trauma in routine practice. In the first sample, only 1 of 14 clients completed the image habituation procedure for homework in the manner described by its authors. In the second ($N = 37$), only 57% complied with an audiotape exposure treatment.

It is common for GPs to receive a letter from a service provider stating that a particular treatment path was agreed upon. But with regards to psychological therapy what has actually happened is that the client has been offered a low-intensity treatment e.g. a group intervention, that can be delivered soon or a high-intensity intervention e.g. individual therapy, that could be delivered at some unspecified future date. Unsurprisingly, the client may opt for the more immediate therapy, but it is doubtful that in this context a true preference is being allowed expression. Further, unless different treatment options are clearly spelt out and efficacy of each expressed in everyday language, then the client is unable to meaningfully choose. Client preferences cannot be given expression unless there is shared decision-making (SDM). Thus, if a client's treatment finishes simply because he/she has had the Agency determined number of sessions or his/her score on a psychometric test has fallen below a certain level at the last administration, this is a violation of evidence-based practice. Such arbitrary determination of treatment endings will likely result in revolving door contacts with mental health professionals and no meaningful change in the client's life. In this connection, Scott (2018) examined 90 clients who went through the UK Government Improving Access to Psychological Therapies Service (IAPT), assessed using the SCID interview, for the effects of a trauma and found that only the tip of the iceberg recovered 9.2%, and of those who initially had PTSD, 16.2% recovered. Care has to be taken in the interpretation of these findings as it was a sample of litigants, but the results were the same whether they were treated by IAPT pre- or post-trauma. In summary, the three-legged stool of EBP collapsed for IAPT clients in that there was no evidence of treatment fidelity to the best research evidence, no evidence of shared decision-making and no evidence that therapists took steps to ensure that they were practising without the operation of a confirmatory bias.

Thus, with regards to any trauma victim one can ask, which population does the client belong to? What would be an appropriate treatment? On what basis is this treatment judged a better prospect for this client than another credible treatment? What would be an acceptable outcome? What would be an appropriate metric? What would be evidence of enduring effectiveness?

The methodological bar for treatment outcome studies has been regularly higher. From an initial acceptance that comparison can be made to an inert waiting list, to the insistence that the comparator should be a credible treatment. Then to Tolin et al.'s (2015) demand that treatments have to have a demonstrated effectiveness outside research centres, delivered by non-specialist clinicians and the study run by and audited by staff not involved in the development of the treatments. But the methodological bar can be so higher that no current studies clear it, so that there is necessarily some trade-off between methodological rigour and the utility of studies.

Comparisons of Trauma-Focussed CBT and Credible Control Groups

The efficacy of a treatment can be gauged by a measure termed the effect size, which is calculated by subtracting the mean post-treatment score of the intervention, from the mean post-treatment score of the comparison group and dividing by the spread of the results, the pooled standard deviation. Hedges' g is the effect size corrected for the number of clients in each group. An effect size of 0.2 is regarded as small, an effect size of 0.5 as moderate and an effect size of 0.8 as large. Usually, a small effect size would be re-garded as clinically insignificant, but in some instances, an effect size of 0.2 may have clinical significance if for example an intervention reduced the risk of suicide. A medium effect size means that the average client in the treat-ment group did better than 69% of the clients in the comparison condition. These are between-group effect sizes which are different to within-group effect sizes and the two are not comparable.

In a study of women suffering from PTSD (Hodgins et al., 2018), the *within*-subject effect size for those in the placebo group was up to 1.5 standard deviations, whether the person was being assessed by a self-report measure or by a clinical interview that yielded a score. By way of example, patients in the placebo group had a mean score of 30 on the PTSD Symptom Scale (Foa et al., 1993) with a mean score of 13 at the end, the spread of scores (standard deviation) was also about 13, yielding a within-subject effect size of 1.3. At first glance, seeing such a change on a PTSD scale would seem to indicate a potent intervention, but not necessarily so. Hodgins et al. (2018) suggest that potential drivers of placebo effects on self-report measures include optimism about treatment efficacy and potentially over-endorsing symptoms at entry into the study to ensure inclusion. The spontaneous recovery and placebo responses rates for PTSD are estimated to be 19–62% (Benedetti et al., 2018). However, clients on a waiting list are subject to a nocebo effect, in that they do not expect to improve until treatment begins. Thus, studies of psychological interventions were the comparison is functioning on a waiting list are a poorer test of the efficacy of treatment than a comparison with a credible active treatment.

The Carpenter et al. (2018) study identified 14 PTSD controlled trials in which CBT was compared with a credible alternative treatment and the overall effect size (Hedges' g) was 0.5. The outcome measures were PTSD symptom measures. Large effect sizes were found in four studies (Blanchard et al., 2003; Bryant et al., 2003; Marks et al., 1998; Rauch et al., 2015). Medium effect sizes were found in four studies (Cottraux et al., 2008; Ehlers et al., 2014; Foa et al., 1991; Markowitz et al., 2015). Small effect sizes were found in six studies (McDonagh et al., 2005; Neuner et al., 2004; Schnurr et al., 2007; Schnuur, 2003; Surís et al., 2013; Resick et al., 2015). It may therefore be concluded that these trauma-focussed CBT interventions contribute something special over and above clients being given a credible rationale for treatment and the provision of support. However, it is not possible to determine the proportion of clients losing their diagnostic status in all of the studies, much less how enduring recovery was likely to be.

Does Trauma-Focussed CBT Make a Real-World Difference?

The trauma-focussed CBT therapies appear equally effective, in that about 1 in 2 of those suffering PTSD lose their diagnostic status by the end of treatment. However, there are wide variations across studies, for PE, 30–97% for cognitive processing therapy and 61–82% for CBT (Jonas et al., 2013). CPT and prolonged exposure were marginally superior compared with non–trauma-focused psychotherapy comparison conditions (Jonas et al., 2013). But the duration of recovery for individuals is unclear from the studies, albeit that mean scores post-treatment are maintained at follow-up. The success of treatments also depends on the population being addressed. Amongst veterans with PTSD approximately two-thirds of patients receiving cognitive processing therapy or prolonged exposure retained their PTSD diagnosis after treatment (range, 60–72%; Steenkamp et al., 2015).

The 14 studies considered by Carpenter et al. (2018) probably constitute the 'best research evidence'. The outcome is discussed in terms of effect size in the Carpenter et al. (2018) study, but whilst such a metric is useful to a clinician it is unlikely to have a 'real world' feel to a client, more concerned with the likelihood of becoming their old-self post-treatment. Springer et al. (2018) suggest that clients should be asked at the outset of treatment what they would regard as 'remission' and consider that perhaps this should be the yardstick rather than the therapist imposed loss of diagnostic status. This would be in keeping with a move to evidence-based practice in which the client's views are given as much credence as the evidence emerging from outcome studies. Using loss of diagnostic status as a criterion for remission (which has to do with end-state functioning rather than response where the focus is on a change of symptoms e.g. 50% reduction) gives the most optimistic evaluation of the efficacy of CBT interventions. With 53.3% of PTSD sufferers, 41.4% of those with GAD, 48% of those with panic disorder/ agoraphobia losing their diagnostic status by the end of CBT. Tolin et al. (2015) have argued that for studies to be credible they should have to clear a 'real world' methodological bar by demonstrating replication in non-research centres with staff not involved in the original research centre. This external validity criteria has been accepted by the Clinical Psychology Division 12 of the American Psychological Association.

Few PTSD studies, if any, would clear the Tolin et al. (2015) bar. For example, Ehlers et al. (2014) sought to demonstrate the external validity of their trauma-focussed CBT by testing its applicability with victims of the Omagh bombing (Gillespie et al., 2002). But no steps were taken to employ 'a gold-standard' diagnostic interview, reliance was entirely on self-report measures and there was no blind assessment post intervention. Thus, the real-world significance of the 14 studies reviewed by Carpenter et al. (2018) is not a settled matter. However, clinicians may find it useful to draw on the details of the studies, with medium or high effect sizes in deciding their applicability to their client.

Springer et al. (2018) point out that the apparent supremacy of CBT for PTSD over this treatment for other disorders may be due to the fact that many of the PTSD studies accepted that there was maintenance of loss of diagnostic status if the person was free of the disorder for just three to four months. They also found that the presence of comorbid depression or substance abuse also adversely affected outcomes. This led these authors to suggest simultaneous treatment of disorders rather than the traditional sequential path.

The study by Ehlers et al. (2014) may be regarded as prototypical of those studies in the Carpenter et al. (2018) meta-analysis with a medium or large effect size for PTSD. In this study, 77% were no longer suffering from PTSD at the end of standard TFCBT treatment, but neither were 43% of those who underwent supportive therapy (yielding a medium effect size). In both treatments, clients had 12 weekly sessions, but it is not clear from the study what the duration of recovery was for those who had 'recovered', although average scores of PTSD severity at 27 weeks and 46 weeks follow-up were maintained. In this study, clients were selected for treatment where 'PTSD was the main problem' but in the routine psychiatric outpatient of those with PTSD, only 1 in 5 (Kiefer et al., 2020) saw the disorder as their main problem. This raises the question of whether the PTSD clients treated in the Ehlers et al. (2014) study can be regarded as typical of those with PTSD in an outpatient setting. It may be noteworthy that 25% of those undergoing treatment had a College/University education, with 68% of those in standard TFCBT classed as professionals or white-collar workers. In the Ehlers et al. (2014) study, dropouts were defined as attending less than 8 sessions, with a dropout rate of just 3.2% in standard TFCBT and 10% in supportive therapy. However, in a meta-analysis of 14 studies (Carpenter et al., 2018), which included Ehlers et al. (2014) study, the average dropout rate was 29% in CBT for PTSD compared to 17% in an active placebo.

Loss of diagnostic status is a necessary condition for believing that a real-world difference in a client's functioning has been achieved. Regrettably in routine practice, traumatised clients rarely achieve this end-point. A study by Scott (2018) of 90 trauma victims, assessed independently with the SCID standardised diagnostic interview, and treated allegedly with CBT, revealed that of those with an initial diagnosis of PTSD (n = 36) 16.2% recovered, for those suffering depression (n = 48) the recovery rate was 14.9%, and for disorders excluding PTSD and depression (n = 49) the recovery rate was 2.2%. This study shows the heterogeneity of trauma responses and that PTSD is not the prototypical response to trauma. Further, the mean number of disorders was 1.6, i.e. most clients had more than one disorder. Caution does however need to be taken with this study in that all were personal injury litigants and the author examined them in the context of being an Expert Witness to the Court, assessing their current and lifetime diagnoses. However, the recovery rates were no different if they were treated before or after litigation. Further litigation is commonplace amongst trauma victims undergoing psychological therapy, e.g. in the Blanchard et al. (2003) study comparing the efficacy of CBT and support therapy with a waiting list, amongst motor vehicle accident survivors with PTSD or severe sub-syndromal PTSD, 60% of the population was involved in litigation.

It is a matter of concern, that in none of the PTSD outcome studies has a metric been used that would be immediately recognisable to a client, such as whether the latter thought that treatment had 'returned me to my usual self' – loss of diagnostic status may be a significantly easier bar to clear. The client would also understand that they had made progress if they could say post-treatment 'I am not yet completely my usual self'. Bruce et al. (2005) used such end-points when assessing the natural history of generalised anxiety disorder, social anxiety disorder and panic disorder. A clinician could higher the meth-odological bar further by insisting that not only should treatment return the client to their usual self but also that they are without any residual PTSD symptoms, lest they relapse. These considerations mean that there may be a greater expectation of the translation of PTSD randomised controlled trials to routine practice than actually occurs on the ground from the client's perspective.

But even when TFCBT is successful in the sense that PTSD clients loose their diagnostic status, about 30% of clients have residual symptoms of each of hypervigilance, exaggerated startle response and insomnia (Larsen et al., 2019) following CPT or PE. Tripp et al. (2020) in a study of veterans found similarly that hypervigilance (47.3%) and sleeping difficulties (63.0%) were the most commonly persisting symptoms for those who no longer met PTSD diagnosis criteria following either PE or drug treatment. In the Tripp et al. (2020) study, post 'recovery' from PTSD 30.6% had an exaggerated startle response and 39% had problems with irritability. The findings of Tripp et al. (2020) and Larsen et al. (2019) make it doubtful whether this subpopulation of 'responders' would actually regard themselves as back to their usual self's. Though perhaps they might regards themselves 'not yet completely my usual self'. But as the descriptions of the TFCBTs below show neither hypervigilance, exaggerated startle response, irritability or insomnia is a target for these interventions. Rather the focus of TFCBTs is on the inability to recall the trauma, because it is held that it is incomplete processing of the trauma that is pivotal in the development of PTSD. Yet, psychogenic amnesia is only initially endorsed by just over two-thirds of those initially undergoing TFCBTs (Larsen et al., 2019) falling to 30–40% at post-treatment and follow-up. By contrast, initial endorsement of hypervigilance and insomnia were each over 80% and exaggerated startle response over 70% (Larsen, et al., 2019). Suggesting that a focus on a state of 'terrified surprise' (hypervigilance plus exaggerated startle response), insomnia and irritability may be an important non-trauma focussed pathway into the treatment of PTSD.

What Do Trauma-Focussed Treatments Look Like?

The trauma-focussed treatments for PTSD, span a spectrum levels of exposure to the traumatic memory ranging from prolonged exposure (Foa et al., 2002) to eye movement desensitisation reprocessing (EMDR). National Institute for Health and Care Excellence (2018) recommended the following trauma-focussed treatments for adult PTSD, prolonged exposure therapy, cognitive processing therapy, cognitive therapy for PTSD, narrative exposure therapy and EMDR. However, American Psychological Association Guideline Development Panel for the Treatment of PTSD (Bufka et al., 2020), made a 'strong recommendation' for variants of cognitive behaviour therapy: cognitive processing therapy, cognitive therapy (CT) and prolonged exposure (PE) therapy. Amongst the psychological therapies, the APA made a 'conditional recommendation' for eye-movement desensitisation reprocessing (EMDR), narrative exposure therapy (NET) and brief eclectic psychotherapy (BEP). The same 'conditional' re-commendation was given to the prescribing of the antidepressants, fluox-etine, paroxetine and sertraline. For some interventions such as psychodynamic therapy, the Panel did not have sufficient evidence to make a recommendation but cautioned that the absence of evidence is not evidence of lack of efficacy. Below CBT variants with a 'strong' recommendation by the APA are first described, followed by two psychological therapies with a 'conditional' recommendation.

Prolonged Exposure

Foa et al. (2002) recommend ten weekly sessions of 90–120 minutes. Treatment begins with psychoeducation about common reactions to trauma, breathing retraining, *in vivo* exposure, imaginal exposure (starting at session 3), processing of imaginal exposure and assigned homework. In session 3, clients close their eyes, visualise the trauma and recount the trauma in the present tense aloud for approximately 30–45 minutes per session. Clients subjective feelings of distress (SUDS), on a scale of 0–100, are elicited every five minutes, with the intention of achieving a reduction in SUDS during the session. At sessions 3 and 10, the whole trauma memory is recounted whereas in the intervening sessions the focus shifts to what is called 'hot spots' and the full memory is not usually recounted. Homework is assigned at each treatment session which consisted of listening to the tape of the imaginal exposure daily and *in vivo exercises*. The next session begins with a review of homework.

Cognitive Processing Therapy

Cognitive processing therapy (Resick et al., 2017) is a 12-session therapy that initially included what was termed 'written exposures'. However, be-cause these 'exposures' were unlike prolonged exposure therapy (repetitions of the trauma for 45–60 minutes to encourage strong emotions, with ratings of distress to monitor habituation within and between sessions) the term was changed to 'written accounts'. The original version of cognitive processing therapy included two written accounts of the index traumatic event and research was conducted on this version until the Resick et al. (2008) dis-mantling study found that the cognitive therapy only version of CPT did just as well 'without exposing clients to the distress of the accounts' (p233 Resick et al., 2017). At the first treatment session, the CPT therapist describes the CPT theory of PTSD, that some people are prevented from recovering be-cause of unhelpful thoughts and that the identification and challenging of these is a key focus of treatment. For homework, clients are asked to write an Impact Statement, a typically one-page summary of why the traumatic event happened, and the consequences of the trauma in terms of their beliefs about themselves, others and the world. At sessions 2 and 3, the Impact Statement is reviewed, and thoughts that interfere with recovery 'stuck points' are noted. For homework, clients monitor their thoughts and feelings in particular noting the content of any event reminiscent of the trauma. Clients are asked to complete self-report measures after each session. The goals for sessions 4 and 5 are to make sure clients can label events, thoughts and emotions and see the connections amongst them. Socratic dialogue is used throughout the sessions to help clients challenge their Stuck Points. A large portion of session 4 is focused on the trauma itself. For homework, clients are asked to complete a Challenging Questions Worksheet each day prior to session 5. About two-thirds of session 5 is spent reviewing the client's completed worksheet before introducing a Problematic Thinking Worksheet, such as possible 'jumping to conclusions', 'mindreading' and 'emotional reasoning'. Homework is then set on Problematic Thinking. For Session 6, Resick et al. (2017) recommend continuing to focus on the index event and associated thoughts. It is recommended that if the client still continues to report nightmares or flashbacks, it is suggested that their content may reveal the part of the event in which the client is still stuck. The therapist is advised to tackle anything that is interfering with the programme such as substance misuse. A Challenging Beliefs Worksheet is then introduced, to facilitate the client generating alternatives to the negative thoughts and rating the believability of the alternatives. For homework, a worksheet is completed each day which is reviewed at session 7. Then, the themes of Safety, Trust, Power/Control, Esteem and Intimacy are introduced as important domains for consideration over the next five sessions. For homework at session 7, the client is given a handout on Safety Issues, with homework addressing this domain on the Challenging Beliefs Worksheet. In sessions 8–10 the focus is on utilising the Challenging Beliefs Worksheet to address Safety, Trust, Power/Control themes. Session 9 begins with a review of the completed Worksheet and the introduction of the handout that addresses Power/Control Issues, then on to the Esteem theme. Session 10 begins with a review of a Trusted Star Worksheet in which Trust is conceptualised in a dimensional rather than binary fashion. The remainder of the session focuses on the way in which the traumatic event has impacted on self-esteem. Session 11 involves looking at Stuck Points with regards to Esteem. Session 12 involves revisiting the client's perception of the impact of the trauma and a new Impact Statement is written that is contrasted with the first. Resick et al. (2017) add that for clients who had experienced frequent childhood abuse there was an advantage in them writing two written accounts of the trauma and comment p233 'It is possible that these clients needed to reconstruct a fragmented set of memories into a coherent narrative in order to benefit from cognitive interventions'. But more generally CPT without written accounts had a lower dropout rate (22%) compared to 34% in the CPT modality that included written accounts.

Cognitive Therapy for PTSD

Cognitive Therapy for PTSD (CT-PTSD) usually involves 12 weekly sessions of 60–90 minutes and up to three optional monthly booster sessions (Ehlers & Wild, 2020). The mean number of sessions is around 10. For sessions that include work on the trauma memory – imaginal reliving, updating memories, or a site visit sessions are usually around 90 minutes, the authors add, p106 'The client needs sufficient time to refocus on current reality...before going home after these sessions'. At the first session, a provisional individualised case formulation is collaboratively developed, as a specific example of the Ehlers et al. (2014) model. The majority of clients start with a few imaginal relivings in session 2 and the information garnered is then used to write a narrative. Though some clients do not do the reliving. Through the imaginal reliving and/ or the writing of the narrative, worse moments in the trauma are identified and put into context so that the 'now' is distinguished from the 'then'. If reexperiencing symptoms persist after successful updating of the client's hot spots and discrimination triggers imagery transformation strategies may be used, one that signifies that the trauma is over. The worst moments of the trauma memories are held to be poorly elaborated and poorly integrated within the context of the trauma and also within relevant previous and subsequent previous and subsequent experiences, p92 'The effect is that people with PTSD remember these parts of the trauma in a disjointed way' (Ehlers & Wild, 2020). Clients are encouraged to let go of maladaptive coping strategies that serve to maintain PTSD, cognitive and behavioural avoidance, excessive precautions (safety behaviours), numbing of emotions (including substance use) and dwelling on the memories (rumination). Towards the end of therapy, the client and therapist distil a summary of what has been learnt, that serves as a template (blueprint) for application in the event of setbacks.

Narrative Exposure Therapy

As in CPT writing about the trauma takes place to aid the processing of the trauma, but in some instances, if the person has difficulty in writing it may be dictated to a trusted confidant. At the end of treatment, the final version of the traumatic experiences is handed over to the client. NET was developed in Africa for populations living with ongoing traumas and in areas where war, rape, killings, armed raids and burning of villages commonly occur. 'The focus of NET is on reconstructing the fragmented memories of traumatic experiences into coherent narrations' (Neuner et al., 2020).

EMDR

National Institute for Health and Care Excellence (2018) recommends that EMDR be delivered individually typically over 8–12 sessions. Treatment begins with psychoeducation about reactions to trauma and proceeds to managing distressing memories and situations; identifying and treating target memories (often visual images) and promoting alternative positive beliefs about the self. Treatment involves repeated in-session bilateral stimulation (normally with eye movements) until the memories are no longer distressing. Bi-lateral tones or sensory input can be used as an alternative to the direct generation of eye movements. Self-calming techniques and strategies for managing flashbacks are practised within and between sessions.

Evidence-Based Practice (EBP)

EBP is a three-legged stool consisting of the best research evidence, clinical expertise and patient preferences. NHS England C De Brun (2013) suggests that EBP represents an integration of the three domains. With regards to the first leg of the stool for PTSD, the Carpenter et al. (2018) studies probably reflect the research, 'best evidence', that is likely to be most germane for routine practice.

The second leg of the stool highlights the importance of the clinician's expertise. The work of Scott and Stradling (1997) reflects one aspect of this expertise, audit, which may be particularly appropriate to evidence-based practice. These authors audited compliance with imaginal exposure in PTSD clients. The audit examined Image Habituation Training (IHT; Vaughan & Tarrier, 1992), in which clients were to record six brief descriptions of aspects of their recurrent intrusive images onto audiotape. Each description was followed by 30 seconds of tape silence during which the client were asked to visualise as intensely as possible the memory that the description evokes. Thus, a taped image habituation sequence lasted a little more than 3 minutes (6 × 30 sec plus the duration of the brief descriptions). Following in-session training, the homework assignment was to listen to the tape for one hour, every day. In the event, only 1 of 14 clients in the Scott and Stradling (1997) study complied with this homework exercise.

In the second audit (n = 37), the imaginal exposure followed that described by Foa et al. (1991), who required clients in their Prolonged Exposure (PE) condition to imagine their trauma as vividly as possible, and describe it aloud in the present tense onto audiotape. But in this study, to enhance likelihood of compliance, they were asked listen to the tape daily for as long as it took them to habituate, as reflected in a decrement in their Subjective Units of Distress (SUDS) rather than the one hour a day, recommended by Foa et al. (1991). Nevertheless, in the Scott and Stradling (1997) study nobody engaged in daily homework practice and only 57% of clients managed to listen to their tape three times a week for three weeks. These audits suggest significant difficulties in translating the imaginal exposure treatments from research centres into routine practice.

But clinician's attitudes to treatment options may be, at least in part, due to their experience of using them in real-world settings. This knowledge forms part of their expertise. A survey of 207 psychologists (Becker et al., 2004) found that only 17% used imaginal exposure to treat PTSD. Whilst 59% believed that using imaginal exposure therapy was likely to increase the client's desire to drop out. Amongst CBT trauma specialists, the figure was nearly 50%. A study of imaginal exposure conducted in routine clinical practice showed a 28% completion rate (Zayfert et al., 2005), which is far lower than the average dropout rate of 27% from randomised controlled trials of CBT (Hembree et al., 2003). Interestingly, most of the dropouts in imaginal exposure in the routine practice, Zayfert et al. (2005) study occurred before the imaginal exposure and it may therefore be that it is anticipation of loss of control with IE that leads to dropping out than the IE per se. More recently, Sijercic et al. (2021) have observed a 33.1% dropout rate, over the course of cognitive processing therapy and nearly half of these individuals dropped out during the first six sessions. To date, TFCBT appears not to be a very marketable commodity. Cognitive avoidance of trauma-related material is, one of the defining characteristics of PTSD, see Table 3.2, of this chapter, so that the client is implicitly not wanting to 'relive' their trauma, but the intent of trauma-focussed therapists is that they facilitate 're-living'. The opposing agendas are likely to make for engagement difficulties that are likely to be more pronounced in routine practice, away from prestigious research centres.

The third leg of the stool highlights the importance of taking into account patient preferences. These can be taken into account by asking patients after their PTSD diagnosis what they would most want to work on. Interestingly when veterans were asked this question (Rosen et al., 2013) 20–25% wanted to improve relationships, with 8–29% identifying estrangement as a primary problem. Whilst 31–37% wanted help with anger and 14–27% wanted help for sleep. The traditional TFCBTs do not have these foci. Interestingly, National Institute for Health and Care Excellence (2018) only recommends targeting symptoms such as insomnia and anger if the person is unwilling to engage in a trauma focussed intervention, client's preferences hold little sway it seems.

Thus, EBP is likely to take a different form from a fundamentalist translation of RCTs for TFCBT. This has implications for supervisors and service providers whose mantra has been that they deliver NICE-approved treatments. Not only is there an absence of fidelity to such protocols in routine practice but also there is a failure to acknowledge the complexity of delivering PTSD treatments. From a service provider's perspective, attracting funding requires a simple positive message to be communicated to paymasters but this can hinder critical reappraisal of service delivery.

References

Abdelghaffar, W., Ouali, U., Jomli, R., Zgueb, Y., & Nacef, F. (2018). Posttraumatic stress disorder in first-episode psychosis: Prevalence and related factors. *Clinical Schizophrenia & Related Psychoses, 12*(3), 105–112B. 10.3371/csrp.ABOU.123015

American Psychological Association. (2017). Clinical practice guideline for the treatment of Posttraumatic Stress Disorder (PTSD) in adults: APA. Available from: http://www.apa.org/ptsd-guideline/ptsd.pdf

Arroll, B., Goodyear-Smith, F., Kerse, N., Fishman, T., & Gunn, J. (2005). Effect of the addition of a "help" question to two screening questions on specificity for diagnosis of depression in general practice: Diagnostic validity study. *BMJ (Clinical Research Ed.), 331*(7521), 884. 10.1136/bmj.38607.464537

Australian Centre for Posttraumatic Mental Health. (2007). Australian guidelines for the treatment of adults with acute stress disorder and posttraumatic stress disorder. Available from: http://www.acpmh.unimelb.edu.au

Becker, C. B., Zayfert, C., & Aanderson, E. (2004). Survey of psychologists' use and attitudes towards exposure therapy for PTSD. *Behaviour Research and Therapy, 42*, 277–292.

Benedetti, F., Piedimonte, A., & Frisaldi, E. (2018). How do placebos work? *European Journal of Psychotraumatology, 9*(Suppl3). 10.1080/20008198.2018.1533370

Blake, D. D., Weathers, F. W., Nagy, L. M., Kaloupek, D. G., Gusman, F. D., Charney, D. S., et al. (1995). The development of a clinician-administered PTSD scale. *Journal of Traumatic Stress, 8*(1), 75–90.

Blanchard, E. B., Hickling, E. J., Barton, K. A., Taylor., A. E., Loos, W. R., & Jones-Alexander J. (1996). One year prospective follow-up of motor vehicle accident victims. *Behaviour Research & Therapy, 34*, 775–786.

Blanchard, E. B., Hickling, E. J., Devineni, T., Veazey, C. H., Galovski, T. E., Mundy, E.,... Buckley, T. C. (2003). A controlled evaluation of cognitive behavioral therapy for posttraumatic stress in motor vehicle accident survivors. *Behaviour Research and Therapy, 41*, 79–96.

Bruce, S. E., Yonkers, K. A., Otto, M. W., Eisen, J. L., Weisberg, R. B., Pagano, M., Shea, M. T., & Keller, M. B. (2005). Influence of psychiatric comorbidity on recovery and recurrence in generalized anxiety disorder, social phobia, and panic disorder: A 12-year prospective study. *The American Journal of Psychiatry 162*(6), 1179–1187. 10.1176/appi.ajp.162.6.1179

Bryant, R. A., Moulds, M. L., Guthrie, R. M., Dang, S. T., & Nixon, R. D. (2003). Imaginal exposure alone imaginal exposure with cognitive restructuring in treatment of posttraumatic stress disorder. *Journal of Consulting and Clinical Psychology, 71*, 706–712.

Bufka, L. F., Wright, C. V., & Halfond, R. W. (Eds.)(2020). Casebook to the APA clinical practice guideline for the treatment of PTSD (pp. 91–121). American Psychological Association. https://doi.org/10.1037/0000196-005

Bush, K., Kivlahan, D. R., McDonell, M. B., Fihn S. D., & Bradley, K. A. (1998). The AUDIT alcohol consumption questions (AUDIT-C): An effective brief screening test for problem drinking. *Archives of Internal Medicine*;158:1789–1795.

Buswell, G., Haime, Z., Lloyd-Evans, B., & Billings, J. (2021). A systematic review of PTSD to the experience of psychosis: Prevalence and associated factors. *BMC psychiatry, 21*(1), 9. 10.1186/s12888-020-02999-x

Carpenter, J. K., Andrews, L. A., Witcraft, S. M., Powers, M. B., Smits, J., & Hofmann, S. G. (2018). Cognitive behavioral therapy for anxiety and related disorders: A meta-analysis of randomized placebo-controlled trials. *Depression and Anxiety*, *35*(6), 502–514. 10.1002/da.22728

Cottraux, J., Note, I., Yao, S. N., de Mey-Guillard, C., Bonasse, F., Djamous- Sian, D.,... Chen, Y. (2008). Randomized controlled comparison of cognitive behavior therapy with Rogerian supportive therapy in chronic post-traumatic stress disorder: A 2-year follow-up. *Psychotherapy and Psychosomatics*, *77*, 101–110.

Cukor, J., Wyka, K., Jayasinghe, N., & Difede, J. (2010). The nature and course of subthreshold PTSD (2010). *Journal of Anxiety Disorders*, *24*, 918–923.

Department of Health and Social Care Press Release Mental Health Recovery Plan March 27th 2021. https://www.gov.uk/government/news/mental-health-recovery-plan-backed-by-500-million

Ehlers, A., Hackmann, A., Grey, N., Wild, J., Liness, S., Albert, I., Deale, A., Stott, R., & Clark, D. M. (2014). A randomized controlled trial of 7-day intensive and standard weekly cognitive therapy for PTSD and emotion-focused supportive therapy. *The American Journal of Psychiatry*, *171*(3), 294–304. 10.1176/appi.ajp.2013.13040552.

Ehlers, A. and Wild, J. (2020). Cognitive therapy for PTSD. In L. F. Bufka, C. V. Wright, & R. W. Halfond (Eds.), *Casebook to the APA clinical Practice Guideline for the Treatment of PTSD*. American Psychological Association

Foa, E. B., Rothbaum, B. O., Riggs, D. S., & Murdock, T. B. (1991). Treatment of posttraumatic stress disorder in rape victims: A comparison between cognitive-behavioral procedures and counseling. *Journal of Consulting and Clinical Psychology*, *59*, 715–723.

Foa, E. B., Riggs, D. S., & Dancu, C. V. (1993). Reliability and validity of a brief instrument for assessing post-traumatic stress disorder. *Journal of Traumatic Stress*, *6*, 459–473.

Foa, E. B., Hembree, E. A., & Dancu, C. V. (2002). *Prolonged exposure (PE) manual Revised version* (Unpublished manuscript).

Gillespie, K., Duffy, M., Hackmann, A., & Clark, D. M. (2002). Community based cognitive therapy in the treatment of posttraumatic stress disorder following the Omagh bomb. *Behaviour Research and Therapy*, *40*(4), 345–357. 10.1016/s0005-7967(02)00004-9

Gillock, K. L., Zayfert, C., Hegel, M. T., & Ferguson, R. J. (2005). Posttraumatic stress disorder in primary care: Prevalence and relationships with physical symptoms and medical utilization. *General Hospital Psychiatry*, *27*, 392–399.

Greenberg, N., Weston, D., Hall, C., Caulfield, T., Williamson, V., & Fong, K. (2021). Mental health of staff working in intensive care during COVID-19. *Occupational Medicine (Oxford, England)*, kqaa220. Advance online publication. 10.1093/occmed/kqaa220

Hembree, E. A., Foa, E. B., Dorfan, N. M., Street, G. P., Kowalski, J., & Tu, X. (2003). Do patients drop out prematurely from exposuretherapy for PTSD? *Journal of Traumatic Stress*, 16, 555–556.

Hodgins, G. E., Blommel, J. G., Dunlop, B. W., Iosifescu, D., Mathew, S. J., Neylan, T. C., Mayberg, H. S., & Harvey, P. D. (2018). Placebo effects across self-report, clinician rating, and objective performance tasks among women with post-traumatic stress disorder: Investigation of Placebo response in a pharmacological treatment study of post-traumatic stress disorder. *Journal of Clinical Psychopharmacology, 38*(3), 200–206. 10.1097/JCP.0000000000000858

International Society of Traumatic Stress Studies. (2019). Posttraumatic stress disorder prevention and treatment guidelines. Available from: http://www.istss.org/ getattachment/Treating-Trauma/New-ISTSS-Prevention-and-Treatment-Guidelines/ISTSS_PreventionTreatmentGuidelines_FNL.pdf.aspx

Jonas, D. E., Cusack, K., Forneris, C. A., Wilkins, T. M., Sonis, J., Middleton, J. C., et al. (2013). *Psychological and pharmacological treatments for adults with Posttraumatic Stress Disorder (PTSD): Comparative Effectiveness Review No. 92. (Prepared by the RTI International-University of North Carolina Evidence-Based Practice Center Under Contract No. 290-2007-10056-I). AHRQ Publication No. 13-EHC011-EF.* Rockville, MD: Agency for Healthcare Research and Quality.

Kessler, R. C., Sonnega, A., Bromet, E., Hughes, M., & Nelson, C. B. (1995). Posttraumatic stress disorder in the National Comorbidity Survey. *Archives of General Psychiatry, 52*(12), 1048–1060. 10.1001/archpsyc.1995.03950240066012

Kiefer, R., Chelminski, I., Dalrymple, K., & Zimmerman, M. (2020). Principal Diagnoses in psychiatric outpatients with posttraumatic stress disorder: Implications for screening recommendations. *Journal of Nervous and Mental Disorders 208*:283–287. doi: 10.1097/NMD.0000000000001131. PMID: 32221181

Kroenke, K., Spitzer, R. L., & Williams, J. B. (2001). The PHQ-9: Validity of a brief depression severity measure. *Journal of General Internal Medicine, 16*, 606–613.

Lang, A. J., & Stein, M. B. (2005). An abbreviated PTSD checklist for use as a screening instrument in primary care. *Behaviour Research and Therapy, 243*, 585–594.

Larsen, S. E., Fleming, C., & Resick, P. A. (2019). Residual symptoms following empirically supported treatment for PTSD. *Psychological Trauma: Theory, Research, Practice and Policy, 11*(2), 207–215. 10.1037/tra0000384

Malet, L., Schwan, R., Boussiron, D., Aublet-Cuvelier, B., & Llorca, P. M. (2005). Validity of the CAGE questionnaire in hospital. *European Psychiatry: The Journal of the Association of European Psychiatrists, 20*(7), 484–489. 10.1016/j.eurpsy.2004. 06.027

Markowitz, J. C., Petkova, E., Neria, Y., Van Meter, P. E., Zhao, Y., Hem- Bree, E., ... Marshall, R. D. (2015). Is exposure necessary? A randomized clinical trial of inter-personal psychotherapy for PTSD. *American Journal of Psychiatry, 172*, 430–440.

Marks, I., Lovell, K., Noshirvani, H., Livanou, M., & Thrasher, S. (1998). Treatment of posttraumatic stress disorder by exposure and/or cognitive re-structuring: A controlled study. *Archives of General Psychiatry, 55*, 317–325.

McDonagh, A., Friedman, M., McHugo, G., Ford, J., Sengupta, A., Mueser, K., ... Descamps, M. (2005). Randomized trial of cognitive-behavioral therapy for chronic posttraumatic stress disorder in adult female survivors of childhood sexual abuse. *Journal of Consulting and Clinical Psychology, 73*, 515–524.

McDonald, S. D., & Calhoun, P. S. (2010). The diagnostic accuracy of the PTSD checklist: a critical review. *Clinical Psychology Review, 30*(8), 976–987. 10.1016/ j.cpr.2010.06.012

National Collaborating Centre for Mental Health. (2019). The Improving Access to Psychological Therapies Manual.

National Institute for Health and Care Excellence. (2005). *Post-traumatic stress disorder (PTSD): the management of PTSD in adults and children in primary and secondary care.* London: NICE. (Clinical Guideline 26).

National Institute for Health and Care Excellence. (2018). *Posttraumatic stress disorder (PTSD).* London: NICE. (Clinical Guideline 116). Available from: https://www.nice.org.uk/guidance/ng116.

National Institute for Health and Care Excellence. (2020). Press release November 10th NICE draft guidance addresses the continuing debate about the best approach to the diagnosis and management of ME/CFS.

NHS England C De Brun (2013). Finding the evidence: Key step in the information production process.

Neuner, F., Schauer, M., Klaschik, C., Karunakara, U., & Elbert, T. (2004). A comparison of narrative exposure therapy, supportive counseling, psychoeducation for treating posttraumatic stress disorder in an African refugee settlement. *Journal of Consulting and Clinical Psychology, 72,* 579–587.

Neuner, F., Elbert, T., & Schauer, M. (2020). Narrative exposure therapy. In L. F. Bufka, C. V. Wright, & R. W. Halfond (Eds.), *Casebook to the APA Clinical Practice Guideline for the treatment of PTSD* (pp. 187–205). American Psychological Association. 10.1037/0000196-005

Osorio, F. L., Loureiro, S. R., Hallak, J., Machado-de-Sousa, J. P., Ushirohira, J. M., Baes, C., Apolinario, T. D., Donadon, M. F., Bolsoni, L. M., Guimarães, T., Fracon, V. S., Silva-Rodrigues, A., Pizeta, F. A., Souza, R. M., Sanches, R. F., Dos Santos, R. G., Martin-Santos, R., & Crippa, J. (2019). Clinical validity and intrarater and test-retest reliability of the Structured Clinical Interview for DSM-5 – Clinician Version (SCID-5-CV). *Psychiatry and Clinical Neurosciences, 73*(12), 754–760. 10.1111/pcn.12931

Prins, A., Bovin, M. J., Smolenski, D. J., Marx, B. P., Kimerling, R., Jenkins-Guarnieri, M. A., Kaloupek, D. G., Schnurr, P. P., Kaiser, A. P., Leyva, Y. E., & Tiet, Q. Q. (2016). The primary care PTSD screen for DSM-5 (PC-PTSD-5): Development and evaluation within a veteran primary care sample. *Journal of General Internal Medicine, 31*(10), 1206–1211. 10.1007/s11606-016-3703-5

Rauch, S. M., King, A. P., Abelson, J., Tuerk, P. W., Smith, E., Rothbaum, B. O., & Liberzon, I. (2015). Biological and symptom changes in posttraumatic stress disorder treatment: A randomized clinical trial. *Depression and Anxiety, 32,* 204–212.

Resick, P. A., Galovski, T. E., Uhlmansiek, M. O., Scher, C. D., Clum, D., & Young-Xu, Y. (2008). A randomised controlled trial to dismantle components of cognitive processing therapy for posttraumatic stress disorder in female victims of interpersonal violence. *Journal of Consulting and Clinical Psychology, 76,* 243–258.

Resick, P. A., Wachen, J. S., Mintz, J., Young-McCaughan, S., Roache, J. D., Borah, A. M., ... Peterson, A. L. (2015). A randomized clinical trial of group cognitive processing therapy compared with group present-centered therapy for PTSD among active duty military personnel. *Journal of Consulting and Clinical Psychology, 83,* 1058–1068.

Resick, P. A., Monson, C. M., & Chard, K. M. (2017). *Cognitive processing therapy for PTSD: A comprehensive manual.* New York: Guilford Press.

Rosen, C., Adler, E., & Tiet, Q. (2013). Presenting concerns of veterans entering treatment for posttraumatic stress disorder. *Journal of Traumatic Stress, 26,* 640–643. 10.1002/jts.21841.

Scheiderer, E. M., Wood, P. K. & Trull, T. J. (2015). The comorbidity of borderline personality disorder and posttraumatic stress disorder: Revisiting the prevalence and associations in a general population sample. *Borderline Personality Disorder and Emotion Dysregulation, 2*, 11. 10.1186/s40479-015-0032-y

Schnurr, P. P., Friedman, M. J., Foy, D. W., Shea, M. T., Hsieh, F. Y., Lavori, P. W., ... Bernardy, N. C. (2003). Randomized trial of trauma-focused group therapy for posttraumatic stress disorder: Results from a Department of Veterans Affairs cooperative study. *Archives of General Psychiatry, 60*, 481–489.

Schnurr, P. P., Friedman, M. J., Engel, C. C., Foa, E. B., Shea, M. T., Chow, B. K., ... Bernardy, N. (2007). Cognitive behavioral therapy for posttraumatic stress disorder in women: A randomized controlled trial. *JAMA, 297*, 820–830.

Scott, M., & Sembi, S. (2006) Cognitive behaviour therapy treatment failures in practice: The neglected role of diagnostic inaccuracy. *Behavioural and Cognitive Psychotherapy, 34*(4), 491–495. 0.1017/S1352465806003055

Scott, M. J., & Stradling, S. G. (1994) Post-traumatic stress disorder without the trauma. *British Journal of Clinical Psychology, 33*, 71–74.

Scott, M. J., & Stradling, S. G. (1997). Client compliance with exposure treatments for posttraumatic stress disorder. *Journal of Traumatic Stress, 10*(3), 523–526. 10.1 023/a:1024805807952

Scott, M. J. (2018). Improving Access to Psychological Therapies (IAPT) - the need for radical reform. *Journal of Health Psychology, 23*(9), 1136–1147. 10.1177/13591 05318755264

Shaw, K., McFarlane, A. C., Bookless, C., & Air, T. (2002). The aetiology of postpsychotic posttraumatic stress disorder following a psychotic episode. *Journal of Traumatic Stress, 15*(1), 39–47. 10.1023/A:1014331211311

Sheehan, D. V., Lecrubier, Y., Sheehan, K. H., Amorim, P., Janavs, J., Weiller, E., Hergueta, T., Baker, R., & Dunbar, G. C. (1998). The Mini-International Neuropsychiatric Interview (M.I.N.I.): The development and validation of a structured diagnostic psychiatric interview for DSM-IV and ICD-10. *The Journal of Clinical Psychiatry, 59 Suppl 20*, 22–57.

Sijercic, I., Liebman, R. E., Stirman, S. W., & Monson, C. M. (2021). The effect of therapeutic alliance on dropout in cognitive processing therapy for posttraumatic stress disorder. *Journal of Traumatic Stress.* 10.1002/jts.22676

Spitzer, R. L., Kroenke, K., Williams, J. B., & Löwe B. (2006). A brief measure for assessing generalized anxiety disorder: the GAD-7. *Archives of Internal Medicine, 166*, 1092–1097.

Springer, K. S., Levy, H. C., & Tolin, D. F. (2018). Remission in CBT for adult anxiety disorders: A meta-analysis. *Clinical Psychology Review, 61*, 1–8. 10.1016/ j.cpr.2018.03.002

Stein, M. B., Walker, J. R., Hazen, A. L., & Forde, D. R. (1997). Full and partial posttraumatic stress disorder: A community survey. *American Journal of Psychiatry, 154*, 1114–1119.

Steenkamp, M. M., Litz, B. T., Hoge, C. W., & Marmar, C. R. (2015). Psychotherapy for military-related PTSD: A review of randomized clinical trials. *Journal of American Medical Association, 314*(5), 489–500. 10.1001/jama.2015.8370

Surís, A., Link-Malcolm, J., Chard, K., Ahn, C., & North, C. (2013). A randomized clinical trial of cognitive processing therapy for veterans with PTSD related to military sexual trauma. *Journal of Traumatic Stress, 26,* 28– 37.

Tolin, D. F., McKay, D., Klonsky, E. D., & Thombs, B. D. (2015) Empirically supported treatment: Recommendations for a new model. *Clinical Psychology: Science and Practice, 22*(4), 317–338. 10.1111/cpsp.12122

Tolin, D. F., Gilliam, C., Wootton, B. M., Bowe, W., Bragdon, L. B., Davis, E., Hannan, S. E., Steinman, S. A., Worden, B., & Hallion, L. S. (2018). Psychometric properties of a structured diagnostic interview for DSM-5 anxiety, mood, and obsessive-compulsive and related disorders. *Assessment, 25*(1), 3–13. 10.1177/1 073191116638410

Tripp, J. C., Norman, S. B., Kim, H. M., Venners, M. R., Martis, B., Simon, N. M., Stein, M. B., Allard, C. B., Rauch, S., & PROGrESS Study Team. (2020). Residual symptoms of PTSD following Sertraline plus enhanced medication management, Sertraline plus PE, and PE plus placebo. *Psychiatry Research, 291,* 113279. 10.1016/j.psychres.2020.113279

Vaughan, K., & Tarrier, N. (1992). The use of image habituation training with posttraumatic stress disorders. *British Journal of Psychiatry, 161,* 658–664.

Weathers, F. W., Blake, D. D., Schnurr, P. P., Kaloupek, D. G., Marx, B. P. , & Keane, T. M. (2015). *The clinician-administered PTSD scale for DSM-5 (CAPS-5) – past month/worst month* [Measurement instrument]. Available at: https://www.ptsd.va.gov/ https://www.ptsd.va.gov/professional/assessment/ adult-int/caps.asp

World Health Organization. (2018). ICD-11 for mortality and morbidity statistics (ICD-11 MMS) version. https://icd.who.int/browse11/l-m/en.

Yeager, D. E., Magruder, K. M., Knapp, R. G., Nicholas, J. S., & Frueh, B. C. (2007). Performance characteristics of the posttraumatic stress disorder checklist and SPAN in Veterans Affairs primary care settings. *General Hospital Psychiatry, 29*(4), 294–301. 10.1016/j.genhosppsych.2007.03.004

Zayfert, C., Deviva, J. C., Becker, C. B., Pike, J. L., Gillock, K. L., & Hayes, S. A. (2005). Exposure utilization and completion of cognitive behavioral therapy for PTSD in a "real world" clinical practice. *Journal of Traumatic Stress, 18*(6), 637–645. 10.1002/jts.20072

Zimmerman, M., & Mattia, J. I. (2000). Principal and additional DSM-IV disorders for which outpatients seek treatment. *Psychiatric Services, 51,* 1299–1304.

Zimmerman, M., Multach, M., Dalrymple, K., & Chelminski, I. (2017). Clinically useful screen for borderline personality disorder in psychiatric out-patients. *British Journal of Psychiatry, 210*(2), 165–166. 10.1192/bjp.bp.116.182121

Chapter 4

Do Treatments Work for the Supposed Reason?

Advocates of trauma-focussed cognitive behaviour therapy (TFCBT) contend that it works because it unlocks arrested information processing. Re-living the trauma is held to be essential and a prelude to the inclusion of corrective information (Foa & Kozak, 1986). The position with regards to EMDR is more equivocal, in that whilst an information processing paradigm is used as an explanation for its efficacy, Lee and Cuijpers (2013) suggest that EMDR does not involve 're-living' but a viewing of the trauma at a distance whilst distracted by bilateral stimulation, avoiding the client being overwhelmed. A basic postulate of TFCBT is that trauma-specific reactions at the time of the event lead to impaired and fragmented memories (see Dalgleish, 2004 for an overview), i.e. that there are problems with the encoding of the traumatic memory. According to Ehlers and Wild (2020) the worst moments of the trauma memories are poorly elaborated and poorly integrated within the context of the trauma. 'The effect is that people with PTSD remember these parts of the trauma in a disjointed way' (Ehlers & Wild, 2020) and their aim is to reduce reexperiencing by elaboration of the trauma memories. Re-living a trauma is inherently a painful experience and one that most people would likely wish to avoid. If however re-living is deemed necessary, there has to be a solid theoretical justification and evidence that a less demanding intervention would not be as effective. In this chapter, the theoretical base for TFCBTs is critically examined, found wanting and a more parsimonious explanation is offered for the efficacy of the intervention. A psychological treatment may be efficacious but if it has problems surmounting an acceptability hurdle it is unlikely to be widely disseminated, the final part of this chapter addresses these problems with regards to TFCBT.

Problems with the Laying Down of the Traumatic Memory?

The basis of the claim that the memory of the trauma is 'disjointed' in PTSD sufferers, relies on a measure of 'disjointedness' (Sachschal et al., 2019), that has four items: '1. I remember different parts like separate scenes. 2. When I

DOI: 10.4324/9781003178132-5

remember a particular upsetting part, it was hard to remember it was then. 3. My memories of the worst moments feel disconnected from/not joined up with/separate from what happened beforehand and afterwards. 4. Some moments come back into my mind unchanged, just as they were'. But the last item does not have face validity as a measure of 'disjointedness', and taken as a whole there is some doubt whether it taps the construct under consideration. Whilst for subjects shown a trauma film (Sachschal et al., 2019), the score on this measure did correlate with distressing intrusions afterwards, this is a questionable analogue for PTSD sufferers.

If there were problems in the encoding of the traumatic memory, then one might expect some physiological correlate at the time which would distinguish those who went on to suffer from PTSD post the incident from those who did not. But no physiological correlate has been identified. It is true, however, that some trauma victims experience peri-traumatic dissociation, e.g. they feel the trauma occurred in slow motion or they felt as if they were looking down on the event. But the correlation between peri-traumatic dissociation and PTSD is small (Thompson-Hollands et al., 2017) and it is forming a negative view of the self in the wake of such experiences that accounts for much of the variance. This suggests that it is a client's negative interpretation of their trauma response rather than the latter per se that should be the salient therapeutic target. This target may involve not only dissociative responses but also 'freezing' at the time of the incident (Bovin et al., 2014).

The development of PTSD in relation to COVID-19 presents a particular challenge to the view that it is problems in the encoding of traumatic memory that is a necessary condition for the development of PTSD. Janiri et al. (2021) found that 30% of COVID-19 patients developed PTSD. These authors used the 'gold-standard' CAPS (Weathers et al., 2018) to establish the PTSD diagnosis. Additional diagnoses were made using the SCID (First et al., 2016) for DSM-5, with 17% meeting criteria for depression, 7% for generalised anxiety disorder, 0.7% for hypomanic episode and 0.2% for psychotic disorders. All 381 patients had attended an Emergency Department, 81% of whom were hospitalised (with an average stay of 18 days), with 50% receiving oxygen therapy and 17% admitted to intensive care. This raises the interesting question, for the significant minority who developed PTSD, when was the traumatic memory laid down, when they first went to the Emergency Department? when they received non-invasive ventilation? The difficulty in clearly highlighting a pivotal moment creates doubt over the centrality accorded to encoding. These doubts are amplified when it is considered that one of the three major predictors in the development of PTSD was the experience of delirium/agitation in the course of COVID-19, a fate suffered by 9% of the sample. The other two predictors of PTSD were a previous psychiatric history and being female.

Whether there was delirium/agitation was determined using the Confusion Assessment Method which has four elements (a) acute onset and fluctuating course as determined by collateral history, (b) inattention – the inability to count back from 20 to 1 is a way of gauging this, although it is blunt, (c) disorganised thinking, and (d) altered levels of consciousness e.g. becoming sleepy/lethargic, vigilance. To meet the DSM criteria (a) and (b) are required together with at least one of (c) and (d).

Interestingly, Janiri et al. (2021) comment that the prevalence of PTSD was identical to that found amongst the 2006 Hurricane Katrina survivors. Both were greater than the 25% found amongst the 2011 Great East Japan earthquake and tsunami survivors and the 20% found amongst residents near the World Trade Centre after the 11th September 2001 terrorist attacks. One could hypothesise that the primary problem for these categories of survivors is what could have/could happen rather than what did happen, which shifts the centre of gravity for PTSD away from problems with encoding.

Fragmented Memories?

The rationale underpinning TFCBTs is that traumatic memories are different to autobiographical memories and have their own unique neural basis. It can be more parsimoniously argued that traumatic memories are maladaptive instances of ordinary autobiographical memory. Bernsten (2021) argues that involuntary memories are commonplace and that whether a particular memory comes to mind depends on the overlap between a retrieval cue and a particular event. By way of example, if a person has been to the Louvre only once before, going a second time will likely evoke memories of the first occasion. Further, involuntary remembering is not specific to traumatic or stressful events. But emotional arousal at the time of memory formation will also enhance the likelihood of all recall, both voluntary and involuntary. Thus, e.g. if a person thought that they were going to die at the time of a trauma, this memory will be easily accessed. Both voluntary and involuntary remembering are enhanced by emotional stress during encoding. Berntsen and Rubin (2014) concluded that evidence for a more fragmented memory amongst PTSD sufferers disappeared when other differences between the latter and non-trauma control group such as education and intelligence were taken into account. Further, the level of reported incoherence was low. Berntsen and Rubin (2014) found that reversing the DSM psychogenic amnesia item to 'trouble forgetting important parts of the traumatic event' resulted in a higher correlation with total PTSD symptoms than 'difficulty remembering important aspects of the traumatic event'. Brewin (2016) has suggested that there are discrepant findings on the relationship between fragmentation and traumatic memory. He acknowledges that no such linkage exists if the focus is on the general trauma narrative. However, Brewin (2016) asserts that the evidence points to a correlation between fragmentation of the worst moments of the traumatic memory and PTSD. Rubin et al. (2016) have fiercely rebutted Brewin's (2016) claim, stressing that in their study they not only looked at general fragmentation but also at the possibility that it was local fragmentation that was salient with regards to PTSD and found no relationship.

These authors conclude that 'the time has come to reconsider' the prevalent beliefs underpinning TFCBT, and which have been dominant for over 45 years.

Episodic memories are not a fixed store of what happened where and when, rather a person experiences a reconstruction each time they are revisited (Clayton & Wilkins, 2017). Each reconstruction is a product of the 'lens' employed on that occasion. Some reconstructions may be more adaptive than others, in that they better help to anticipate future events. From the perspective of mental time travel (MTT) (see Rahman & Brown (2021) for an extensive discussion), it is not easy to incorporate the notion that is obligatory for the therapist to assist the client to incorporate 'corrective information' into a 'fear structure' for therapeutic progress to be made (Foa & Kozak, 1986). Such fear structures are held to consist of the stimulus for the fear, the response and the meaning associated with it. Emotional processing is the modification of such structures. But emotions beyond fear such as guilt, horror, anger, shame and disgust are often part of PTSD, suggesting that the tapestry of emotions that need addressing is much richer.

Although there are strongly overlapping regions in the brain involved in remembering and imagining (Addis, 2018), there are some differences and what is remembered tends to be more graphic than what is imagined. Further, the imagining is more cognitively demanding. But one of the functions of memory appears to be to help anticipate future events. The consciousness of the self in subjective time is involved in both remembering the past and imagining the future. Thus, the view of self is likely to have a chronology, making it an important, albeit neglected therapeutic target.

Whither Arrested Information Processing?

The notion that arrested information processing plays a pivotal role in the development of PTSD, is reflected in the inclusion of psychogenic amnesia, operationalised as gaps in the memory of the trauma, as one of the symptoms of PTSD in the DSM. But of the 20 symptoms comprising PTSD in the DSM-5 (American Psychiatric Association, 2013), it is one of the least frequently endorsed (Weathers et al., 2018), further it has an extremely low correlation 0.17 with overall PTSD score (only recklessness also had such a low correlation). Whereas the other 18 symptoms had mean correlations of 0.51 with the severity of PTSD. This lead (Weathers et al., 2018) to reflect that 'it may be that these items are important but relatively rare symptoms of PTSD, or it may be that they are simply not representative of the PTSD construct'. This suggests that whatever gaps in traumatic memory there may or may not be, they do not play a pivotal role in the development of PTSD.

Further Foa and Kozak (1986) assert that the client has to be enabled to process the memory of the trauma, at the right level, not too much that they feel overwhelmed but not too little that that memory is not activated. It is held that it is the emotional processing of the traumatic memory at the right level that allows corrective information to be included in the posited fear structure. But this appears akin to trying to drive at the right speed through an area without any speed limit signs being visible before one gets there. If indeed the therapist has to ensure an optimal level of the client's emotional processing this makes the approach less easy to disseminate and may make clinicians reluctant to employ the intervention.

Difficulties in Identifying the Active Ingredients in TFCBT

All trauma-focussed therapies developed in randomised controlled trials contain multiple interventions, and it may be that to the extent that they do work, they do so for reasons other than the proposed theoretical justifications. Identifying the active ingredients for change becomes even more difficult when, as is often the case in routine practice, amalgams of the TFCBTs are distilled and delivered. For example, Blanchard et al. (2003) delivered CBT to PTSD and severe sub-syndromal PTSD clients, that consisted of progressive muscle relaxation, writing a detailed description of their accident, reading it aloud at each session and at home three times a day 'to force the participant to think about the accident, rather than to avoid the thoughts'. For homework, clients were asked to complete graded exposure in vivo exposure to fear arousing cues on the road. Simultaneously, clients were taught to identify negative self-talk, cognitive fallacies and how to dispute them. For the second session, clients were encouraged to invite a supportive partner to the session. Near the end of treatment, clients were asked to reinstate activities and there was a focus on anger issues. For CBT, of those with an initial diagnosis of PTSD, 71% recovered by post-treatment, the comparable figure for those undergoing supportive therapy was 43% (of those on the waiting list 15% recovered). But the CBT programme though effective for most was so multifaceted that drawing any conclusion on the active ingredient is well-nigh impossible. It may be that there is some commonality amongst the trauma-focussed therapies, such as the client testing out whether their fears are groundless, that is the active ingredient. Blanchard et al.'s (2003) study hints that the provision of support may indeed be an active ingredient for change, albeit one that is not usually systematically addressed in TFCBT. That the trauma-focussed therapies all produce much the same level of effectiveness despite very differing doses of exposure to the traumatic memory, raises the possibility that exposure per se may not be necessary. This latter suggestion runs counter to what has been an article of faith for 50 years.

The Credibility Gap Between TFCBT and Clients

There is a gap between the deliberations of the clinicians/theoreticians behind trauma-focussed CBT and the narrative of clients. Clients do not volunteer that there is something 'disjointed' in how they look at the trauma. As I write it is the 15th Anniversary of the July 7th London bombing, of the 700 people physically injured, few would think that they somehow got the events of the day wrong, or would this be an uppermost topic in any Survivor group. Similarly, the Auschwitz, survivor, Edith Egger (2017), who afterwards became a clinical psychologist, was askance at the idea of deliberate re-living of the trauma 'Work through it? I lived it, what other work is there to do? ... I've broken the conspiracy of silence. And talking hasn't made the fear or flashbacks go away. In fact talking seems to have made my symptoms worse... we can choose to be our own jailors or we can choose to be free'. She did revisit Auschwitz but her sister, with whom she went through the Concentration camp, declined.

References

Addis, D. R., (2018). Are episodic memories special? On the sameness of remembered and imagined event simulation. *Journal of the Royal Society of New Zealand*, *48*(2–3), 64–88.

American Psychiatric Association. (2013). *Diagnostic and statistical manual of mental disorders* (5th ed.). Washington, D.C.: APA.

Berntsen, D., & Rubin, D. C. (2014). Involuntary memories and dissociative amnesia: Assessing key assumptions in posttraumatic stress disorder research. *Clinical Psychological Science*, *2*(2), 174–186. 10.1177/2167702613496241

Berntsen, D. (2021). Involuntary autobiographical memories and their relation to other forms of spontaneous thoughts. *Philosophical Transactions of the Royal Society of London. Series B, Biological Sciences*, *376*(1817), 20190693. 10.1098/rstb.2019.0693

Blanchard, E. B., Hickling, E. J., Devineni, T., Veazey, C. H., Galovski, T. E., Mundy, E., Malta, L. S., & Buckley, T. C. (2003). A controlled evaluation of cognitive behavioural therapy for posttraumatic stress in motor vehicle accident survivors. *Behaviour Research and Therapy*, *41*(1), 79–96. 10.1016/s0005-7967(01)00131-0

Bovin, M. J., Dodson, T. S., Smith, B. N., Gregor, K., Marx, B. P., & Pineles, S. L. (2014). Does guilt mediate the association between tonic immobility and posttraumatic stress disorder symptoms in female trauma survivors?. *Journal of Traumatic Stress*, *27*(6), 721–724. 10.1002/jts.21963

Brewin, C. R. (2016). Coherence, disorganization, and fragmentation in traumatic memory reconsidered: A response to Rubin et al. (2016). *Journal of Abnormal Psychology*, *125*(7), 1011–1017. 10.1037/abn0000154

Clayton, N., & Wilkins, C. (2017). Memory, mental time travel and the Moustachio Quartet. *Interface Focus*, *7*(3), 20160112. 10.1098/rsfs.2016.0112

Dalgleish, T. (2004). Cognitive approaches to posttraumatic stress disorder: The evolution of multirepresentational theorizing. *Psychological Bulletin, 130*(2), 228–260. 10.1037/0033-2909.130.2.228

Egger, E. (2017). *The choice*. London: Rider.

Ehlers, A., & Wild, J. (2020). Cognitive therapy for PTSD. In L. F. Bufka, C. V. Wright, & R. W. Halfond (Eds.), *Casebook to the APA clinical Practice Guideline for the Treatment of PTSD*. American Psychological Association.

First, M. B., Williams, J. B. W., Karg, R. S., & Spitzer, R. L. (2016). *Structured Clinical Interview for DSM-5 Disorders – clinician version (SCID-5-CV)*. Arlington, VA, American Psychiatric Association.

Foa, E. B., & Kozak, M. J. (1986). Emotional processing of fear: Exposure to corrective information. *Psychological Bulletin, 99*(1), 20–35.

Janiri D., Carfì, A., Kotzalidis, G. D., et al. (2021). Posttraumatic stress disorder in patients after severe COVID-19 infection. *JAMA Psychiatry*. Published online February 18, 2021. 10.1001/jamapsychiatry.2021.0109.

Lee, C. W., & Cuijpers, P. (2013). A meta-analysis of the contribution of eye movements in processing emotional memories. *Journal of Behavior Therapy and Experimental Psychiatry, 44*(2), 231–239. 10.1016/j.jbtep.2012.11.001

Rahman, N., & Brown, A. D. (2021). Mental time travel in post-traumatic stress disorder: Current gaps and future directions. *Frontiers in Psychology, 12*, 624707. 10.3389/fpsyg.2021.624707

Rubin, D. C., Berntsen, D., Ogle, C. M., Deffler, S. A., & Beckham, J. C. (2016). Scientific evidence versus outdated beliefs: A response to Brewin (2016). *Journal of Abnormal Psychology, 125*(7), 1018–1021. 10.1037/abn0000211

Sachschal, J., Woodward, E., Wichelmann, J. M., Haag, K., & Ehlers, A. (2019). Differential effects of poor recall and memory disjointedness on trauma symptoms. *Clinical Psychological Science: A Journal of the Association for Psychological Science, 7*(5), 1032–1041. 10.1177/2167702619847195

Thompson-Hollands, J., Jun, J. J., & Sloan, D. M. (2017). The Association between peritraumatic dissociation and PTSD symptoms: The mediating role of negative beliefs about the self. *Journal of Traumatic Stress, 30*(2), 190–194. 10.1002/jts.22179

Weathers, F. W., Bovin, M. J., Lee, D. J., Sloan, D. M., Schnurr, P. P., Kaloupek, D. G., Keane, T. M., & Marx, B. P. (2018). The clinician-administered PTSD Scale for DSM-5 (CAPS-5): Development and initial psychometric evaluation in military veterans. *Psychological Assessment, 30*(3), 383–395. 10.1037/pas0000486

Chapter 5

A New Paradigm

People are disturbed not so much by events but by whether they allow themselves and their personal world to be defined by the traumas. A key function of memory is to allow us to anticipate the future. Each time the trauma is revisited, there is the potential for it to be remembered with different implications for today. There are dots laid down by our history but they can be joined up in different ways. Discussion of trauma is necessary to gauge the extent to which the trauma victim sees it as central to their self-definition and perception of their personal world. However, there is no virtue in a repeated re-living of the first account of the trauma, which can result in a re-traumatisation and dropping out of treatment. It is important to determine whether clients are more concerned about what could have happened/could happen as opposed to what did happen. In constructing the narrative of the trauma, it is important to elicit (a) whether others give the same history of the incident, (b) whether the client is conscious of the developmental level at which they were operating at the time of the trauma, (c) whether the client believes that they must remember all details of the trauma, (d) what the client takes their response to the trauma to mean about them now and (e) how the current sense of self/personal world differs from that pre-trauma.

Evidence is presented that the centrality accorded to the trauma relates to the severity of post-traumatic stress disorder (PTSD) symptoms, albeit that both reciprocally interact with each other. This means that treatment can proceed along a self-identity axis, daring to engage in pre-trauma behaviours and along a connectedness axis, in which the narrative regarding others and in particular significant others is re-activated. It is suggested that a hallmark of PTSD is a state of 'terrified surprise', a combination of exaggerated startle response and hypervigilance, which is misinterpreted as a threat from the local environment. In this new perspective, the client's pre-trauma view of themselves and their personal world is validated. This emphasis on the client's resources differs from the deficit-driven 'incomplete processing' approach of trauma-focussed therapy, thereby reducing the power differential between client and therapist.

Restorative cognitive behaviour therapy (RCBT) is about restoring the trauma victim to a sense of their former selves or rebuilding a sense of self.

DOI: 10.4324/9781003178132-6

The process is akin to restoring an old property to its former glory or constructing a rebuild on the site. As such the prime focus is on the self, rather than how the property became dilapidated. There is clear water between RCBT and trauma-focussed CBT (TFCBT). To the extent that TFCBT works, it may do so because of its inadvertent impact on the sense of self rather than a re-processing of the traumatic memory.

RCBT addresses the sense of 'I am not me anymore', a common utterance amongst trauma survivors. The focus of RCBT is on restoring a sense of continuity with the 'I'. Reasserting that the victim did not die either physically or psychologically in their trauma. There is a capitalising on the client's pre-trauma functioning and that therapy is a quest for its rediscovery. But in instances where the client believes that they have never functioned well, a 'rebuild' is undertaken.

In RCBT, there is no opposition between the client's goals and the agenda of the therapist. Most debilitated traumatised clients would not choose to talk about their trauma, in RCBT this is taken as a normal, natural response to a horror. By contrast in TFCBT, the client is assured that their response to the trauma is 'normal' but the agenda of the therapist is to help them properly process the traumatic memory. Not only is this a double standard but also there is an inherent challenge to the therapeutic alliance as clients and therapists are wanting to tug in opposite directions. This is likely to result in therapeutic non-starts or dropping out of treatment. Further, the TFCBT is likely to demand a significant level of expertise from the therapist to counter the differing agendas. Beierl et al. (2021) have suggested that the working alliance (agreed tasks, goals and bond) may be particularly important in the treatment of PTSD because the trauma-focussed treatments have relied upon encouraging clients to overcome their avoidance of talking or thinking about the trauma. In the study by Beierl et al. (2021) of clients undergoing trauma-focussed CBT, it was found that both clients and therapists working alliance ratings after session 1 predicted PTSD symptoms at the end of treatment. Though, as in other studies of the predictive value of the working alliance, the amount of variance accounted for was small to medium, 13–28%, depending on whether it was the therapist's or client's perspective on the alliance. Thus, developing a working alliance appears important in the treatment of PTSD but is not of overriding importance. Nevertheless, a treatment that presents no inherent hurdles to the working alliance must be considered favourably. RCBT provides less of a challenge to the working alliance and is thereby likely to be much easier to disseminate.

Mental Time Travel

In RCBT, it is held that traumatic memory is not different to ordinary autobiographic memory i.e. there is no qualitative difference between everyday memories and those of a trauma. All memories have a commonality in that one of their functions is to help us anticipate future events. My track record of failures to rectify computer problems has taught me that it is far better to hand such matters over to my wife, when they occur! Mental time travel travelling backwards to particular experiences and then forward imagining their implications for today is part of normal functioning. Indeed, we develop the capacity to remember the past and anticipate the future around the same age. Whilst there is a great deal of overlap in the neural structures involved in remembering and anticipating, there are some differences. What is remembered tends to be more graphic, with more sensory input, whilst what is anticipated is less colourful. We remember a particular event/s when there is some overlap between a current situation and a historical event. Passing Goodison Park, the home of Everton FC, reminds me of first going there in the boy's pen as a ten-year-old. However, this is not any different to a trauma victim being reminded of being assaulted by the sight of a group of youths walking towards him. In order to imagine the worst, the reminder does not have to be physically identical, in this example, it may be young men not youths who perpetrated the assault, but in the imagining both are put in the same category, i.e. there is conceptual as well as perceptual processing involved in imagining. It may be that the imagining is not adequately contextualised, e.g. the victim of a serious road traffic accident may contemplate with 'horror' the thought of driving again, such that they do not purchase a new car, rather than contemplating a road map for driving, visualising initially simply switching the engine on in the drive, then when accomplished, visualising reversing the car into the road, etc.

Clients are often distressed that the memory of a traumatic event continues to intrude long after they or significant others think it should. However, from an evolutionary perspective, it makes sense to have a daily forced journey back to trauma and to then move forward and gauge its relevance, if any, for today. Once the relevant question is addressed the client can move on. Thus, e.g. if a refugee or battered spouse is undergoing therapy but is still in a dangerous environment this may well nullify any treatment gains. Ensuring the safety of the victim is the first essential.

Mental Time Travel and Disorders

Mental time travel (chronesthesia) is not confined to a particular disorder such as PTSD. For example, a depressed client may engage in mental time travel to say bullying at work that led them to give up their job. A client with a specific phobia about driving since a serious road traffic accident, may find that when they attempt to drive, they remember the car tailgating them before impact, causing them to alter their driving style.

Historically, mental time travel is not a feature given any significance in the CBT treatments for depression, specific phobias or adjustment disorders. It is often noted, however, that a first panic attack may occur at the time of the trauma or shortly after, but the salience of this memory is not usually a therapeutic focus.

Though CBT is heralded as the first line treatment for depression and the anxiety disorders by NICE, in none of the studies has there been a demarcation of how clients with significant mental time travel differ in outcome from those for whom MTT is not a significant issue. Thus, e.g. studies of the CBT treatment of specific phobias, by Wolitzky-Taylor et al. (2008) extol the virtues of CBT claiming that those undergoing the treatment are better than 85% of those undergoing a comparison treatment (but with no indication of the proportion that lost their diagnostic status or for how long). But arguably those with a phobia about having an MRI scan, dental, needle, dog, spider or snake phobia are very different to those who develop a trauma-induced phobia. The average number of sessions in the outcome studies was three with 46% of the studies examining only one treatment session. But the author's experience is that when a specific phobia is work-related or the result of a serious road traffic accident many more sessions are required. For example, for those traumatised by a work-related trauma many may have serious doubts that an employer has taken sufficient steps to prevent a recurrence of the trauma should they return to work. Those with a trauma-induced phobia often suffer financially because of their inability to return their place of work and become either unemployed or their employment opportunities become much more limited. The extant studies do not take into account that mental time travel is an element of trauma-induced phobias and that treatment is not as straightforward as NICE claims.

A similar argument can be adduced for body dysmorphic disorder (BDD), though CBT treatment is claimed to be effective (Krebs et al., 2017), in that 50% of those treated show a response, many do not remit. Further generalising from these studies is problematic as the subjects in the studies do not have an acquired disfigurement. Trauma victims may suffer a minor physical disfigurement after their trauma, but such that significant others do not believe it detracts from their overall appearance whilst the person themselves may regard their appearance as 'gross'. In such instances, a DSM-5 defined diagnosis of BDD, an exaggerated concern over a minor physical anomaly may be appropriate. However, bullying and teasing by a member of the opposite sex are important predictors of BDD in the Krebs et al. (2017) studies. Thus, MTT to such experiences in adolescence may be a feature of BDD, but this aspect has not been a focus in the CBT treatment. The latter has consisted of exposure e.g. mixing socially and response prevention e.g. not using excessive camouflage. For those with a trauma-induced BDD there is likely to be a particular MTT trip. Interestingly, the DSM-5 classifies BDD under 'obsessive-compulsive and related disorders'. There is clearly room for new treatment strategies. The presence of an acquired disfigurement, will serve as a reminder of a trauma and therefore serve to maintain PTSD symptoms.

MTT is an integral part of PTSD, but it is a return ticket, its function is not to revisit the trauma for its own sake, but to gauge any implications for today. In particular, whether the trauma should dictate how the self, others and the world are viewed.

Centrality of Event/s

The extent to which an individual perceives a traumatic event as central to their identity and life story can be gauged by the Centrality of Event Scale (CES), which contains statements such as 'This event has become a reference point for the way I understand myself and my world', 'this event permanently changed my life' 'I feel that this event has become part of my identity' (Berntsen & Rubin, 2006). It has been found that the CES correlates not only with measures of PTSD symptoms in relation to a specific traumatic event (a mean correlation of 0.5) but also with symptoms of depression and anxiety (Gehrt et al., 2018). Whilst aspects of autobiographical memory, vividness (0.4), emotional intensity (0.4) and physical reaction (0.3) were also significantly correlated with the CES score (Gehrt et al., 2018). But a study by Robinaugh and McNally (2011) suggests that it is the perception of the trauma as central to one's future that may be more damaging than the perception of trauma as central to one's current self. In terms of treatment, this makes it crucially important to challenge the client's perception of the relevance of the trauma to today, tomorrow and the foreseeable future.

Earlier Tversky and Kahneman (1973) had noted the way in which shortcuts (heuristics) are used to process information, sometimes sacrificing accuracy for speed/effortless processing. In particular, they highlighted the operation of the availability heuristic, in which a memory is so vivid e.g. of a serious road traffic accident, that it exaggerates the likelihood of the recurrence of the incident. The vividness and availability of the autobiographical memory may dictate future actions, e.g. the frequency of subsequent driving, rather than the statistical likelihood of recurrence. The more available memories are more likely to be made more central.

Gehrt et al. (2018) also found a stronger association between the CES and grief and the CES and shame compared to other non-trauma-related measures of negative affect and maladaptive thoughts. Both grief and shame link to identity and PTSD symptoms. Gehrt et al. (2018) comment that 'rather than being poorly integrated and hard to access', as advocates of TFCBT contend (e.g. Dalgleish, 2004), the traumatic memory appears to be highly accessible and this elevated accessibility is robustly related to PTSD symptoms. But correlation does not equal causality and more research is needed to clarify the direction of causality. However, a study by Greenblatt-Kimron et al. (2021) of Holocaust survivors, their offspring and grandchildren with a comparison triad who did not experience this trauma, found that the way in which centrality was accorded to the Holocaust was an intergenerational predictor of debility. Secondary traumatisation refers to symptoms of distress and behaviours that result from close or extensive contact with a traumatised individual and event centrality was a distinctive mechanism for this.

Although a salient memory is a necessary component of event centrality, not everyone who could volunteer a vivid description of a trauma makes it central. It may be that pre-existing factors such as rumination may play a part but as yet there are no definitive answers on the processes involved.

The Dynamic Between Memory and View of Self

'It's no use going back to yesterday, because I was a different person then' so states Alice in Lewis Carroll's Alice's Adventures in Wonderland (Carroll, 1965). The implication is that to remember you have to be the same person as at that time. Chronesthesia is a form of consciousness that makes us aware of the passage of time, travelling backwards and forwards, revisiting the past in order to best anticipate events. Alice appears to have experienced an extreme disruption of this form of consciousness, but there appears to be a greatly diluted version of it occurring in those who develop PTSD. Oftentimes, the complaint of the PTSD sufferer is that 'I am not me anymore' and it is difficult to access experientially how they functioned pre-trauma, though they can recall their activities and behaviours pre-trauma. It is rather like getting old, you are out walking recalling that you would once have run for and caught a bus nearby but alas not now, it seems as if you are a different person. But there can be an accessing of the pre-trauma self, by an at least partial re-engagement in pre-trauma activities, it is not so much reclaiming life as experiencing a continuity of self that trauma cannot negate, 'I am still me'. Ordinarily, there is a reciprocal interaction between remembering and view of self, thus if one has just satisfactorily completed a difficult task, for the moment at least, one might think of oneself in a positive light and call to mind similar achievements.

In the BBC TV Programme, 'The Repair Shop' people bring in artefacts that are in a great state of disrepair but were associated with either a particular cherished time in the person's life and/or a very valued person. Invariably, when the craftsmen restore the item to its former glory, e.g. making a wartime accordion playable again, the owners are deeply moved. In PTSD, it is as if mental objects of the opposite valence are accessed with devastating emotional consequences, but each time they are re-visited they are re-constructed and this can be done in a manner that renders them less pernicious. As the White Queen in Alice Through the Looking Glass observed, 'it's a poor sort of memory that only works backwards'.

Terrified Surprise

The cardinal features of PTSD are often thought to be flashbacks, nightmares and avoidance but these are not specific to the condition, clients who develop specific phobias post-trauma can also be troubled by intrusions and avoidance. But clinically, a state of 'terrified surprise', a combination of hypervigilance and exaggerated startle response, appears to be most prototypical of PTSD sufferers – constantly on the edge of their seat and easily alarmed. Larsen et al. (2019) found that over 80% of their PTSD sample showed initial hypervigilance and over 70% an exaggerated startle response. Clients who develop non-PTSD disorders post-trauma, rarely engage in the ubiquitous checking involved in hypervigilance, though they may check more in a specific domain related to their trauma such as driving. Similarly, in non-PTSD disorders that may emerge post-trauma clients may report that they are more easily startled but not to the extent that they get angry or warn other people to signal their approach. Even amongst treatment responders, to cognitive processing therapy and prolonged exposure, 30% of Larsen et al. (2019) study still exhibited hypervigilance and an exaggerated startle response at long-term follow-up. In a study by Tripp et al. (2020), residual symptoms of hypervigilance amongst responders were even higher at almost one-half (47.3%) hypervigilance with two-third (63%) of responders having sleeping difficulties. It may be that the insomnia is a consequence of the hypervigilance. Whether this is the case there could be additional benefit in focussing on terrified surprise in psychoeducation about PTSD and in its treatment.

Whilst loss of diagnostic status may be indicative of a response to treatment, this may be a necessary but insufficient condition for a return to real-world or best functioning. It may be that focussing on terrified surprise at the outset of treatment would offer an alternative, potentially more productive line of treatment. Alternatively, a focus on terrified surprise might be appropriate for the subsample of responders to TFCBT for whom this is an issue, necessitating some additional treatment.

Maples-Keller et al. (2019) have suggested that trauma-potentiated startle response is a better psychophysiological index of response to treatment than either skin conductance or heart rate. They found that responders to psychological treatment for PTSD showed greater differences to non-responders on trauma potentiated startle response than on either of the other physiological measures. Further, all the PTSD patients initially showed the trauma-potentiated startle response. Trauma-potentiated startle was assessed via electomyographic recordings of the *orbicularis oculi* muscle that mediates eyeblink responses to acoustic stimuli. Essentially, the degree of blinking at trauma-related sounds distinguished responders from non-responders. Maples-Keller et al. (2019) suggest that the trauma-potentiated startle response is such a good indice because the eye-blinking response connects directly to the brain's amygdala (alarm) that plays a pivotal role in the fear response.

Arguably, a state of terrified surprise is a hallmark of PTSD. It may be that PTSD develops because the trauma victim misattributes their sense of terrified surprise to aspects of their current environment. This in turn leads to avoidance of sources of the perceived threat and a withdrawal. Importantly, the client unwittingly prevents themselves from learning that there are no significant dangers in their personal world.

Beyond the Intra Psychic

Interpersonal traumas are more likely to trigger PTSD than impersonal ones (Kessler et al., 1995), suggesting that it may be the personal narrative about connectedness, that acts as a 'lightning conductor' to the disorder, rather than extreme trauma per se. Feelings of detachment or estrangement from others (D6) is one of the diagnostic symptoms for PTSD in DSM-5. If coupled with the DSM-5 symptom of 'irritable behaviour and angry outbursts' (E1) important relationships may be fractured. Thus, a PTSD treatment that begins with a focus on facilitating post-trauma connectedness may seem particularly germane to some clients.

TFCBTs do not have a specific focus on the social domain. One of the consequences appears to be that even amongst those that recover from PTSD with TFCBT a significant minority are left with interpersonal difficulties. The Larsen et al. (2019) study showed that amongst treatment responders to CPT or PE approximately 30% had problems with detachment at long-term follow-up, with 20% of responders having problems with irritability, suggesting that despite helpful treatment there had not been a restoration or building of social connectedness for a significant minority of beneficiaries. A deficit in perceived social support has been found to be particularly related to the presence of complex PTSD (Simon et al., 2019) and poor perceived social support had already been implicated as an important risk factor for the onset and maintenance of PTSD.

In a study by Ehler's et al. (2014), one group of PTSD sufferers were provided with emotion-focussed supportive therapy (EFST). In EFST, clients were engaged in a conversation about the emotional effects of their trauma, the difficulties it may have caused and possible solutions. Whilst clients were free to talk about any aspect of their trauma, the therapist made no attempt to elaborate on the details. Therapists did not engage in cognitive restructuring, helping them to discriminate triggers or direct them into how to change their behaviour. As homework, clients kept a daily diary of their emotional responses to the events of the week that was discussed at the following session. With EFST, 43% of clients no longer met the criteria for PTSD after therapy. EFST has two strengths (a) it is a therapy that could be easily disseminated and (b) it is a therapy that would be readily acceptable to therapists and clients because of its non-trauma focus. It is likely that there would have been added benefit to the EFST if cognitive restructuring had been an added ingredient. But Ehler's et al. (2014) report that 'After normalizing PTSD symptoms, the therapist gave the rationale that the trauma had left the patient with unprocessed emotions and that therapy would provide them with support and a safe context to address their unresolved emotions'. This raises a conundrum, how if a client's reactions to the trauma were normal can there be unprocessed emotions? The credibility of this rationale is likely to be diluted further in routine practice where the therapist does not have the backing of a prestigious research study. This underscores the need for research studies to be replicated in routine practice by those who have not developed the protocol. Nevertheless, the Ehler et al.'s (2014) study does provide a tantalising hint that providing support to PTSD clients without elaboration of the traumatic memory can yield significant results.

There is further suggestive evidence of the benefit of an interpersonal focus in the treatment of PTSD from a study by Markowitz et al. (2015). In this study, Markowitz et al. (2015) compared interpersonal psychotherapy (ITP), prolonged exposure therapy and relaxation therapy, ITP and PE were equally effective. The first half of IPT emphasised affective attunement, recognising, naming, and expressing one's feelings in non-trauma-related interpersonal situations; the remainder addressed typical IPT problem areas (e.g. role disputes, role transitions). IPT addressed not trauma but its interpersonal aftermath, and no homework was assigned. ITP was (a) more effective for those with depression and PTSD, (b) found to have a lower drop-out rate amongst those with comorbid depression, (c) more acceptable to those who had suffered childhood or adult sexual trauma, and (d) was initially preferred to the other options. But like Ehler et al.'s (2014) EFST, IPT awaits replication in routine settings by clinicians not involved in the development of the protocols.

The interpersonal approaches introduce another, non-traditional pathway into the treatment of PTSD. For some sufferers, it may be their preferred pathway into addressing their PTSD difficulties. But caution is needed, as to date the interpersonal interventions, as stand-alone interventions are only possibly efficacious, but they could be an active ingredient in a broader restorative CBT (RCBT) approach.

Negative Alterations in Cognition and Mood

DSM-5 (American Psychiatric Association, 2013) changed the diagnostic criteria for PTSD to include two symptoms related to cognition (a) the development of negative belief about the self, others or the world and (b) blame of self or others for the cause or consequences of the trauma. The DSM-5 also included, as a symptom of PTSD, the development of a persistent negative emotional state, that was not present in the earlier version of the DSM. The DSM-5 cites fear, horror, anger, guilt or shame as examples of this negative affect. Aaron Beck (see Abela & D'Alessandro, 2002) had suggested that a negative view of self, the world and future was associated with depression. It might therefore be expected that a measure of post-traumatic cognitions would correlate as much with depression as with PTSD. Wells et al. (2019) found this to be the case, using their nine-item Post-traumatic Cognitions Inventory (PTCI-9; Wells et al., 2019). The correlation between the PTCI-9 total score and PTSD score as measured by the CAPS (Weathers et al., 2015) was significant, with an $r = 0.41$, but modest, leading Wells et al. (2019) to comment that 'post-traumatic cognitions are an aspect of PTSD but they are not representative of the entire PTSD diagnosis and are only one of several determinants (e.g. startle response, disrupted extinction of learning) of PTSD'. The PTCI-9 has three subscales. negative cognitions about self, negative cognitions about the world and self-blame (each composed of three items) example items from the respective subscales are 'I feel I don't know myself anymore', 'people can't be trusted', 'the event happened because of the way I acted'. Given that treatment changes in post-traumatic cognitions preceded changes in PTSD (see Ehlers & Clark, 2000) addressing PTCI-9 type cognitions may be important, not only for the amelioration of PTSD but also for trauma-related depression. But although targeting negative alterations in cognition is an important focus, it probably should not be an exclusive target.

The Presentation of a Credible Rational for RCBT

Restorative CBT (RCBT) has an inherent face validity – returning the client back to being themselves again. The goal is not to erase the traumatic memory, but rather to become mindful of it but not to such an extent that it significantly interferes with their functioning. There are thus no marketing hurdles in the dissemination of RCBT. There is a very wide range of starting points for the treatment depending on the client's preferences e.g. better managing important relationships, anger. In this way, the RCBT is personalised. In instances where the trauma has been the final tipping point into the development of a personality disorder, it may be more a question of a rebuild CBT rather than restoration CBT, both of which reflect the acronym RCBT.

Treatment in RCBT is personalised further by the recognition that most clients suffer from more than one disorder post-trauma and that all need to be addressed, taking into account any physical limitations such as pain arising from the trauma. Thus, it is not a question of the client squeezing themselves into a trauma or pain centres standard ministrations but the therapist personalises treatment to comprehensively address client need.

Different Stories for Different Disorders

The possible reactions to stress are almost infinite and it is unlikely that the disorders recognised in DSM-5 comprehensively cover all instances of significant functional impairment following a trauma. This is likely to be particularly true of disorders falling under the umbrella of the DSM-5 'Trauma and Stressor Related Disorders' whose only commonality is the term 'stress'. But identifying a specific disorder/s gives a pathway to the CBT treatment of that disorder. The beginning of the journey is marked by explaining to the client how they came to get 'lost' and the directions that they can take. In RCBT, a narrative/storytelling approach is used as much as possible to convey messages. Politicians/religious leaders commonly use metaphors to convey their messages knowing that they are more likely to move people rather than relying on some logical explanation. CBT can be conducted at two levels the Beckian level of discrete automatic thoughts or at 'chunkier' level of metaphors/roles. Most clients find the latter more acceptable but some prefer the scientific/logical approach epitomised by Beck. It is not a question of either metaphor or logical reasoning but of utilising both, the particular admixture employed by the therapist should depend on the particular client, making treatment personalised.

Adjustment Disorder and Specific Phobias

Adjustment disorders and specific phobias can go undiagnosed, at least in part because the person regards their reactions to the trauma as normal. Initially, they may employ their own coping strategies and expect time, as with their physical injuries, to be a great healer. Oftentimes, they do not pathologise their reaction and are in effect waiting for the storm to pass. It is important to distinguish being in the storm e.g. Nursing staff working through the pandemic, from storm damage which can only be properly assessed post the storm. Adjustment disorders and specific phobias are descriptors in the domain of storm damage.

But when such cases come to the notice of professionals they are most often given descriptors such as 'post-traumatic symptoms', 'possible depression' or if multiple physical enquiries have not revealed a source for their difficulties, 'a somatic disorder'. Unfortunately, such labels are often 'sticky', passed on without question and the danger is that psychological treatment is built on these 'fuzzy' constructs.

The importance of risk-taking to recovery can be highlighted using metaphors such as (a) COVID-19, which has involved calculated risk-taking for everyone, e.g. a medic going to work but not in Intensive Care and therefore not provided with full Personal Protective Equipment (PPE), running a risk of infection and (b) car driving with its inherent risks, the tentativeness of the learner driver, the fearfulness of the newly qualified driver and the veteran who gets from 'A' to 'B' without knowing how they got there. Thus, the CBT is restorative but not without the cost of graded risk-taking. The choice of story used should be matched to the client, e.g. a Care Home Worker is likely to relate more easily to the COVID narrative but the key point is to negate risk aversion, this latter means increased tolerance of uncertainty.

A first step in the assessment is to clarify the coping strategies employed and their utility. What has been gained by employing the strategies and what has been lost? This is a prelude to distilling 'maybe better ways of playing it', building in a review date, giving space for naturally occurring readjustments to occur. But, if there is ongoing avoidance of engaging in a pre-trauma activity, this may restrict their work life and/or social functioning. The therapist can suggest it need not become the established 'new norm' and a new road map can be established in which the client gradually dares to do what they did before, 'to get back to their old selves'. But first, they have to practice being a child again, daring to do things to get their confidence. The ill-effects of a child never having the opportunity to do dares can be readily appreciated by most clients. Behaving more like a child with respect to what they avoid involves mental time travel, recalling their own dares that may not have been approved of by parents. As such it introduces an element of fun/humour into efforts to restore themselves. Children or grandchildren can be invited to monitor their completion of dares and decisions made about appropriate sanctions for not doing the homework! For the more scientifically minded client, dares can be regarded as an acronym for **d**on't **a**void **r**ealistic **e**xperiment**s** and are the behavioural experiments of traditional CBT, testing out the validity of hypotheses about fear. The 'dares' implicitly challenge the weighting given by the client to the likely losses of approaching normal behaviour and help to crystalise possible gains. So that the client realises that ultimately there is more to be gained from constructive risk-taking than loss. But this is only feasible in an environment that could be regarded as safe for the community.

With traditional exposure therapy for specific phobias, the response rate is about 50% (Loerinc et al., 2015) but a study by McGlade and Craske (2021) suggests that this can be enhanced by imaginary rehearsal between sessions. In this procedure, clients are asked (a) to remember what was involved in the 'dare', (b) to consider the gap between their expectations when they did a 'dare' with the actual experience and (c) to summarise what they had learnt from the experience by distilling two or three differences between the expectations and the experiences. This new memory of what happens in the feared situation may thereby be rendered more accessible than the original traumatic memory.

Post-traumatic Stress Disorder

Therapists can be guided by the simple model of Adult PTSD (Scott, 2020) in Fig. 5.1.

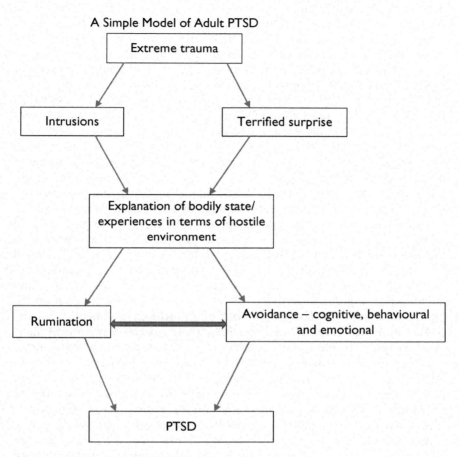

Figure 5.1 A Simple Model of Adult PTSD.

In Fig. 5.1, extreme trauma, produces intrusions of the event, in the form of flashbacks and/ or dreams of the trauma. If this is coupled with a state of terrified surprise, comprising of hypervigilance and an exaggerated startle response, it can lead to an explanation of the bodily state e.g. tension and experiences e.g. flashbacks, in terms of a hostile environment. This in turn can lead to widespread avoidance. This avoidance likely has three dimensions (1) emotional – seeking to avoid re-experiencing anything reminiscent of the emotions that occurred at the time of the trauma, (2) cognitive – blocking thoughts or images of the trauma and (3) behavioural – avoiding anything reminiscent of the trauma. Avoidance is maintained by ruminating about the trauma: how it may have been prevented, 'what ifs', how they may have acted differently, the consequences of the trauma. Rumination is the act by which the trauma is made central to the client's life, the lens through which the personal world is viewed. It has been found to be a strong predictor of PTSD symptoms (Murray et al., 2002) and may also set the scene for avoidance. There is likely a reciprocal interaction between avoidance and rumination. The above model is described as 'simple' because it shows only the development of PTSD, but it is in fact part of a cyclic process, in which the low mood associated with PTSD gives greater access to negative memories, a phenomenon known as mood-dependent recall (Kenealy, 1997), this serves to perpetuate the PTSD. The use of alcohol/drugs to cope with an enduring state of 'terrified surprise', gives a temporary lift in mood, followed by a significant deterioration, which in turn leads to rumination on all misfortunes. The above model is also 'simple' in that it has the most relevance to adults and adolescence, capable of abstraction. With regards to pre-adolescent children, it is more likely that the child feels a pressing need to be attached to a caregiver, is angry at any perceived threat to this attachment and is fearful when he/she considers themselves alone. The child likely has an implicit magical, if erroneous, belief in the care-givers ability to protect. Thus, the intermediary between intrusions/terrified surprise and avoidance in Fig. 5.1 is a perception of abandonment, rather than an explanation of bodily symptoms in terms of a hostile environment.

At a biological level, at least in adults, there is likely a reciprocal interaction between the pre-frontal cortex (PFC), located at the front of the brain and the amygdala, which is located more centrally (Shin et al., 2004). In PTSD, the amygdala (brains alarm) has become hypersensitive but in principle, the PFC can do an override, such that distressing responses to reminders are diluted, reminding the person that the danger is over. Within this model, there is no need for the client to re-experience the trauma per se, simply for the PFC to send a corrective verbal/visual message about the current threat. The new interpretation overrides but does not eliminate the earlier interpretations of stimuli as threatening. The medial prefrontal cortex, amygdala and hippocampus are especially involved in this process (Sotres-Bayon et al., 2006).

Relating the PTSD Story to Clients

The brain's alarm (amygdala) plays a key role in the development and maintenance of PTSD. The amygdala becomes hypersensitive, reacting strongly to any reminder of the trauma. It works on a perceptual matching rather than whether the reminder is conceptually the same. The amygdala's responsiveness to possible threats can be demonstrated by the therapist directing his forefinger towards his/her eye and commenting that he/she blinks despite knowing that he/she would not poke their finger into their eye, the blinking response is connected to the operation of the amygdala. In essence,

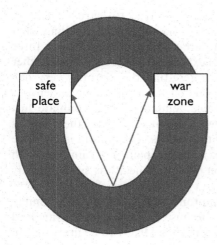

Figure 5.2 Amygdala.

Source: (dodgy alarm).

the PTSD client is described as operating with a 'dodgy alarm', each ringing of the alarm is treated as a true burglary rather than a faulty piece of equipment. It is likened to ringing the police station every time a neighbour's alarm goes off, rather than reflecting, perhaps with some irritation, that the neighbour is simply not good at DIY. Drawing the dodgy alarm as in Fig. 5.2 (the amygdala is almond-shaped) helps the client appreciate that he/she is not losing their mind but that there is an everyday explanation for the core of their difficulties.

Prior to their trauma, the client felt in a 'safe place' (the 10-O'clock position) but since their trauma, their alarm is in the 'war zone' (the 2-O'clock position), in which they are operating with 'war zone glasses' seeing danger everywhere. Minor dangers are imbued with significant threats. The client is in a state of terror, hypervigilant for danger often repeatedly checking things. In the 2-O'clock position, the client is likely very easily startled by unexpected, noises or movements and operates in a state of 'terrified surprise'. The goal of therapy is to remove this sense of being constantly on the edge of their seat, expecting something bad to happen even in benign settings such as sitting in a waiting room. It can be explained that with the alarm in the 2-O'clock position it is easily triggered such that minor irritation, e.g. being in a queue can cause a major outburst e.g. leaving without getting what you were waiting for. The goal of therapy is to reset the alarm. However, this can only be achieved by deliberately tripping the alarm, by a dare, experiencing the discomfort but learning experientially that there is no present danger. In which case, the alarm is nudged anticlockwise, gradually approaching the 12-O'clock position, where the sense of threat is less, perhaps a Field Hospital, but not yet with the security of the safe place depicted by the 10-O'clock position. The client is encouraged to learn from each nudge by Imagery Rehearsal (McGlade & Craske, 2021), i.e. recalling what they did, what they learnt from the last dare and crystalising two or three differences between their expectation and experience. This facilitates further dares. It is explained that the process of resetting the alarm is very like learning to drive two steps forward and one back, so that some patience is necessary. There are inevitably unexpected reminders that debilitate just when the client has been functioning well. Because of this, the client is counselled against being hypercritical of themselves. The mantra is the same as for trying to achieve fitness with exercise 'no pain, no gain'. As with achieving physical fitness, the restoration of mental health is similarly only possible by a gradual approach.

Fig. 5.2 can be used to explain key symptoms of PTSD such as insomnia, impaired concentration and detachment. Because of the threat level involved in being in a 'war zone' sleep and concentration are likely to be impaired. In addition, there is likely to be a strong sense of disconnection from others, because they are talking the language of a safe place and the client that of a war zone – communication is like that of two people who do not understand each other's language. The client wishes to retreat into their own world (bunker) and not be contacted, this can be represented as in Fig. 5.3.

Although the client is determined to constantly seek the sanctuary of the bunker, they experience boredom and isolation when there. The idea behind Figs. 5.2 and 5.3 is as Einstein said that 'everything should be made as simple as possible, but not simpler'.

Panic Disorder

A panic attack may occur at the time of an extreme trauma, it can signal the re-emergence of a previous period of suffering from panic disorder. But it

Figure 5.3 The Bubble/Bunker.

may also be the trauma victims first experience of a panic attack. Some trauma victims have no history of panic disorder and a panic attack may first occur many months post-trauma. In the wake of an extreme trauma, the amygdala (brain's alarm) is implicated in the genesis of the panic attacks. Having been rendered hypersensitive by the extreme trauma, the alarm is set off by any unusual but not abnormal bodily sensation, if these sensations are catastrophically misinterpreted it leads to the persistence of panic disorder (Clark et al., 1999). Thus, a hypersensitive alarm can be triggered externally by any reminder of the trauma but also internally by unusual but not abnormal bodily sensations. Psychoeducation of a traumatised client with panic disorder begins with an explanation of the pivotal role of the amygdala in its development and the role of catastrophic misinterpretation of bodily sensations in its maintenance. Avoidance of situations in which panic attacks have occurred, or are believed likely to occur, stops the client's learning that there is no inherent threat in such situations. Sometimes, panic disorder clients engage in safety behaviours e.g. always ensuring that they are accompanied, but this prevents learning that there is no internal or external threat to their physical integrity. If situations are avoided because of a fear of panic attacks and the person worries about when the next attack will be they will likely also meet the DSM-5 (American Psychiatric Association, 2013) diagnostic criteria for Agoraphobia. For clients with both PTSD and panic disorder, reference to Fig. 5.1 offers a user-friendly way of describing their difficulties. It is a visual aid for decatastrophising unusual bodily sensations. Such 'decatastrophisation' can be underlined further by having the client replicate the attacks by for example vigorous exercise, and learning experientially that the development of such symptoms is not sinister.

Depression

Depression is a common accompaniment of PTSD, with over 50% of the latter cases also suffering from the former. But post-trauma depression may occur in its own right, often a person's physical injuries mean that they are not able to perform the occupational or social role that they performed previously. The loss of a valued role may lead to depression (Champion & Power, 1995), particularly amongst individuals whose sense of worth is bound up with their occupational role. But it may also be the case that a person's injuries prevent them from engaging in important pastimes e.g. cycling, which in turn may have been a major social occasion with friends. Post-trauma depressed clients often have a limited range of activities that they can engage in. This, therefore, means encouraging the client to make additional speculative investments. The client can be given the narrative, of having a sum of money, avoiding 'putting all your eggs in one basket' and seeking to develop a wide-ranging investment portfolio. In this way, ensuring that there are checks and balances in place for the fluctuating profits from any one investment. It can be explained that for the traumatised depressed client, the temptation is to see the world as not worth investing in and to do the equivalent of trying to preserve capital by sticking monies under the carpet, which in turn becomes the victim of inflation. The therapeutic task is to encourage the client to timetable in a variety of small investments, and not to wait until they feel like making an 'investment'.

It can be the case that historically one particular investment in the client's life worked extraordinarily well pre-trauma and there were few if any other investments. In addition, the client may have become very attached to say a particular pre-trauma role and used it to define their identity (an overvalued role; Champion & Power, 1995). This may make it particularly difficult for the client to consider other investments. Therapeutically, there is a conversation to be had about fusing together the sense of worth with a particular role. In essence, the lens of the role is being regarded as central for the determination of worth. The therapist can enquire about what lens they used prior to acquiring the role to gauge their worth and what lenses they use for evaluating the worth of significant others. The therapeutic message to be conveyed is that it is entirely arbitrary to choose a particular role to define worth/identity.

Substance Abuse

Increased substance use post-trauma is commonplace, the client's rationale is often that it helps them get to sleep since. But although it may help them get to sleep quicker, there is no improvement in the quality of the sleep. It should be explained to the client that alcohol is a depressant and that after an initial euphoria they will find it harder to motivate themselves to do everyday tasks, e.g. cleaning, and the guilt at not performing basic roles, enhances depression. Referring to Fig. 5.1, it can be suggested that 'pickling the alarm in alcohol' prevents resetting it. A client's sense of self-efficacy can be enhanced by suggesting a postponement of the time they usually start drinking by say 30–60 minutes, the duration of the postponement is much less important than the realisation that they have some degree of control, that can be gradually amplified. The increased substance use is usually accompanied by increased irritability and alienation from significant others. Occasionally, the client's increased substance use is kept secret but more commonly it has become all too obvious to significant others. Most usually, the increased substance use is a coping strategy for the ongoing sense of vulnerability/threat.

If a client has had no days without excessive substance use since the trauma or if withdrawal symptoms have been so severe that they resumed excessive use, the client should be encouraged to seek medication from his/ her GP to make withdrawal easier. Traditionally, substance abuse services have been separated from psychological therapy services, this has led to attempts to treat disorders sequentially. But concurrent treatment may lead to better results.

Pain and Disfigurement

Like substance abuse services pain management services, at least in the UK, are usually located separately from psychological therapy services, resulting in a sequential, stepwise approach, but many clients default between steps. Whilst it is useful to have a Pain Management specialist to manage medication, the associated psychological therapy service is usually not broad enough in focus to treat a psychological disorder, rather the focus is somewhat narrower on the management of pain. It can be explained to the client that because pain and emotion affect each other, it is useful to have a focus on both in therapy. To clarify the reciprocal interaction of pain and emotion, the client can be invited to consider having a bad headache, then receiving a telephone call that they have won the National Lottery, for a time at least the person would not be noticing their headache. This example also makes it clear that at least for mild and moderate levels of pain distraction is useful. But it is unlikely that a distraction strategy will eradicate the pain rather the most likely scenario is that it will reduce the severity.

Sullivan et al. (1998) found that the total score on their Pain Catastrophising Scale (PCS) predicted the pain intensity, perceived disability and employment status over and above any anxiety and depression and controlling for the initial intensity of pain. The PCS has three sub-scales, rumination, magnification and helplessness. The rumination score was the best predictor of pain and disability. The items comprising the rumination subscale 'I anxiously want the pain to go away', 'I can't seem to keep it out of my mind, 'I keep thinking about how much it hurts' and 'I keep thinking about how badly I want the pain to stop', would appear to reflect according to the pain a centrality. An exemplar of helplessness would be a client who believes that the pain is always intense and unmanageable. As an antidote to this clients can be encouraged to monitor their activities and levels of pain, rating the latter on a 0–10 point scale where a 10 is the worst pain imaginable. This usually reveals that sometimes their pain is worse than others and that the severity can be affected by what they do e.g. a hot bath, singing to favourite music.

Clients with pain can be inclined to make pain central to their life by waiting to feel relatively pain free before becoming active. This in turn tends to lead to 'blitzing' activities on 'good days', then feeling greater pain on succeeding days, 'until the sun comes out again' when they again 'blitz'. Thus, a repeating cycle of 'boom and bust' is set up, that is reflected in major shifts in mood. A more adaptive strategy is to teach the client to pace themselves i.e. to just do what is achievable on a regular basis, akin to driving a car at its most efficient speed, albeit inevitably straying just above and below the optimum speed. This results in a steadying of mood. But pain/disability may mean that the client becomes unable to discharge an important role such as looking after the physical needs of their severely disabled child. Whilst priority in such circumstances must be in doing what is best for the child this can come at a considerable emotional cost for the parent/carer, with the possibility of sliding into depression.

Disfigurement to varying degrees is a possible consequence of extreme trauma. There is always the danger that the victim defines their worth in terms of the disfigurement. The therapeutic task is to help the client relinquish the centrality accorded to appearance. To some extent, this can be achieved by encouraging the client not to cover up the disfigurement, but there is often an abiding concern that others will evaluate them negatively. When others ask about the origins of the disfigurement, this can cause acute embarrassment and a wish to escape. The treatment options are curtailed if significant others say that they would make similar attempts at concealment if they were disfigured in the same way as the victim. Clients can be helped to look at their disfigurement or disability more objectively, by asking (a) how pre-trauma they would have reacted to a person with such a disfigurement/disability and (b) whether they would have used it as a litmus test of the person's worth. This can then lead to an elaboration of what it is about a person, that makes them valued and whether these characteristics died in their trauma. It may be concluded that in the client's culture appearance is overvalued and a counter-cultural position is needed for a person to celebrate being themselves no matter what exigencies befall them – essentially fostering a notion of intrinsic worth.

The diagnostic label of body dysmorphic disorder (BDD) can be used to denote an exaggerated concern about a minor physical anomaly but the treatment literature on BDD does not relate to a population with acquired disfigurement/disability and so its applicability is in doubt. Traditional treatment for BDD involves exposure and response prevention. There is the added difficulty with the BDD diagnosis as to what constitutes a 'minor anomaly', is it minor to the client, parents, the clinician or the wider culture? Matters are complicated further in that a disfigurement/disability acquired pre-adolescence may acquire a heightened significance many years later in the context of potential intimate relationships, i.e. the significant functional impairment is delayed.

References

Abela, J. R., & D'Alessandro, D. U. (2002). Beck's cognitive theory of depression: A test of the diathesis-stress and causal mediation components. *The British Journal of Clinical Psychology, 41*(Pt 2), 111–128. 10.1348/014466502163912.

American Psychiatric Association. (2013). *Diagnostic and statistical manual of mental disorders* (5th ed.). Washington, D.C.: APA.

Beierl, E. T., Murray, H., Wiedemann, M., Warnock-Parkes E., Wild, J., Stott, R., Grey, N., Clark., D. M. & Ehlers, A. (2021). The relationship between working alliance and symptom improvement in cognitive therapy for posttraumatic stress disorder. *Frontiers in Psychiatry*, 12, 602648. 10.3389/fpsyt.2021.602648.

Berntsen, D., & Rubin, D. C. (2006). The centrality of event scale: A measure of integrating a trauma into one's identity and its relation to post-traumatic stress disorder symptoms. *Behaviour Research and Therapy*, 44, 219–231.

Carroll, L. (1965). *Alice's adventures in wonderland*. London, UK: Macmillan Press.

Champion, L. A., & Power, M. J. (1995). Social and cognitive approaches to depression: Towards a new synthesis. *The British Journal of Clinical Psychology*, *34*(4), 485–503. 10.1111/j.2044-8260.1995.tb01484.x.

Clark, D. M., Salkovskis, P. M., Hackmann, A., Wells, A., Ludgate, J., & Gelder, M. (1999). Brief cognitive therapy for panic disorder: A randomized controlled trial. *Journal of Consulting and Clinical Psychology*, *67*(4), 583–589. 10.1037//0022-006x.67.4.583.

Dalgleish, T. (2004). Cognitive approaches to posttraumatic stress disorder: The evolution of multirepresentational theorizing. *Psychological Bulletin*, *130*(2), 228–260. 10.1037/0033-2909.130.2.228.

Ehlers, A., & Clark, D. M. (2000). A cognitive model of posttraumatic stress disorder. *Behaviour Research and Therapy*, *38*(4), 319–345. 10.1016/s0005-7967(99)00123-0.

Ehlers, A., Hackmann, A., Grey, N., Wild, J., Liness, S., Albert, I., Deale, A., Stott, R., & Clark, D. M. (2014). A randomized controlled trial of 7-day intensive and standard weekly cognitive therapy for PTSD and emotion-focused supportive therapy. *The American Journal of Psychiatry*, *171*(3), 294–304. 10.1176/appi.ajp.2013.13040552.

Gehrt, T. B., Berntsen, D., Hoyle, R. H., & Rubin, D. C. (2018). Psychological and clinical correlates of the Centrality of Event Scale: A systematic review. *Clinical Psychology Review*, 65, 57–80. 10.1016/j.cpr.2018.07.006.

Greenblatt-Kimron, L., Shrira, A., Rubinstein, T., & Palgi, Y. (2021). Event centrality and secondary traumatization among Holocaust survivors' offspring and grandchildren: A three-generation study. *Journal of Anxiety Disorders, 81*, 102401. Advance online publication. 10.1016/j.janxdis.2021.102401.

Kenealy P. M. (1997). Mood-state-dependent retrieval: The effects of induced mood on memory reconsidered. *The Quarterly Journal of Experimental Psychology A, Human Experimental Psychology*, *50*(2), 290–317. 10.1080/713755711.

Kessler, R. C., Sonnega, A., Bromet, E., Hughes, M., & Nelson, C. B. (1995). Posttraumatic stress disorder in the National Comorbidity Survey. *Archives of General Psychiatry*, *52*(12), 1048–1060. 10.1001/archpsyc.1995.03950240066012.

Krebs, G., Fernández de la Cruz, L., & Mataix-Cols, D. (2017). Recent advances in understanding and managing body dysmorphic disorder. *Evidence-based Mental Health*, *20*(3), 71–75. 10.1136/eb-2017-102702.

Larsen, S. E., Fleming, C., & Resick, P. A. (2019). Residual symptoms following empirically supported treatment for PTSD. *Psychological Trauma: Theory, Research, Practice and Policy, 11*(2), 207–215. 10.1037/tra0000384.

Loerinc, A. G., Meuret, A. E., Twohig, M. P., Rosenfield, D., Bluett, E. J., & Craske, M. G. (2015). Response rates for CBT for anxiety disorders: Need for standardized criteria. *Clinical Psychology Review, 42*, 72–82. 10.1016/j.cpr.2015. 08.004.

McGlade, A. L., & Craske, M. G. (2021). Optimizing exposure: Between-session mental rehearsal as an augmentation strategy. *Behaviour Research and Therapy, 139*, 103827. Advance online publication. 10.1016/j.brat.2021.103827.

Maples-Keller, J. L., Rauch, S., Jovanovic, T., Yasinski, C. W., Goodnight, J. M., Sherrill, A., Black, K., Michopoulos, V., Dunlop, B. W., Rothbaum, B. O., & Norrholm, S. D. (2019). Changes in trauma-potentiated startle, skin conductance, and heart rate within prolonged exposure therapy for PTSD in high and low treatment responders. *Journal of Anxiety Disorders, 68*, 102147. 10.1016/ j.janxdis.2019.102147.

Markowitz, J. C., Petkova, E., Neria, Y., Van Meter, P. E., Zhao, Y., Hembree, E., Lovell, K., Biyanova, T., & Marshall, R. D. (2015). Is exposure necessary? A randomized clinical trial of interpersonal psychotherapy for PTSD. *The American Journal of Psychiatry, 172*(5), 430–440. 10.1176/appi.ajp.2014.14070908.

Murray, J., Ehlers, A., & Mayou, R. A. (2002). Dissociation and post-traumatic stress disorder: Two prospective studies of road traffic accident survivors. *The British Journal of Psychiatry: The Journal of Mental Science, 180*, 363–368. 10.11 92/bjp.180.4.363.

Robinaugh, D. J., & McNally, R. J. (2011). Trauma centrality and PTSD symptom severity in adult survivors of childhood sexual abuse. *Journal of Traumatic Stress, 24*(4), 483–486. 10.1002/jts.20656.

Scott., M. J. (2020). Post traumatic stress disorder: An alternative paradigm. *American Journal of Applied Psychology, 9*, 1–6. 10.11648/j.ajap.20200901.11.

Shin, L. M., Orr, S. P., Carson, M. A., Rauch, S. L., Macklin, M. L., Lasko, N. B., … Pitman, R. K. (2004). Regional cerebral blood flow in the amygdala and medial prefrontal cortex during traumatic imagery in male and female Vietnam veterans with PTSD. *Archives of General Psychiatry, 61*(2), 168–176.

Simon, N., Roberts, N. P., Lewis, C. E., van Gelderen, M. J., & Bisson, J. I. (2019). Associations between perceived social support, posttraumatic stress disorder (PTSD) and complex PTSD (CPTSD): Implications for treatment. *European Journal of Psychotraumatology, 10*(1), 1573129. 10.1080/20008198.201 9.1573129.

Sotres-Bayon, F., Cain, C. K., & LeDoux, J. E. (2006). Brain mechanisms of fear extinction: Historical perspectives on the contribution of prefrontal cortex. *Biological Psychiatry, 60*(4), 329–336. 10.1016/j.biopsych.2005.10.012.

Sullivan, M., Stanish, W., Waite, H., Sullivan, M., & Tripp, D. A. (1998). Catastrophizing, pain, and disability in patients with soft-tissue injuries. *Pain, 77*(3), 253–260. 10.1016/S0304-3959(98)00097-9.

Tripp, J. C., Angkaw, A., Schnurr, P. P., Trim, R. S., Haller, M., Davis, B. C., & Norman, S. B. (2020). Residual symptoms of posttraumatic stress disorder and alcohol use disorder following integrated exposure treatment versus coping skills treatment. *Journal of Traumatic Stress, 33*, 477–487. 10.1002/ jts.22552.

Tversky, A., & Kahneman, D. (1973). Availability: A heuristic for judging frequency and probability. *Cognitive Psychology*, *5*, 207–232.

Weathers, F. W., Blake, D. D., Schnurr, P. P., Kaloupek, D. G., Marx, B. P., & Keane, T. M. (2015). *The Clinician-Administered PTSD Scale for DSM-5 (CAPS-5) – Past Month/Worst Month* [Measurement instrument]. Available from https://www.ptsd.va.gov/ https://www.ptsd.va.gov/professional/assessment/adult-int/caps.asp.

Wells, S. Y., Morland, L. A., Torres, E. M., Kloezeman, K., Mackintosh, M. A., & Aarons, G. A. (2019). The development of a brief version of the posttraumatic cognitions inventory (PTCI-9). *Assessment*, *26*(2), 193–208. 10.1177/1073191111 6685401.

Wolitzky-Taylor, K. B., Horowitz, J. D., Powers, M. B., & Telch, M. J. (2008). Psychological approaches in the treatment of specific phobias: A meta-analysis. *Clinical Psychology Review*, *28*(6), 1021–1037. 10.1016/j.cpr.2008.02.007.

Part II

Applying the Centrality Framework

Introduction

In Part 2, of this volume, the reader is introduced to a variety of characters whose vantage point on their trauma and coping responses radically changed during their discourse with the clinician.

1. Terry was abused by a teacher at school, subsequently, his relationships were fraught and he had carried a post-traumatic stress disorder label for most of his adult life.
2. Mary was preoccupied that she and her daughter could have been killed when they collided with an HGV, her subsequent fear of driving meant that she felt unable to apply for a permanent teaching post at another school. Attendance at a trauma stabilisation group was recommended but she was only able to make two sessions, because of her job and childcare demands. Treatment via a video link was arranged.
3. Ann was with her Mum on a bus which braked sharply, they were both thrown about, her agoraphobia intensified, and she began binge eating.
4. Simon thought he was going to die when he was attacked by a group of young men, had a panic afterwards and became effectively housebound.
5. Paul was hit by a crane on a building site he was subsequently unable to do manual work and was concerned that he was letting down his children. Matters were compounded by his abuse of alcohol and the lower back pain that he had suffered since. He had dropped out of a pain management group.

Their journey back to their old selves/best functioning is narrated in the following chapters. These cases are amalgams of actual cases, covering a wide spectrum of traumas. They can serve as templates that can be drawn upon in constructing a treatment plan for almost any trauma victim. However, it is not painting by numbers, artistry in their creative use is called for and there likely will be gaps that call for clinical ingenuity.

DOI: 10.4324/9781003178132-7

The clients are assisted on their journey by reference to various sections of the self-help book, *Moving On After Trauma* (Scott, 2008). The first chapter highlights the common reactions to trauma, and the reader can follow the journey of any of the 19 characters that they might identify with through treatment. In the second chapter of *Moving On After Trauma*, the reader is introduced to the 'dodgy alarm', 'the bubble' and a pictorial representation of the emotional numbness experienced by many traumatised clients. Thus, the first two chapters of *Moving On After Trauma* are primarily concerned with psychoeducation. Later chapters deal with the management of mood, restoring relationships and the management of pain and disfigurement. The book is a useful adjunct to restorative CBT. Familiarity with it during treatment, helps the client to feel that they are not as abnormal as they thought and it can be a reference for clients post-treatment. Importantly, it also helps the client's support network to understand what he/she is going through thereby facilitating social support.

The formulation is held to be the bridge between assessment and treatment (Macneil et al., 2012) and to involve consideration of the five P's, presenting problem, predisposing factors, precipitating factors, perpetuating factors and protective/positive factors. The trauma is a particular exemplar of a precipitating factor. But a focus on the 'presenting problem' is in practice not as simple as it sounds, as Macneil et al. (2012) illustrate a person meeting the criteria for a diagnosis of borderline personality disorder may variously have problems with maintaining employment, erratic friendships and physical health complications from self-harm. Despite this, the UK Government Improving Access to Psychological Therapies (IAPT) programme use a 'problem descriptor' to determine treatment (IAPT Manual, 2019). IAPT uses problem descriptors to determine what treatment to give to whom. But problem descriptors are a rule of thumb to determine treatment. In randomised controlled trials, treatment was based on a reliable diagnosis, which would typically take an hour or more to determine. IAPT has come up with a problem descriptor shortcut of undetermined reliability and which it seeks to legitimate by asking the therapist to provide an ICD-10 code. The IAPT Manual considers it as a best practice if a service provides an ICD-10 code for at least 80% of cases. But this would leave one in five people with rudderless treatment. When clients are assigned an ICD-10 code, it is usually a single code and a Manager may advise that another code is appropriate rather than the one the clinician selects. Whilst the IAPT Manual advises that more than one code can be appropriate, it also advises that treatment should be dictated by the principal problem, this likely has the effect of making for single awards of ICD-10 codes.

The IAPT Manual claims that ICD-10 codes are the basis of the NICE recommended treatments, but they are not. Most of the mental health trials considered by NICE are based on the more reliable and stricter DSM criteria. Notwithstanding this ICD-10 provides diagnostic criteria for each disorder, but IAPT also contends that it does not make diagnosis. It is therefore difficult to escape the conclusion that IAPT pays lip service to ICD-10 codes for its' own credibility. Despite this, the IAPT Manual insists that the treatment protocol should follow the identified problem but the protocols have never been matched to problems but to disorders.

There is no empirical basis for highlighting the importance of one problem over another. The therapist may resolve matters by translating 'Presenting Problem' as the 'Chief Complaint', in order to highlight a particular treatment pathway. But this translation may represent an imposition of the clinician's definition of the situation. Clients can be involved by asking them how they would like things to be different in the various domains. Whilst this is acknowledging the client's preferences, a leg in the three-legged stool that comprises evidence-based practice, it still does not direct treatment along any particular pathway. It is rather like a group of Ramblers out for a Sunday walk, discussing where to next, the pub in the next village, the completion of the walk etc. Further, as the work of Kiefer et al. (2020) indicates the chief complaint/presenting problem is often a non-trauma-related disorder even though a trauma-related disorder is present. Persons (2015) helpfully points out that 'the disorder-focussed literature provides cognitive-behavioural conceptualisations of disorders that can be used as templates for formulating and designing treatment for individual cases'. But predisposing factors such as intolerance of uncertainty, addiction to approval, low self-esteem and abusive childhood may help flag up additionalpathways. However, the weighting to be given to the likely multiplicity of predisposing factors is not clear. Being directed by the first 2P's is akin to a lost motorist, stopping to ask people the way, rather than relying on his/her SatNav, albeit that the latter is by no means infallible. The nature of the third P, though an important consideration for the client's story does not inevitably point in a specific treatment direction, e.g. if the client experiences an extreme trauma such as torture, it does not inevitably mean that they will need treatment for PTSD. The range of factors that may perpetuate the 'Presenting problem' is extensive including cognitive, behavioural and emotional avoidance, absence of perceived social support, financial/health problems and substance abuse. The very breadth of information generated by the first 4P's can induce a 'freeze' response in a therapist or a headlong flight into action, that minimises the complexity of the data. Organisationally, the imperative may be to be seen to do something. The fifth 'P' is protective/positive factors, given that social support (or at least perceived social support) is a predictor of outcome in disorders such as PTSD and depression, it may be important to include significant others in treatment to act as therapists in the community.

The above considerations suggest that overall 'formulation' is a somewhat fuzzy process and that the likely effect on the outcome would be uncertain. Flinn et al. (2015) identified four studies relating to the inter-rater reliability of cognitive-behavioural formulations and found that in one study there was virtually no reliability (a kappa between 0 and 0.1), in two studies the kappa was between 0.1 and 0.6 (slight to moderate reliability) and in one study there was substantial reliability (a kappa between 0.81 and 1.0). The British Psychological Society (2011) suggested that the very modest inter-rater reliability of formulation might be improved by grounding it with a more comprehensive assessment system, such as including review of records so that there are multiple sources of data to draw upon. In this context, drawing upon the results of a standardised semi-structured diagnostic interview as Persons (2015) recommends may give a firmer base so that it is not so much formulation that is seen as pivotal between assessment and treatment, but 'case' formulation i.e. in what way is the individual a specific exemplar of the disorder in question. In this way, there would not be a single formulation but a case formulation for each disorder. If say three disorders were identified, each represented on x, y and z axes and each at right angles to each other, then the individual would occupy a particular point in a 3D space. The progression (trajectory) of the client through therapy would be charted by interventions that were applied simultaneously, but each of them would be a treatment strategy pertinent to the identified axis. A similar, but simpler charting could apply to a client with two identified disorders i.e. the client could be conceived as being located at a particular point in a 2D space. The charting prevents the relegation of co-morbid disorders but is more difficult if the co-morbidity is more.

Comorbidity is the norm in routine practice, a study of attendees at a UK Government IAPT service (Hepgul et al., 2016) found that 58% had three or more current emotional disorder diagnoses and 14% two current emotional disorder diagnoses. This comorbidity is even more extensive when personality disorders are considered. In routine practice, clients are not screened for the presence of a personality disorder, but Zimmerman et al. (2005) found that in a population of psychiatric outpatients almost one-third had one or more of the DSM-5 personality disorders. The prevalence of avoidant personality disorder in the Zimmerman et al. (2005) study was 14.7%, borderline personality disorder 9.3% and antisocial personality disorder 3.6%. Hepgul et al. (2016) found similar levels of the prevalences of the two personality disorders that they assessed for, 4% for antisocial personality disorder and 16% for borderline personality disorder. The prevalence of any personality disorder in those with major depression was 51.3%, generalised anxiety disorder 63.9% and panic disorder 55.6% (Zimmerman et al., 2005). Without knowing the base rates for accompanying disorder, the clinician is working in a therapeutic tunnel. Treatment that focusses on just one disorder is likely to leave the client short-changed. But so is a treatment that takes no account of the possible presence of a personality disorder. Missing both comorbid emotional disorders and personality disorders is likely to have deleterious consequences. This may be reflected by the fact that in the study by Hepgul et al. (2016) almost four in ten (38%) of those presenting were on their second or more IAPT episode, with a median duration of illness of seven months. The formulation and diagnosis are not once and for-all-time events, rather they are provisional hypotheses that might well have to be reviewed if progress is not made.

References

British Psychological Society. (2011). *Good practice guidelines on the use of psychological formulation.* Leicester, UK: Author.

Flinn, L., Braham, L., & das Nair, R. (2015). How reliable are case formulations? A systematic literature review. *The British Journal of Clinical Psychology, 54*(3), 266–290. 10.1111/bjc.12073.

Hepgul, N., King, S., Amarasinghe, M., Breen, G., Grant, N., Grey, N., Hotopf, M., Moran, P., Pariante, C. M., Tylee, A., Wingrove, J., Young, A. H., & Cleare, A. J. (2016). Clinical characteristics of patients assessed within an Improving Access to Psychological Therapies (IAPT) service: Results from a naturalistic cohort study (Predicting Outcome Following Psychological Therapy; PROMPT). *BMC Psychiatry, 16*, 52. 10.1186/s12888-016-0736-6.

IAPT Manual. (2019). The improving access to psychological therapies manual National Collaborating Centre for Mental Health.

Kiefer, R., Chelminski, I., Dalrymple, K., & Zimmerman, M. (2020). Principal diagnoses in psychiatric outpatients with posttraumatic stress disorder: Implications for screening recommendations. *Journal of Nervous and Mental Disorders, 208*, 283–287. 10.1097/NMD.0000000000001131. PMID: 32221181.

Macneil, C. A., Hasty, M. K., Conus, P., & Berk, M. (2012). Is diagnosis enough to guide interventions in mental health? Using case formulation in clinical practice. *BMC Medicine, 10*, 111. 10.1186/1741-7015-10-111.

Persons, J. B. (2015). Developing and using a case formulation to guide cognitive-behaviour therapy. *Journal of Psychology and Psychotherapy, 5*, 179. 10.4172/21 61-0487.1000179.

Scott, M. J. (2008). *Moving on after trauma.* London: Routledge.

Zimmerman, M., Rothschild, L., & Chelminski, I. (2005). The prevalence of DSM-IV personality disorders in psychiatric outpatients. *The American Journal of Psychiatry, 162*(10), 1911–1918. 10.1176/appi.ajp.162.10.1911.

Chapter 6

Re-visiting the Implications of the Trauma

It is the norm for people not to want to talk about their worst experiences. The evidence is that most people experience an extreme trauma at some point in their life and clinicians should therefore expect that people do not want to talk about their trauma. It is not appropriate to view a reluctance to talk about an extreme trauma as evidence of pathology. From an evolutionary perspective, it is unlikely that a maladaptive coping response should have been so universally adopted. Thus, as clients seek to provide a context for their distress, upset in the assessment interview is likely to be par for the course. This requires a light touch, rather than an exhortation 'to get it all out, talk it through, fully process it'.

In this chapter, a client's first take on their trauma, its implication for their view of themselves and their personal world is explored. This is followed by the distillation of an alternative narrative, created by questioning the validity, utility and authority by which the account is held. The alternative narrative is canvassed as the better window through which to view themselves and their personal world and its similarities to the pre-trauma perspective are underlined. Thus, repairing the ruptured sense of 'I'.

The classic dictum underlying cognitive behaviour therapy is that 'men are disturbed not by things, but by the views which they take of things', this is attributed to the Stoic Philosopher Epictetus, (The Enchiridion Epictetus translated by Higginson (2020)). Epictetus discussed this in the context of death, but there is no special case made for extreme trauma i.e. there is no anticipation that the response to such events would be qualitatively different from other adversities. Epictetus was born into slavery and endured a permanent physical disability. In essence, the Stoic philosophers were 'centralists' in taking the person's view of matters as playing a pivotal role in distress. Unlike the trauma-focussed CBT theorists, the ancient Stoic philosophers did not see the distress as originating in the particulars of the adversity.

An extreme trauma can mark the beginning of a new chapter in a person's life, and the ensuing story can have a nightmarish quality. To such an extent that the person may become suicidal. A reliable risk assessment has

DOI: 10.4324/9781003178132-8

therefore to be an integral part of the assessment of any trauma victim and is addressed next. But care has to be taken that the vividness of the trauma, complete with sensory details, can make it an easily accessible explanation of all that follows, when it may be only a partial explanation, given the client's pre-trauma history.

Risk Assessment

A risk assessment is held to be a component of a 'good assessment' (IAPT Manual, 2019 p23), whatever the diagnosis. But there is no guidance in the IAPT Manual as to how risk is to be assessed. Vail et al. (2012) observed 'that IAPT clinicians did not have set procedures or questions for assessing mental health risk, and were flexible in the approaches they adopted. They often relied on their own clinical judgement and experience about how to approach the topic of mental health risk'.

Routinely, the IAPT Service administers the PHQ9 (Kroenke et al., 2001), item 9 on this measure, is referred to as the suicide item, and is scored from 0 to 3, in response to the question, 'How often have you been bothered by thoughts that you would be better off dead or of hurting yourself in some way?' Possible responses include 'not at all' (0), 'several days' (1), 'more than half the days' (2) and 'nearly every day' (3) over the past two weeks. A score of 1–3 would at face value indicate suicide risk, and Na et al. (2018) found that 41.1% of patients on a depression register scored greater than 0. This would mean a very high proportion of clients are at risk and in need of monitoring/support, placing a very heavy burden on Emergency Mental Health Assessment Units and A & E Departments. However, Scott (2018) examined 90 cases going through IAPT and found that in only three cases, there was mention of risk in the documentation. Thus, in practice, item 9 is rarely the springboard for action.

The question posed by item 9 is itself ambiguous, mixing passive thoughts of death and the desire for self-harm in a single response item. Further, the past two-week time-frame of the PHQ-9 is unnecessarily restrictive, the persons long-term history has to be carefully considered because there is a 25–30% chance that after one suicide attempt there will be another in 1–2 years (DSM-5; American Psychiatric Association, 2013). In the Na et al. (2018) study, the same subjects were asked the following:

1.   Have you started to work out or worked out details of how to kill yourself? Do you intend to carry out this plan?
2.   Have you made a suicide attempt – purposely tried to harm yourself with at least some intention to end your life?
3.   Have you taken any steps to prepare to kill yourself or actually started to do something to end your life or were stopped before you actually did anything?

When a positive response to any of the above three questions (which are part of the gold standard for indicating suicidal behaviour) was taken as indicative of potential suicide, the proportion of potentially suicidal subjects was only 13.4%, i.e. three times less. Thus, the use of the PHQ-9 by itself is not a reliable indicator of suicidal behaviour.

The semi-structured standardised diagnostic interviews DIAMOND (Tolin et al., 2018) and the MINI (Sheehan et al., 1998) each contain their own suicide screens, which permit a determination of low, moderate and severe risk of suicide. The QuickSCID-5 (First & Williams, 2021) has an Overview section in which questions are asked about active and passive suicidal behaviour.

Overview

It emerged from an open-ended overview that Terry was sexually abused over a period of months by a teacher at school when he was aged 12. Afterwards, he gave up his involvement with musical instruments and became disruptive in class. By age 15, he was using cannabis and by 19 cocaine, his substance abuse continued for a decade. In his late 20s, he disclosed to a psychiatrist that he had been abused. However, though he often had thoughts that he would be dead in his 20s, he had not made a suicide attempt or had he planned one and been interrupted. He had never been considered a suicide risk. It was concluded that he had post-traumatic stress disorder in relation to the abuse and that he was also suffering from depression. He was prescribed antidepressants and helped with managing withdrawal symptoms from cocaine and cannabis. Terry had support from a female cousin and was in a long-term relationship with a supportive partner with whom he had two children. However, he was very anxious around people and minimised social contact. Terry worked as a taxi driver interspersed with lengthy periods of lethargy. He said that he had had several goes at counselling but to no avail, though the therapists were 'nice enough'.

Diagnostic Interview

Having completed the SCID Overview (First et al., 2016) interview, the therapist went through the diagnostic modules that were indicated by the open-ended interview, PTSD and depression. Terry said that he had 'flashbacks' of his abuse, but when asked how often he said they are always there, the therapist (Th) sought to clarify matters:

Th: By flashbacks, I was meaning pictures of the abuse popping into your mind, sometimes for no reason.

Client: I just go off on one thinking about it.

Th: How do you mean 'go off on one'?

Client: Well, I am ok one minute, then I start thinking about what happened, if interrupted, I'm like a bear with a sore head, then later I feel so guilty.

Th: What about nightmares of the abuse?

Client: As I am going asleep, I sometimes think about it and I have had problems with sleep since then.

Th: Are you woken by nightmares of the abuse?

Client: I was for months after it happened and started wetting the bed, I was so embarrassed, my brother mocked me for it, he told friends at school, I never lived it down.

In the above exchange, Terry's concerns appear more to be with depressive rumination about the abuse rather than the symptoms of intrusion that relate to PTSD, but he was avoidant of social situations. He thought himself worthless – 'ashamed, should have done something about what happened' – i.e. he was suffering from trauma-related guilt. Terry saw adults as a threat, had problems with irritability and insomnia. In many respects, he appeared prototypical of a person with PTSD, but he was not in a state of terrified surprise. At the time of his assessment, there was building work going on outside the office, the conversation was punctuated by the sound of an electric drill, but Terry had no exaggerated startle response and simply observed that the structures being erected reminded him of when he used to work on a building site, losing the job for poor attendance. He had no hypervigilance. In his previous counselling, he was told that he needed to work through his abuse and express all his feelings about it. But he found knowing that he would have to discuss the abuse put him off attending and after attending he usually felt worse and dropped out. The therapist commented:

Th: Don't want to go down same route as previous therapists, but got to find ways of stopping stuff from the past getting in the way of your life.

Client: I think I have been broken by what happened.

Th: But maybe not broken beyond repair.

Client: How do you mean?

Th: What is there to stop you spending a few minutes playing the keyboard or drawing as you did before the abuse?

Client: It seems so trivial compared to all I've got going on, have difficulty getting enough money to pay for the petrol to get down here.

Th: We could space out the sessions a bit more if that would help?

Client: I could see making myself making excuses if they are too spaced out.

Th: Like what

Client: That you are not really interested.

At this stage in the interview, the therapist is fairly clear that a trauma-focussed CBT treatment would not be appropriate and that it is doubtful that Terry meets the criteria for PTSD. The therapist shares this with him:

Th: I don't think that post-traumatic stress disorder is the right description for what you are suffering.

Client: I have Googled it and it seems right.

Th: You have certainly got some of the symptoms of PTSD but not the whole package and it may be why previous talking therapy hasn't worked for you.

Client: That's a bit of a relief but I was reading about this Complex PTSD that those who have been abused suffer.

Th: But there are key bits of the Complex PTSD jigsaw missing such as flashbacks/nightmares and terrified surprise, that even though some bits of the jigsaw fit, such as irritability and insomnia, it is not the overall picture. My take is that you do look at life through the lens of the abuse and this greatly affects your relationships and what you think of yourself. I thought we might make a start, by you doing some little things that can remind you that you are still you despite the abuse.

Client: Some drawing and keyboard playing.

Th: Yes, restoring and updating you for starters, maybe bring in your partner so she can help with the update. I think I know a useful direction to start but the direction might be clearer after our next session.

In this first session, the therapist is keen to point that whilst no definitive diagnosis has yet been made, there is nevertheless a useful footpath along which to start the therapeutic journey. Further, it is one that is substantially different from previous therapeutic efforts with Terry. Although the prime focus of the first interview is assessment, assessment and treatment are interlocking strands throughout restorative CBT (RCBT) treatment. Thus, even in this first session, there is the distillation of homework, involving the rediscovery of pre-trauma pleasures.

At the end of the session, the therapist felt that it had been an unusually exhausting and felt somewhat negative towards him. The therapist began to mull over Terry's comment about (a) therapists 'not being really interested', (b) a theme of at least ambivalence to engaging in previous treatments and (c) not persisting with treatment or work. Whilst the therapist felt that depression was clearly present and felt justified in this because Terry had been on and off antidepressants for almost 30 years, there was a sense in which this was not the whole story. At the next interview, the therapist was pleased and surprised that Terry had spent some time playing his keyboard and enjoyed it. However, he said that his partner could not make the appointment because of work commitments. The therapist re-iterated his invitation for her to attend because he had a sense that his interpersonal difficulties were at the heart of his problems.

With this in mind, the therapist asked Terry's permission to clarify, what the pattern of his relationships was. For this, the therapist used the questions in the SCID-5-PD interview (First et al., 2016) for avoidant personality disorder:

Th: Do you believe that you're not as good, as smart, or as attractive as most other people?

Client: Yes

Th: Tell me about that.

Client: Never held down a job for any length of time, flit and float, but I was good at school, well at least before the abuse. Look at me now, so overweight could have a heart attack, a slob smoking cigarettes, well she only allows me to smoke in the garden for the sake of the kids.

Th: So you suffer the cold of the garden for the kids.

Client: Yes, I suppose so, I drop them off at school and collect them because she is working.

Th: Have you avoided jobs or tasks that involved having to deal with a lot of people?

Client: Yes, I try and drop the kids off at school at the last moment so I don't have to talk to other parents in the school playground, sometimes they end up late because I cut it too fine.

Th: Is it because you just don't like to be around people or is it because you are afraid of being criticised or rejected?

Client: I just don't do people.

Th: How far back does that go?

Client: All my adult life, in teenage years just did drugs.

Th: What about before that?

Client: I was a happy kid always got on with my cousin still do.

In the above exchange, the diagnostic questions for an avoidant personality disorder are slotted in very naturally into the conversation. The therapist is not content with monosyllabic responses but seeks examples of what might be an avoidant personality disorder pattern, such as avoiding taking the initiative in social relationships.

Avoidant personality disorder is the most common of the personality disorders, occurring in 14.7% of psychiatric outpatients, followed by borderline personality disorder 9.3% with almost a third meeting diagnostic criteria for at least one of the 10 DSM personality disorders (Zimmerman et al., 2005). A UK study by Hepgul et al. (2016) of the clinical characteristics of clients attending the Improving Access to Psychological Therapies (IAPT) found that 16% had a borderline personality disorder. Yet, a personality disorder descriptor was not mentioned at all in the records of 90 IAPT-treated clients in a study by Scott (2018). A service cannot meet the needs of an unidentified population.

The SCID-5-PD offers both categorical e.g. avoidant PD/not avoidant PD and dimensional characterisations of personality disorder e.g. for avoidant PD the scale goes from 0 to 14. The dimensional approach recognises that there is no qualitative difference between those with and without a personality disorder and that we are all located at varying points on the scales that comprise each of the ten personality disorders described in the DSM. Terry furnished many examples of a 'pervasive pattern of social inhibition, feelings of inadequacy and hypersensitivity to negative evaluation, beginning by early adulthood and present in a variety of contexts' (First et al., 2016) such that he met criteria for avoidant personality disorder. This was relayed to Terry thus:

Th: It seems that you always expect people to be critical of you and you do a runner when they get near.

Client: It seems daft when you put it like that, makes me think of the Road Runner, Bugs Bunny cartoons the kids have been watching on their Tablet, but you are right.

Th: *Laughing* if you are the 'Road Runner' who is after you?

Client: Can't remember the name of the character who does the chasing, I was ok when I was the kid's age, but it all changed with the bedwetting and being skitted in school.

Th: It seems that you see the people you meet as the teenagers that skitted and bullied you in disguise?

Client: It seems crazy, if it hadn't been for that teacher, I wouldn't be in this mess.

Th: The mess is that you developed an avoidant personality disorder but the good news that we should be able to teach how to stop it getting in the way and become more like your pre-abuse self.

Client: It is like I don't know him, it was someone else.

Th: Well, you have clearly changed since then, your bigger, heavier, deeper voice but you are still you.

Client: Felt a bit like that doing keyboard and drawing.

In the above conversation, the therapist has presented Terry with a working model of how his difficulties have arisen. There is a normalising of his symptoms by using the diagnosis of avoidant personality disorder. But the use of a personality disorder diagnosis does not imply that is a permanent immutable feature of a person, albeit that this was the original conceptualisation of these disorders. The model shared with Terry is so simple that it carries fairly obvious treatment implications. Further, the personality disorder descriptor has not alienated him. An alternative diagnosis of social anxiety disorder was considered and rejected because Terry did not think that any particular aspect of him was under scrutiny and evaluation by others. Thus, the treatment foci were on his depression and avoidant personality disorder.

Treatment

Beck (2015) has noted that the personality disorders are distinguished by their differing cognitive content with the exception of borderline personality disorder where a cognitive process, dichotomous thinking, is held to be the hallmark. He has identified a cognitive profile for each personality disorder, summarised under the headings **View of Self** *(Core beliefs) e.g. for Avoidant PD 'socially inferior', 'I'm unlovable',* **View of Others** *(core beliefs) e.g. for Avoidant PD critical, demeaning 'they look down on me',* **Conditionallpredictive and imperative beliefs** *e.g. for Avoidant PD 'if people notice me, they will reject humiliate me'* **Overdeveloped strategies** *e.g. for Avoidant escape and* **Underdeveloped strategies** *e.g. for Avoidant social risk-taking.*

Terry's functioning is aptly described by the mentioned earlier exemplars of Beck's cognitive profile of avoidant personality disorder. Treatment was guided by this cognitive profile. Terry's view of himself as 'unlovable' was based on his conclusion that he should have stopped the abuse earlier by reporting to the teacher. He used his feelings of guilt and shame as the litmus test of his worth. The therapist explained that trauma-related guilt (TRG) is common after extreme trauma, such as surviving a car accident in which a fellow passenger died, but that these are bogus guilt feelings because no choice is involved. In a similar way, his TRG should be regarded as a 'mental cold' irritating but of no significance. However, his guilt/shame feelings remained central to his sense of self. The therapist suggested that he was too naive at the time to be able to do anything other than he did, but this had no impact on the session, but at the next session he reported:

Terry: Looked at a picture of myself taken around the time of the abuse, I was just a skinny kid.

Therapist: Doing the mental time travel, going back to then, there was never a Terry with the knowledge you have now as an adult.

Terry: No, I probably still believed in Father Christmas.

Therapist: Maybe when you feel low see a set of traffic lights on red, shout stop, when the lights go to amber ask yourself, 'am I picking up a way of looking at myself from the past, that doesn't really make sense today?'

Terry: Bit like thinking Father Christmas could deliver all the presents this Christmas.

Therapist:	Yes, before you move off ask yourself, based on all the evidence what would be a better way of looking at yourself?
Terry:	It is like I have hung myself for a minor traffic offence.
Therapist:	Yes, when the lights go to green do something that would give you a sense of achievement or pleasure.
Terry:	I could draw some traffic lights as a reminder, but also maybe of Father Christmas deliveries or maybe of me hanging the young Terry, hmm that's a bit gruesome.
Therapist:	They say a picture is worth a thousand words, doing some drawings on these seems a great idea.
Terry:	Could even get the kids to do some traffic lights.
Therapist:	Could get them to use them on you when you are getting angry over nothing, it's just Stop, Think, Go.

In this exchange, the therapist is using imagery as much as cognitive re-structuring to bring about change. The RCBT uses narrative as much as challenging logical reasoning. Importantly, the target is not the details of the abuse per se but what the client takes it to mean about functioning today. The hallmark of the personality disorders is managing interpersonal distance. This can make the management of the therapeutic alliance particularly difficult and therapy is often more protracted, as the following dialogue reveals.

Terry:	Thanks for getting back to me when I missed the sessions, the first one I missed because I couldn't afford the petrol. Then I just got depressed, financial problems, relying on my partner.
Therapist:	You can rely on your partner.
Terry:	Yes, she's good, don't know how she puts up with me, I don't even see the traffic lights, go off like a firework.
Therapist:	How do you know that there can't be other good people out there?
Terry:	Well, there's my cousin who I grew up with.
Therapist:	What about doing some dares with people, to give them a chance (social risk-taking).
Terry:	Instead of spending all my time in my bunker where I'm as bored as hell
Therapist:	Perhaps, start in the school playground just commenting on the weather to other parents.
Terry:	As you say it, it doesn't seem that big a deal but to me it's massive.
Therapist:	Maybe get your partner, to keep a record of your social dares, she could also give you yellow or red cards if you don't use the traffic lights.

Terry: (laughing) For a red card, I could have to sit on the naughty step at the bottom of the stairs, the kids would love that.

Therapist: Learning to use the traffic lights for anger is like learning to do hill starts when learning to drive, one week you can do it, the next week you can't, but if you persevere you gradually get there.

Terry: I am an all or nothing person either I get it right or it's rubbish.

Therapist: Trouble is that is not useful for learning anything as it is almost always 2 steps forward and one back, got to budget for this.

In the above conversation, Terry's negative view of others is addressed as well as the sabotaging of his connecting with others because of irritability. There is also a dual focus on his depression and avoidant personality disorder. A history of child abuse is common amongst client's presenting in routine practice, a study by Hepgul et al. (2016) found that 21% presented with moderate or severe sexual abuse and 16% with moderate or severe physical abuse. If the therapist does not ask about abuse it is unlikely to be declared and the therapist may rest content with an identified disorder such as depression which comprises only a partial description of the client's difficulties. However, it cannot be assumed that because a client has been abused they must have a personality disorder, simply that enquiry needs to be made about the latter possibility.

After ten sessions of treatment spanning eight months, a follow-up review was arranged two months later to check that Terry's recovery from depression had been maintained. Self-report measures, usually refer to functioning in the previous two weeks and are subject to demand characteristics. There is a danger with self-report measures that they can present a glowing image of the client's functioning if administered at a 'good' point in the natural waxing and waning of symptoms. In keeping with the DSM-5 criteria (American Psychiatric Association, 2013), for remission his functioning in the previous two months was used as the appropriate time frame to rule out natural fluctuations.

References

American Psychiatric Association. (2013). *Diagnostic and statistical manual of mental disorders* (5th ed.). Washington, D.C.: APA.

Beck, A. T. (2015). *Theory of personality disorders in cognitive therapy of personality disorders* (3rd ed.). A. T. Beck, D. D. Davis, & A. Freeman (Eds.), New York: Guilford Press.

First, M. B., Williams, J. B. W., Karg, R. S., & Spitzer, R. L. (2016). *Structured clinical interview for DSM-5 disorders – clinician version (SCID-5-CV)*. Arlington, VA: American Psychiatric Association.

First, M. B. & Williams, J. B. W. (2021). *Quick structured clinical interview for DSM-5 disorders*. Washington, D.C: American Psychiatric Association.

Hepgul, N., King, S., Amarasinghe, M., Breen, G., Grant, N., Grey, N., Hotopf, M., Moran, P., Pariante, C. M., Tylee, A., Wingrove, J., Young, A. H., & Cleare, A. J. (2016). Clinical characteristics of patients assessed within an Improving Access to Psychological Therapies (IAPT) service: Results from a naturalistic cohort study (Predicting Outcome Following Psychological Therapy; PROMPT). *BMC Psychiatry*, *16*, 52. 10.1186/s12888-016-0736-6

Higginson, T. W. (2020). *The enchiridion epictetus*. New York: Liberal Arts Press.

IAPT Manual. (2019). The Improving Access to Psychological Therapies Manual National Collaborating Centre for Mental Health.

Kroenke, K., Spitzer, R. L., & Williams, J. B. (2001). The PHQ-9: validity of a brief depression severity measure. *Journal of General Internal Medicine*, *16*(9), 606–613. 10.1046/j.1525-1497.2001.016009606.x

Na, P. J., Yaramala, S. R., Kim, J. A., Kim, H., Goes, F. S., Zandi, P. P., Vande Voort, J. L., Sutor, B., Croarkin, P., & Bobo, W. V. (2018). The PHQ-9 Item 9 based screening for suicide risk: A validation study of the Patient Health Questionnaire (PHQ)-9 Item 9 with the Columbia Suicide Severity Rating Scale (C-SSRS). *Journal of Affective Disorders*, *232*, 34–40. 10.1016/j.jad.2018.02.045

Scott M. J. (2018). Improving access to psychological therapies (IAPT) - the need for radical reform. *Journal of Health Psychology*, *23*(9), 1136–1147. 10.1177/13591 05318755264

Sheehan, D. V., Lecrubier, Y., Sheehan, K. H., Amorim, P., Janavs, J., Weiller, E., Hergueta, T., Baker, R., & Dunbar, G. C. (1998). The Mini-International Neuropsychiatric Interview (M.I.N.I.): The development and validation of a structured diagnostic psychiatric interview for DSM-IV and ICD-10. *The Journal of Clinical Psychiatry*, *59*(*Suppl 20*), 22–57.

Tolin, D. F., Gilliam, C., Wootton, B. M., Bowe, W., Bragdon, L. B., Davis, E., Hannan, S. E., Steinman, S. A., Worden, B., & Hallion, L. S. (2018). Psychometric properties of a structured diagnostic interview for DSM-5 anxiety, mood, and obsessive-compulsive and related disorders. *Assessment*, *25*(1), 3–13. 10.1177/1 073191116638410

Vail, L., Adams, A., Gilbert, E., Nettleingham, A., & Buckingham, C. D. (2012). Investigating mental health risk assessment in primary care and the potential role of a structured decision support tool, GRiST. *Mental Health in Family Medicine*, *9*(1), 57–67.

Zimmerman, M., Rothschild, L., & Chelminski, I. (2005). The prevalence of DSM-IV personality disorders in psychiatric outpatients. *The American Journal of Psychiatry*, *162*(10), 1911–1918. 10.1176/appi.ajp.162.10.1911

Chapter 7

When the Trauma Highlights a Pre-existing More Pernicious Problem

The simplicity of a referral, e.g. a phobia about driving since a road traffic accident, can lift a therapist's spirits in that the latter may feel it is straightforward and within his/her comfort zone to treat. This makes it tempting for the therapist to operate with a recency heuristic, giving greater weighting to anything that is furnished early on in the interview and prematurely getting into action to resolve the 'simple' therapeutic target. But detailed questioning about a range of disorders can hint at a personality disorder problem. There is a therapeutic disincentive to such detailed enquiry because the therapist does not want to open a can of worms that he/she may perceive as (a) beyond his/her therapeutic resources, (b) more time demanding than he/she and/or employing agency will accept and (c) may involve unnecessary labelling of the client. These difficulties and the way forward are illustrated in the following case example.

Mary

After the accident, Mary became too fearful to apply for a permanent teaching post because it would likely involve driving further afield. She had been involved in a Motorway collision with a Heavy Goods Vehicle, as their car spiralled out of control she thought she and her daughter who was accompanying her were going to die. Since the accident, she kept driving to a minimum. Initially, at the prompting of her GP, she self-referred to the Government IAPT service. Following a 30-minute telephone interview, she was informed that a Stabilisation Group would be most appropriate for her and six weeks later she began the course. Mary managed to attend only two sessions because of work and childcare demands. She said that she found the sessions 'helpful' in that she did manage to attend a group, something she had avoided all her life but was given no diagnosis. However, there is insufficient evidence that such Trauma Stabilisation Groups result in a loss of diagnostic status and that those entering TSGs fared better than those on a waiting list or having treatment as usual (Lewis et al., 2020). Subsequently, she referred herself to a therapist for video link consultations.

DOI: 10.4324/9781003178132-9

After the open-ended part of the MINI semi-structured interview (Sheehan et al., 1998), the therapist moved on to investigate the diagnostic possibilities of depression, panic disorder, substance abuse, post-traumatic stress disorder and social anxiety disorder. The results for all these disorders were negative, but whilst conducting the PTSD interview there were some odd findings:

Therapist: Apart from this accident, has there been any other major negative life events?

Mary: No.

Therapist: Were you abused as a child?

Mary: *(after a long pause)* Yes.

Therapist: Was that physical or sexual abuse?

Mary: Sexual, but I don't really want to go there.

Therapist: Ok, I just want to ask some further questions about the possible effects of the accident on you, how do you feel about yourself?

Mary: I don't feel bad about myself in relation to the accident but I have never been fond of myself, don't take selfies or like looking in the mirror.

Therapist: How do you view other people?

Mary: I've always kept away from them, even with my daughter's father, I wouldn't tell him what music I liked.

Therapist: Why?

Mary: I don't really know, think it goes back to the abuse by a family member, I was told what would happen if I told anyone about it. I think in the end my husband got fed up with me being a closed book and I would give him grief for being too open with other people. I just stick with my daughter and the cats, don't get me wrong I can perform ok in a work situation as a locum teacher, but I have never been able to cope with the small talk over lunch or something like that.

Therapist: Do you feel disconnected from others?

Mary: Yes, but that goes way back before the accident.

Therapist: Since the accident do you avoid driving?

Mary: As much as possible only do essential driving, to and from work and go to the shops. But I am stymied if a permanent position comes up and it's any distance away.

The therapist's notes from the first session indicated that the client's primary concern was not the accident per se but what could have happened, her daughter's life cut tragically short, her cats left unattended and uncared for. The client likely met diagnostic criteria for a specific phobia about driving, but oddly this could not be confirmed by the MINI (Sheehan et al., 1998) as it does not have a module on specific phobia. Inspection of the notes also suggested that the client had an avoidant personality disorder. At the next session, the therapist confirmed the presence of a specific phobia using the SCID interview (First et al., 2016) and avoidant personality disorder with the SCID interview for personality disorder (First et al., 2016).

It was agreed that the therapeutic targets would be her preoccupation with 'horror videos' in relation to the accident, her phobia about driving and the avoidant personality disorder. The client felt that her avoidant personality disorder had ruined her life because it affected everything, whereas the effects of her phobia were more limited. Rather than being affronted by the personality disorder label, she was relieved that her interpersonal difficulties had a name and there was a way around them. At the next session, her 'horror videos' were addressed. Thus, it is not only disorders that are the target for treatment, but in keeping with, the three-legged stool for evidence-based practice (NHS England C De Brun, 2013), the client's wishes are taken into account and 'horror videos' became the starting point for treatment. In this way, the therapeutic alliance was fostered.

Treatment

Mary unlike Terry could not recall her life before the abuse, so that RCBT in her case referred to re-building CBT rather than restorative CBT. The treatment of Mary began with what she considered of great importance, flashbacks of the accident.

Therapist: What is it about the accident that gets to you?

Mary: It could have been curtains for both of us.

Therapist: So, it is not what actually happened on the motorway?

Mary: Well, I do sometimes think of not being able to control the car, feeling helpless.

Therapist: Is it more what did happen or more what could have happened that gets to you or a bit of both?

Mary: Both.

Therapist: In percentage terms, how much of each is it that disturbs you?

Mary: 60% what could and 40% what did.

Therapist: How do those get in the way?

Mary: Now as I approach the car, I feel sick I imagine our funeral service, what would be sung. If I can get out of getting into the car I will.

Therapist: So, what most disturbs you most is a 'horror video' of what could have happened rather than a 'reality video' of what did happen?

Mary: Yes, I suppose so.

Therapist: So, most of the 'pain' is coming from somewhere different to the accident itself?

Mary: I hadn't thought of it that way.

Therapist: It is rather like going to your GP with a pain in your thigh, the GP examines it and says nothing wrong with your thigh but I think you have got a trapped nerve in your back. The 'horror video' has become the central lens through which you view life, occasionally you might swap it for the 'reality video' of the accident. But either of your videos put you out of the game and we will need to work on both.

The above dialogue illustrates that it is problematic for the therapist to assume that what is currently most debilitating will be the memories of the 'worst moments' in the trauma. The therapist then went on to address the relevance of the 'horror videos'.

Therapist: Imagine that your daughter had to run to catch the bus from school today and arrived home safely. Just before bed she is upset and you ask her what is troubling her and she says 'I could have tripped running across the road for the bus and been killed by a car', what would you say to her?

Mary: But you didn't trip and you didn't get hit?

Therapist: What if she replied 'but I could have'.

Mary: I'd probably be tempted to say 'it's late, don't be stupid', but that's not good enough is it?

Therapist: Isn't it? What might be missing?

Mary: A bit of affection and I might gently remind her 'I've told you loads of times not to run across roads, there is always another bus'.

Therapist: So what you have done is to teach her not to take the 'horror video' seriously, there is no need to let it stop her getting to sleep?

Mary: Yes, it is like when she was upset by nightmares when she was little.

Therapist: Could you practice doing exactly the same over the 'horror video' of you both dying in the accident?

Mary: I could do, but why does it keep happening?

Therapist: It's just the brain's way of protecting you, just checking out each day, that what you fear most isn't going to happen today. If you keep calm and simply answer the concern raised each time you will settle down in the way in which a child does after re-assurance.

Mary: I'll give it a go, it's a completely new way of coming at it.

Therapist: It is always difficult to know in advance how long it will take practicing this 'radical apathy' for the 'horror videos' before they wither away. It is often two steps forward and one back, likely becoming more 'urgent' if something untoward happens on the road, but if you just keep going you can get there.

In the above exchange, the therapist has set out a roadmap for recovery that budgets for likely setbacks. In this way, the client is inoculated against the almost inevitable setbacks. The stage is also set for increased risk-taking as a driver and as a passenger. This parallels the increased social risk-taking necessary to address her avoidant personality disorder. Thus, the two disorders, a specific phobia and avoidant personality disorder are tackled simultaneously and seamlessly. Both would feature in homework assignments.

Homework is a key feature of RCBT and most of the session is spent discussing the previous sessions homework and negotiating an appropriate homework assignment. Without this focus on homework, sessions can become simply crisis support sessions. But this is not to say that on occasion the focus on homework might not be suspended because of a crisis e.g. unexpected bereavement. The homework assignments are a crystallisation of the new learning in the session, a summary, for application outside the session, in the real world of the client's life. Client's typically have impaired concentration, so it is unlikely that they will retain the essence of what is discussed in therapy for application between sessions. Without engagement with homework assignments, it is unlikely that there will be meaningful, lasting change in the client's life. This makes it imperative (Cox et al., 1988) to give the client a concise written summary of the session, together with the specifics of the homework task i.e. the 'what', 'where', 'when'. The therapist keeps a copy of the assignment, so that the next therapy session can begin with the review of homework. In this way, a continuity between sessions is assured. Kazantis (2021) presents homework 'as a primary means of facilitating generalisation and maintenance of skills' but from a client's point of view its' importance derives from whether it is perceived as being instrumental in restoring 'normal' functioning. Checking this out with the client before assigning the homework is crucial. On a practical note, the therapist has found it useful to write session notes and homework assignments on a Tablet PC, making it easy to print off the latter at the end of a session. Alternatively, with the COVID crisis, much treatment is online or via the telephone and the homework can be sent via e-mail or text message after the session.

The homework assignment that was negotiated with Mary at the end of the fifth session is shown in Table 7.1.

In the setting of homework, it is important to capitalise on the client's strengths, in Mary's case, she had successfully achieved academically so that it is not so much learning a new skill but extending the range of action of an already existing skill. In eliciting the details of the operation of this 'old' skill, the therapist is able to borrow on the graphic imagery of the 'gremlin' to match the equally vivid imagery of the 'horror video'. Thus, there is a matching in kind rather than relying entirely on the logical proposition that

Table 7.1 Mary's Homework Assignment

1. When approaching the car, focus on the task in hand, ignore the 'horror video' of the 'coulds', being relayed by your 'gremlin'. This was the type of 'gremlin' who used to play up when preparing for exams you managed to sideline him then and can now. Note how your expectations are much the same as you have had in the recent past when you have been going to get into a car but the video of what actually happens (the reality video) is quite different.
2. Do as many dares as you can fit in your week, don't be bothered about the distance you go, or whether you feel relaxed afterwards. The important point is to dare yourself to adopt the style of driving you had before the accident and notice the difference between your expectations and the experience. You could think of the train driver telling you to 'mind the gap' as you step from the train (expectation) to the platform (experience).
3. Do as many dares as you can fit into your week socially e.g. eat lunch with colleagues in the staffroom rather than going to your car to eat. Watch out for (a) the historical narrative you use e.g. they can tell I am uncomfortable, they will find fault, (b) how you go on a fishing expedition afterwards to find something to criticise yourself for e.g. a piece of tomato slipped out of my sandwich as I was eating it. Again, notice the gaps between expectation and experience.

given that she had driven for ten years without a serious road traffic accident the chance of a recurrence was at least 1 in 10 × 365 or about 1 in 4,000. It is not a question of using graphic imagery or logical disputation but of using both.

The above homework differs markedly from the traditional CBT approach to treating phobias in which at the outset of therapy a hierarchy of avoided situations is collaboratively constructed. The subjective units of distress (SUDS), usually on a scale of 0–100, (where 100 is maximum distress), experienced at each rung of the 'ladder' is noted and the client is typically instructed to stay at the particular 'rung' until the SUDS have reduced by 50%. Whereas in a classic behavioural approach the concern would be that the client should habituate to what is feared i.e. a 100% reduction before moving from the particular 'rung'. Further, clients are told that if a particular 'step' is too much, all is not lost, because intermediate steps can be introduced. Thus, a cognitive element is introduced into what was initially a classic behavioural approach. Arguably, the RCBT approach suggested above offers more agency to the client and takes a better account of the client's history and mental time travel.

The homework set in Table 7.1 stresses a commonality in approaching problems as diverse as a specific phobia and avoidant personality disorder to construct a coherent narrative about treatment. Treatment is not just about 'zapping' particular symptoms in turn.

Later sessions of Mary's treatment were devoted to her disclosing personal information about herself, starting with at lunchtime at school letting her political views be known in the wake of the forthcoming General Election. This led to the disclosure that intimacy with her ex-husband had been sabotaged by cued flashbacks of the abuse that she had suffered from a family member, but she had not disclosed this to him. Mary conceded that her ex-husband's reaction to disclosure probably would not have been negative and indeed she felt 'sorry' for him, but this served to maintain her low self-esteem. Nevertheless, it was agreed that it might be important to schedule further sessions when there was any prospect of an intimate relationship, something that she had long since given up on. This highlights the more general issue that in treating a client with a personality disorder, one is more likely involved long term, albeit with long intervals in between. The danger of this with some personality disorders such as borderline personality disorder is that it becomes unrelenting crisis intervention, which is of very limited help to the client and a poor use of the therapist's resources.

References

Cox, D. J., Tisdelle, D. A. & Culbert, J. P. (1988). Increasing adherence to behavioral homework assignments. *Journal of Behavioral Medicine, 11*, 519–522 10.1007/BF00844844

First, M. B., Williams, J. B. W., Karg, R. S., & Spitzer, R. L. (2016). *Structured clinical interview for DSM-5 disorders – clinician version (SCID-5-CV)*. Arlington, VA: American Psychiatric Association.

First, M. B., Williams, J. B. W., Benjamin, L. S., & Spitzer, R. L. (2016). *User's guide for the SCID-5-PD (structured clinical interview for DSM-5 personality disorder)*. Arlington, VA: American Psychiatric Association.

Kazantzis, N. (2021). Introduction to the special issue on homework in cognitive behavioral therapy: New clinical psychological science. *Cognitive Therapy and Research, 45*, 205–208. 10.1007/s10608-021-10213-9

Lewis, C., Neil, P., Roberts, N. P., Andrew, M., Starling, E. & Bisson, J. I. (2020). Psychological therapies for post-traumatic stress disorder in adults: Systematic review and meta-analysis, *European Journal of Psychotraumatology, 11*(1), 1729633, DOI: 10.1080/20008198.2020.1729633

NHS England C De Brun. (2013). Finding the evidence: Key step in the information production process.

Sheehan, D. V., Lecrubier, Y., Sheehan, K. H., Amorim, P., Janavs, J., Weiller, E., Hergueta, T., Baker, R., & Dunbar, G. C. (1998). The Mini-International Neuropsychiatric Interview (M.I.N.I.): The development and validation of a structured diagnostic psychiatric interview for DSM-IV and ICD-10. *The Journal of Clinical Psychiatry, 59*(Suppl 20), 22–57.

Chapter 8

The Client's Account Is Not Necessarily Veridical

Oftentimes, others are present at the time of the incident and can provide a corrective to the client's account. But significant others can also unwittingly make matters worse by suggesting a different course of action would have been more appropriate (hindsight bias) or that they had a 'lucky' escape (ignoring base rate). These cognitive illusions can affect clinicians as much as the public, Lilienfeld and Lynn (2015) give the example of a therapist assuming success because of client improvement on a self-report measure, ignoring the bias (heuristic) of regression to the mean. The trauma does not speak for itself it is a social construction. The character depicted in this chapter shows the difficulties that can arise when psychologically naive clients isolate themselves with their trauma narrative. The therapeutic task is to make the trauma narrative a semi-permeable membrane open to adaptive modification.

The case of Ann illustrates that there can be huge therapeutic gains from accompanying the client in their mental time travel to and on the return journey from their trauma. But significant others may have made the same return trip to and from the trauma or to a not too dissimilar extreme trauma. Precisely because they are 'significant others' they are credible sources of persuasion and offer the prospect of looking at the trauma through another window on reality. The therapist is only one source of persuasion and in some instances the least potent in the client's restoration of themselves. In assessing a client's resources, it is important to include their social resources and draw upon these.

Ann

She had missed two of her assessment appointments because of an increase in the frequency of her panic attacks since an incident that occurred when she was travelling on a bus with her mother. At the third scheduled appointment, during the Overview interview for the QuickSCID-5 (First & Williams, 2021), Ann said that the bus braked sharply to avoid a car, she and her mother had just stood up to get off and were thrown down the aisle

DOI: 10.4324/9781003178132-10

of the bus. Ann said that she landed in the well of the bus where passengers board, could see the traffic 'whizzing' past, and was fearful of the doors opening and being thrown out. She said that she had panic attacks when she tried to leave home.

Diagnostic Interview

The diagnostic interview part of the QuickSCID-5 (First & Williams, 2021) gives largely single questions to ask about each of the questions that comprise the DSM-5 disorders, and it can be used simply as a screen for disorders in which simple 'yes' or 'no' responses are required. Alternatively, it can be used as a diagnostic interview in which examples of the presence of the symptoms are elicited to determine whether a symptom should be considered present at a clinically significant level. In addition, follow-up questions are asked for clarification of responses. In Ann's case, the interview was conducted in this latter manner.

As part of the interview, the therapist asked, 'Have you had at least two attacks like this that came out of the blue, i.e. in situations where you didn't expect to be nervous or uncomfortable'. Ann's response was in the affirmative and she cited examples of triggers (a) relatives from another part of the country visiting and (b) when she was weeding her front garden. Had she been unable to furnish such examples, the QuickSCID-5 (First & Williams, 2021) would have directed the therapist to a consideration of agoraphobia rather than go on to enquire about the various symptoms that may be manifest in a panic attack. In addition to meeting diagnostic criteria for panic disorder and agoraphobia, she met the criteria for PTSD.

Treatment

Treatment began with a focus on her panic symptoms and the therapist said that he wanted to see if a simple exercise could produce the symptoms she feared. In the first treatment session, she was asked to stand and breathe deeply and quickly and raise her hand if she became uncomfortable. This she did after a minute, and she went to sit down, the therapist asked her not to sit and stand a little longer, after a further 30 seconds, the therapist said she could stop deep breathing. Again, when she went to sit down he asked her to stand a little longer whilst he asked her some questions. The therapist then explored her expectations and experiences at the various stages of the hyperventilation challenge. Inducing panic symptoms and having the person discover that nothing terrible happens, the hyperventilation challenge has been an important component of randomised controlled trials for panic disorder (Meuret et al., 2005). The dialogue went as follows, as she stood:

Therapist:	What went through your mind when I asked you to stand and do the exercise?
Ann:	I don't want to do this, but you are here so it must be ok.
Therapist:	What went through your mind when you raised your hand?
Ann:	I don't like this, this could go pear-shaped.
Therapist:	Pear-shaped in what way?
Ann:	I could lose control or have a heart attack or something or make a show of myself.
Therapist:	Did you?
Ann:	I felt bad.
Therapist:	But did what you expected happen?
Ann:	No.
Therapist:	What do you make about that?
Ann:	I am a 'drama queen', always have been.
Therapist:	At the end of the breathing excercise, you went to sit down and I stopped you, what was going through your mind to want to sit down?
Ann:	I felt shaky, thought I could collapse.
Therapist:	Did you collapse?
Ann:	No, I am still standing.
Therapist:	What do you make of that?
Ann:	I make it a drama right through, as a kid I remember standing on wet sand and thinking it might be sinking sand and hurried to the dry sand.
Therapist:	What would have happened if you hadn't gone to the dry sand.
Ann:	Nothing, the other kids were just playing around.
Therapist:	It seems that you do safety things that aren't necessary, because you imagine horrors and take them seriously. In therapy, we could look at teaching yourself not to take the imagined catastrophes seriously, becoming the dare devil you never became as a kid!

In the above transcript, the therapist has helped the client learn experientially that there is a gap between expectations and experience with regards to panic attacks, rather than giving didactic instruction on the development and maintenance of panic disorder. The salient catastrophic cognitions are (a) more likely to be accessed when they are 'hot' and (b) alternative narratives are likely to be more accessible if constructed in an emotional state that is congruent with the distress experienced during the panic. The therapist then helped the client construct an alternative narrative for use at the first signs of a panic attack. But problems arose when the therapist suggested she should employ such a strategy when she began gradually approaching avoided situations by herself, it seemed impossible to negotiate such a homework. The conversation continued:

Ann:	I won't be able to do it.
Therapist:	Why?
Ann:	Because I would be by myself.
Therapist:	But earlier on in this session, you brought on a panic attack and nothing happened?
Ann:	That's different, you were with me.
Therapist:	How did I stop your worse fears from happening?
Ann:	You just did.
Therapist:	But what did I do exactly?
Ann:	Even before the accident, I would often get my Mum to go places with me, so I wouldn't have an attack. That's why I was on my way to town with my Mum on the day of the accident.
Therapist:	But you had a big panic attack at the scene, didn't you?
Ann:	Yes.
Therapist:	So how does having someone with you make a difference?
Ann:	I just feel safer.
Therapist:	So your goal is always to get to a feeling of safety?
Ann:	I suppose so, I didn't do what other kids did, like going on fairground rides.
Therapist:	Do you think you missed out?
Ann:	Yes.
Therapist:	Do you think you still miss out?
Ann:	Probably.
Therapist:	Perhaps, we could look at gradually doing what most others do, like your Mum, rather than always "hunting for a feeling of safety".
Ann:	Yes, that's different, becoming independent.

The above extract indicates that the negotiation of homework is not an easy task, it is straightforward for the therapist to set homework that he/she can clearly see would make a worthwhile difference, but without being sensitive to the clients barely expressed reservations about the task. Unless the client's concerns about lack of capacity are addressed, there is likely to be non-compliance with homework that may sour the therapeutic alliance. The homeworks set in this instance related not only to the client's panic disorder but also to PTSD, the obstacles to the latter are crystallised in the following dialogue:

Ann:	I don't like talking or thinking about the incident.
Therapist:	What do you do when the memory comes to mind?
Ann:	Go and eat.
Therapist:	How much do you eat?
Ann:	I was 10 stone before the accident and now I'm 13 stone, I look 'gross'.

Therapist: Do you binge eat?
Ann: Yes.
Therapist: When you binge, how long does it go on for?
Ann: A couple of hours.
Therapist: How often does that happen?
Ann: A couple of times a week.

The therapist then went through the seven questions in the QuickSCID-5 (First & Williams, 2021) that comprise enquiry about binge eating disorder and the client met the criteria. But, as is often the case this diagnosis was missed at the assessment appointment because the client had simply said that she distracts herself by playing on her phone when she has flashbacks and no further enquiry was made. Whilst this is also true, the client's sense of disgust and loss of control probably prevented her from volunteering the eating problems that had developed post the incident. Thus, assessment is an ongoing process and not confined to the initial assessment. But it does demand a resilience on the part of the therapist, in this example trying to focus on the intrusions related to PTSD but in so doing unearthing another 'therapeutic bomb'. The dialogue continued:

Therapist: Maybe you might tackle the binge eating, by say only eating at the dining room table with a knife and fork and eating what will fit on a small plate.
Ann: My granddaughter would think I'm mad eating crisps and chocolate with a knife and fork.
Therapist: Would that matter if she thought you were mad?
Ann: No, she thinks I'm mad anyway, the way I carry on, we could have a laugh about it.
Therapist: Rather than bingeing in secret?
Ann: Yes.

In the above dialogue, the client was making their self-worth conditional on their control of eating. But the therapist implies that eating behaviour need not be central to the client's identity, but sharing a difficulty with a significant other, using humour, might be more important. The session continued:

Therapist: Do you keep the incident secret?
Ann: Certainly do, it is horrible, don't want my granddaughter getting scared to get the bus to school.
Therapist: But if you really believed it was dangerous you would not be letting her get the bus?
Ann: Well, I get her to give me a ring when she gets to school, sometimes she forgets and I go ballistic.

Therapist: But if you truly believed there was real danger you wouldn't be letting her get the bus.

Ann: If it was down to me, I wouldn't let her get the bus, but my mother tells me not be so stupid.

Therapist: Your Mum was on the bus with you, on the day of the incident?

Ann: Yes.

Therapist: How come your Mum isn't bothered about travelling by bus and you are?

Ann: She's just different, not a 'drama queen' like me.

Therapist: That you let your granddaughter get the bus despite your fears suggests maybe you agree with your Mum's view more than your own gut reaction.

Ann: Maybe I do.

In this dialogue, the therapist is weaning the client off seeing her particular take on the incident as necessarily more valid/useful than her mother's. The exchange continues:

Therapist: How does your granddaughter feel about getting the bus?

Ann: She's not bothered.

Therapist: So you have got your Mum and granddaughter looking at travelling by bus totally differently to yourself, what do you make of that?

Ann: I'll live longer!

Therapist: But would you 'live'?

In this exchange, the therapist is preparing the ground, cognitively for tackling the client's behavioural avoidance that is part of the PTSD. However, the client's avoidance of talking about the intrusions leaves open the possibility that they may sabotage any behavioural task. In the next exchange, the focus is not on the intrusions per se but on how the client manages the intrusions:

Therapist: It seems that you try to keep the flashbacks a 'secret' from yourself, by eating a lot and playing on your phone, but has that worked?

Ann: It does for a bit but they keep coming back.

Therapist: Why not try to give them a special time, when you write about them for a few minutes a day, literally write them off and your banned from picking at them at other times, because though you say you don't want to go over the incident you are like a dog worrying a bone over them, the picking is worse than the sore itself.

Ann: I don't know whether I could do that.

Therapist: Why not?

Ann: I might get too upset.

Therapist: Well, try just writing a couple of sentences in the next few minutes and see if it is that bad?

Ann: A bit like doing the panic attack?

Therapist: Exactly, just as you can train yourself not to be bullied by the panic attacks you can train yourself not to be bullied by the flashbacks.

Ann: Ok.

At the next therapy session, matters took an unexpected turn, the client's mother had seen her writing and asked to read what she had written. But her mother challenged her account of the incident, in that she said she never did fall into the well of the bus, rather when she was thrown forward, she did hit the front window of the bus and then fell backwards collapsing next to where the driver sits and he could not open his door to help at first. The client was nonplussed by her mother's differing account of the incident and she conceded that the latter might have a better take on the significance of the incident for today. This paved the way for her making bus journeys, first accompanied then alone.

References

First, M. B. & Williams, J. B. W. (2021). *Quick structured clinical interview for DSM-5 disorders.* Washington, D.C.: APA.

Lilienfeld, S. O. & Lynn, S. J. (2015). Error/biases in clinical decision making. In R. L. Cautin & S. O. Lilienfeld (Eds.), *The encyclopaedia of clinical psychology* (1st ed.). London: John Wiley & Sons. DOI: 10.1002/9781118625392.wbecp567

Meuret, A. E., Ritz, T., Wilhelm, F. H., & Roth, W. T. (2005). Voluntary hyperventilation in the treatment of panic disorder--functions of hyperventilation, their implications for breathing training, and recommendations for standardization. *Clinical Psychology Review, 25*(3), 285–306. 10.1016/j.cpr.2005.01.002

Chapter 9

Capitalising on the Client's Credible Model of Persuasion

The significant others in a client's life have their own history and it is more likely than not that at least one of them has encountered an extreme trauma. Client's can thus learn how others have coped post-trauma and it may serve as a template for managing their own difficulties. At first sight, it may seem better if the significant others trauma is almost identical to their own, but this may be too overwhelming and they learn from others experiences when there is little or no emotional arousal arising from them.

Simon

Simon had been on a night out with a cousin in City Centre bars, as they were leaving a bar, he met an old school friend who stopped to chat, whilst his cousin went on ahead towards a taxi rank. A few minutes later Simon followed alone, he heard footsteps running behind him, turned and was assaulted by a group of about five young men. He thought that he was going to die. After what seemed to him to be an 'eternity' he made it to his feet, began running with his assailants in hot pursuit, he felt sure that they would catch him but in the event, he escaped by running back into the club he emerged from and the staff summoned the police and ambulance service.

During the Overview interview for the QuickSCID-5 (First & Williams, 2021), he related many of the symptoms of PTSD and also screened positive for depression. His depression chiefly related to his being unable to work as a locksmith since the attack, in part because of a fear of going to stranger's homes but in part that there had been damage to his Ulnar nerve in his right arm in the attack, so his right hand had become clawed, making it difficult to use the tools he had used in his work. He had been prescribed the anti-depressant Sertraline by his GP, and the latter had given him the telephone number of the Improving Access to Psychological Therapies (IAPT) service, which he rang and a telephone assessment was arranged. He said that the therapist said that he probably had post-traumatic stress disorder and would benefit most from a Stabilisation Group but there was a 2-month wait for the next group. Simon duly attended and found that there were initially 15

DOI: 10.4324/9781003178132-11

people in the group and two therapists. He said everybody was asked to talk about how they had come to the group, but before it was his turn he was distressed by the distress of a lady following an armed robbery at her home. Simon said that by the time it was his turn he felt even less like talking about his assault and 'glossed' over it. He returned for a second session but was dissuaded from doing so by his partner who said that he was not 'mad' and she had been to therapy groups in the past and they were 'a waste of time'. After the second session which he described as 'therapists drawing diagrams on whiteboards, about fight or flight', he dropped out.

Diagnostic Interview

At the interview, the DIAMOND (Tolin et al., 2018) a semi-structured interview was used and it was discovered that Simon had periodically abused alcohol since the assault and this was affecting his relationship with his partner. He added however that his relationship with his partner had always been precarious because she had used cocaine to help with her own mental health problems. Simon said that he stuck with her to 'protect' their six-year-old son. He had made fleeting attempts to work since the incident, but was fearful of meeting strangers and was finding it took him much longer to perform his tasks as a locksmith because of his injury. Simon said that he was very stressed by a recent visit to his GP, to consider the renewal of his antidepressant medication, the waiting room was full, he felt threatened and went and stood outside looking in until his name appeared on the screen. He said that he was then unnecessarily abrupt with his GP because he just wanted to 'escape' as soon as possible. The diagnostic interview confirmed the presence of PTSD and depression.

Treatment

Treatment began by talking Simon through Fig. 5.1 (The Adult Model of PTSD), Fig. 5.2 (The Amygdala (brain's alarm)) and Fig. 5.3 (The Bubble/bunker) of Chapter 5, using the text accompanying the figures as a template. The therapist commented that the flashbacks/dreams usually fade with time, unless the person continues to behave as if they are in a 'war zone'. The dialogue went as follows:

Simon: Like me in the Dr's
Therapist: Yes, you felt you had to 'escape'.
Simon: It sounds crazy, other people have become the enemy and I just wanted to get home to my 'bunker' as soon as possible.
Therapist: Who was in the Surgery at the time?
Simon: It was the morning surgery, so mainly elderly people.
Therapist: But you saw them as a threat?

Simon:	I didn't really think about who was there.
Therapist:	Sounds as if you had an amygdala hijack, responding to your internal alarm going off, rather than sorting out whether there is a real and present danger.
Simon:	A bit like Tony Blair waging war on Saddam Hussein without checking first of all whether he actually had weapons of mass destruction.
Therapist:	Going by your dodgy alarm makes you 'wage war' on a 'just in case' basis.
Simon:	If I was a politician I would be sacked.
Therapist:	If PTSD clients were politicians, they would have us all on permanent lockdown, would you vote for them?
Simon:	I go 'ballistic' enough over little things not being right, without thinking of politicians!

In this exchange, the therapist is suggesting that the client consider a new narrative about his modus operandi since the assault. In the first instance, the therapist gradually moves the client away from their highly charged post-trauma story to consider a parallel political situation with no personal implications (the Iraq War), then moving forward in time to suggest that important features of this event are salient to today. Thus far, the therapist has not sought to have the client elaborate on the details of their trauma. The dialogue has taken place at the macro level of roles adopted, rather than the micro-CBT level of individual negative thoughts. Roles are a construction comprising a wide set of thoughts and beliefs. In terms of cognitive behaviour therapy, it is equally valid to work at the macro as opposed to the micro level. Which is most appropriate at a particular point in time depends on the clinical judgement of the therapist, taking into account the client's background. Homework was set for Simon, to determine whether his local environment was any more threatening than his GP's waiting room. He also agreed to try a few more locksmith's jobs and test out whether the householder's were as dangerous as he feared. The next session began with a review of homework:

Therapist:	How did it go checking out whether it is a 'war zone' in your local community?
Simon:	After seeing you last, I was just about to go out, when through the window I saw John next door in his garden and I thought 'better leave it until he goes into his house', so I waited half an hour, but was kicking myself because I knew that I was being stupid.
Therapist:	Don't you get on with John?
Simon:	He's a really nice old guy, loves to talk but I think he is just lonely since his wife died a few years ago.

Therapist:	So, what was the problem in going out?
Simon:	I can't stand small talk since the assault and he will ask me how my hand is doing and I'll start then thinking of the assault. But I did go out a few times since our last session and I did a locksmith job for a friend who is a locksmith who got a call just as he was driving away on holiday and he rang me to see if I could do it.
Therapist:	How did the job go?
Simon:	It was an elderly lady who found she had lost her keys when she returned from shopping, a neighbour who has a key was on holiday and her daughter who lives nearby had also gone on holiday, it is that time of year. I took forever doing the job.
Therapist:	Was the lady bothered?
Simon:	No, not only did she make me a cup of tea, but she put madeira cake, biscuits and a fruit tart on a plate for me.
Therapist:	So what was the problem?
Simon:	It wouldn't have been an easy job at the best of times, because of a double mortice lock, but it probably took twice the time because of my weak grip with my right hand and I fumble more.
Therapist:	But the lady didn't know that and wasn't bothered?
Simon:	But when I fumble, it reminds me of the assault, then I get angry that I'm not doing it as quickly as I used to.
Therapist:	One of the main things I wanted to look at in your therapy, is how you look at everything through the lens of the assault, how you make it central, for example all your thoughts on working relate to the assault. You could look through a different set of binoculars and say, I have still got good contacts in the locksmith trade, if a job takes twice as long who is bothered.
Simon:	But if I take longer it is a loss of income.
Therapist:	Would that be a big deal?
Simon:	Probably not, but it gets to me.

In the above exchange, there is a more traditional CBT focus in that the therapist is drilling down to find the particular thoughts that are operating that sabotage his occupational functioning and encouraging a reconstruction. For homework, the client was asked to monitor his mood, note any dips in mood and to try and 'pick the lock' of any bothersome thought he could find such as 'I'm taking too long'. In delivering CBT, the therapist is concerned to use metaphor that the client is very familiar with, rather than presenting CBT in a way that is most familiar to students on CBT training courses. The aim is to make the CBT truly culturally sensitive. But intrusions related to the assault continue to be an issue, oftentimes triggered by some reminder, and can affect both social and occupational functioning. In the following exchange, the therapist explains the use of the MOOD chart

Table 9.1 MOOD Chart

Monitor	bserved thinking	Objective Thinking	Decide
mood/intrusions.	'What was I saying to myself'.	'what would be a more helpful way of thinking'.	'decide what to do and do it. Don't ruminate, but don't block concerns'.
Mood dipped doing the job.	This is ridiculous that I take this long doing a job now.	Who is complaining? The customer is happy enough.	Don't pick at my incapacity, concentrate on picking at the lock. Now is not the time and place for sorting out job issue/finances will do later when I've got space.

(Table 9.1) that can be used to both monitor and respond to intrusions and manage mood.

Therapist: What I would like to do is a slow-motion action replay of the times when you are getting upset in a situation and look at how things might have worked out better. For this, we can use the MOOD chart (Table 9.1) the first column, the "M" of mood, is about Monitoring what has just happened, for example's sake, we could put down your dip in mood doing you last job, the first 'O' refers to Observed thinking' i.e 'what you said to yourself at the time', and you might have put in 'I'm taking far too long', the second 'O' stands for Objective thinking i.e 'what would be the most helpful way of thinking here?' and in that column you might put 'nobodies complaining about the time I'm taking, it will probably get better with time' and the 'D' of MOOD is about deciding what to do and do it, and in this column you might put 'just concentrate on what I've got to do, don't start ruminating about how my performance compares to before the assault, now isn't the time for sorting out job options/finances I will leave that to a special time when I sort it out with pen and paper'.

Simon: It's like putting everything through a filter to stop it getting under your skin, instead of just reacting.

Therapist: Obviously, you can't always write the MOOD chart down, but you can use the same framework in any situation, whether it is just having had flashbacks of the assault or being woken by a dream of it.

Simon: The second and third columns are just making sure you think everything through before you move off, a bit like being at the traffic lights on amber.

Therapist: Yes, the final column is 'green' going off in a direction, not just sitting there 'ruminating' with maybe other motorists beeping you. The temptation in post-traumatic stress disorder is to 'stew' on anything to do with the trauma or to block it, both of which are as bad as each other.

Simon: I don't get it, anyone would want to block what is horrible!

Therapy: Yes, but the harder you try to push something away the more it springs back, it is as if the memory of the assault is on elastic band the harder you push it away the more it springs back.

Simon: That's true all the drinking I've done to block it just makes the memories worse the next day.

Therapist: You have to control the memory, by deciding on the time place and manner of addressing it or it will control you.

Simon: A bit like son pestering me to do things.

Therapist: Yes.

In the above dialogue, the therapist is acknowledging the detrimental role of rumination and avoidance, suggesting ways around these dysfunctions. For homework, the client said that he would have a special time for writing and thinking about the assault 'so I don't allow it to take over my whole life'.

Rumination has been found to be a strong predictor of subsequent PTSD symptoms (Murray et al., 2002) but is not specifically addressed in trauma-focussed CBT. It refers to the client going endlessly over the incident, how they may have prevented it, and a pre-occupation with thoughts such as "what if..." and perhaps also of revenge. The 'time and a place' strategy directly targets rumination.

At the next session, this was reviewed:

Simon: I wrote about it a couple of times (and he handed the therapist what he had written in his notebook).

Therapist: What strikes me reading this is that you made a difference even in very difficult circumstances.

Simon: How do you mean?

Therapist: You outran them and escaped.

Simon: Never thought of it like that, always been a good runner.

Therapist: So you weren't as helpless as you thought you were. Maybe you should give yourself credit for making a difference.

Simon: It turns it on its head a bit.

Therapist: It is possible to look at even horrors in a way that they don't totally take over your life.

The written exercise was not set as a homework in a trauma-focussed context of habituating to the traumatic memory or of elaborating the trauma memory. The rationale for the homework was that (a) that there is no need for the traumatic memory to dominate the day – there is an implicit message not to 'pick' at the traumatic memory but to address it at an appropriate time and place and (b) it is important to determine what implications the client sees the trauma as having for today and to review the perceived implications. The next therapy session began thus:

Simon: After our last session, I was talking to my Dad about having escaped in the assault, and he was telling me how over 30 years ago he was at the Hillsborough Football Disaster, he was in the Leppings Lane area of the ground and managed to climb up into the stands to avoid being crushed to death. He always commemorates the anniversary but he's never let it get in the way of life, he took me camping as a kid, spoilt me really.

Therapist: You could copy him by not putting the horror central to life, refusing to let it take over, maybe even taking your son camping and running.

Simon: Sounds good, but probably wouldn't go down well with partner, as if we go away she will say we are abandoning her might need some careful negotiation.

The above exchange underlines that others in a client's circle are probably more credible sources of persuasion than the therapist and should be harnessed as an important resource. But significant others can also have a negative impact. During the next treatment session, problems managing cued, distressing recall of the trauma were addressed:

Simon: Thought I was doing good, took my son out twice to play football in a nearby park. The first time was fine and my son was delighted, creating good memories. But the second time, there were some teenagers messing about on their bikes, I began thinking of the assault, then of a nightmare I had had, in which I'm running away from the assailants and I stumble and fall and they are breathing down my neck and I woke up then in a sweat and couldn't get back to sleep. I was then in such a state and went home but then thought I had 'failed'.

Therapist: Failed in what way.

Simon: Well I let my son down.

Therapist: Did he think that?

Simon: Well know, he was just glad to have been out with me.

Therapist: So in what way had you failed?

Simon: I had let the memory of the incident take over my life.

Therapist: It seems a reasonable goal not to let the memory dictate your life, but you might have to do it in stages.

Simon: How do you mean?

Therapist: Well imagine when your son is a few years older at school and he is getting bullied, to begin with he would likely run away from the bullies, but you might advise to try staying for a few minutes in the vicinity of the bullies but 'blank' them. To begin with, he might only manage this for 30 seconds, but you would praise him, because it is a start.

Simon: I see if he has got to gradually learn to handle bullying, I should do the same thing with being bullied by the memories. But I'm not sure what I could have done differently.

Therapist: Well, you could use the traffic light routine when you want to take flight, see the lights on red, when the lights go to amber you could delay your response by say bending down and tying your shoelace, the playing a game of 'spot the difference' between the trigger, in this case the teenagers and the assault. Then go off in a direction where you are restoring life to what it was like before, a 'stop', 'think through', 'go' process.

Simon: I was upset by the local teenagers on the field where I was with my son, but I suppose the differences were these were teenagers and not young men, it was daylight, not the early hours of the morning and there were other families around. I like the shoelace idea.

Therapist: What actually disturbs you are the horror videos you play, whether awake or asleep and it is not the details of the assault that decides your actions. As we have discussed previously the assault is irrelevant to your everyday life, it only becomes relevant if you choose to look at life through that lens.

Simon: Yes, other families, were just flying kites and picnicking, not 'seeing' any danger.

Therapist: Disturbed sleep suggests unsorted business in the day, if you have avoided situations in the day, you are likely to be on 'sentry duty' at night and your mind can easily 'go dancing' once you are asleep. So that having a special sort out time in the day for anything related to the trauma that bothers you can pay dividends at night. But you have to make sure that beyond this time you are not ruminating/agonising, in a sort of daydream, about your concerns, if you do, this will keep you depressed.

In this chapter, the case example underlines that the client does not exist in a vacuum, that significant others can influence their narrative both positively and negatively. The therapeutic task is to identify what, if any, aspects of the client's social milieu can be used as catalysts to effect change. This can involve inviting a significant other into at least some of the therapy sessions but even when this is not viable, it is possible to capitalise on perspectives taken by others. The significant others can offer a different window through which to view the trauma, oftentimes relegating the importance given to the latter but without dismissing it.

References

First, M. B. & Williams, J. B. W. (2021). *Quick structured clinical interview for DSM-5 disorders*. Washington, D.C.: APA.

Murray, J., Ehlers, A., & Mayou, R. A. (2002). Dissociation and post-traumatic stress disorder: Two prospective studies of road traffic accident survivors. *The British Journal of Psychiatry: The Journal of Mental Science, 180*, 363–368. 10.11 92/bjp.180.4.363

Tolin, D. F., Gilliam, C., Wootton, B. M., Bowe, W., Bragdon, L. B., Davis, E., Hannan, S. E., Steinman, S. A., Worden, B., & Hallion, L. S. (2018). Psychometric properties of a structured diagnostic interview for DSM-5 anxiety, mood, and obsessive-compulsive and related disorders. *Assessment, 25*(1), 3–13. 10.1177/1 073191116638410

Chapter 10

Forsaking the 'Warzone Glasses' for Pre-trauma Specs

Clients can become imprisoned by fear post-trauma. They may lock themselves up in their 'bunker' for 'safety'. On the rare excursions outside, they may wear 'warzone glasses' and see danger in situations that the general population see as innocuous. Their behaviour is usually met by incredulity by those who accompany them, increasing their reluctance to make contact or go out. Their 'pre-trauma' self seems that of another person, an alien being, of no relevance to the 'now'. Operating on the maxim 'you become what you play at', the clinicians task is to gradually encourage such clients to dare to do what they would have done previously e.g. checking on safety only as often as they would have done before the trauma. Some roles may no longer be possible and the clinician's task is to help the client construct meaningful alternative roles. This is particularly difficult as a common complaint of post-trauma clients is that they have lost their confidence. But identification of individuals in their social mix who might be an asset for a specific purpose can result in a re-engagement in the construction of a valued role. Equally, it may be important to nullify the effects of a particular individual in their social world who would effectively sabotage construction. It is important to harness not only social support for a client but also instrumental support.

Paul

Paul was hit in his ribs by the bucket of a crane on a building site, thrown to the ground, and thought he was going to die because of his inability to breathe. He was taken by ambulance to the hospital where he was an inpatient for ten days. Paul felt that his life had become 'unrecognisable', he was no longer able to work on building sites or go to the gym, his estranged partner complained about his missing maintenance payments. He felt that he was letting his daughters down. Paul was angry that the crane driver had been given virtually no training.

DOI: 10.4324/9781003178132-12

Diagnostic Interview

Paul was screened for the most common disorders using the Gateway Diagnostic Interview Questionnaire (GDIQ) (see Table 3.1). This suggested further enquiry be made about PTSD, depression and alcohol dependence. He met DSM-5 (American Psychiatric Association, 2013) criteria for PTSD and depression but from his account, it was unclear whether he met the criteria for alcohol dependence. In the earlier DSM-IV-TR (American Psychiatric Association, 2000) version, he would probably be given a diagnosis of substance abuse but this ceased to be a category in DSM-5 (American Psychiatric Association, 2013). Since the incident, he was increasingly drinking at home, rather than going to the pub to socialise. He was very irritated that the first questions from acquaintances in the pub were about how his compensation claim was going, rather than about his well-being. Paul protested 'I just want my life back'. He did, however, have the support of two long-standing friends. He had attended a pain management group but dropped out after two sessions.

Treatment

Paul was troubled by flashbacks and nightmares of seeing the bucket come towards him. It was agreed that these would be a first focus in treatment. He said that the bucket seemed to take 'forever' to hit him. Paul was angry at himself for not having got out of the path of the bucket. The following dialogue ensued:

Paul: I just stood there, but seemed to be looking down on what was happening, the next thing I know I'm on the ground, struggling to breathe.

Th: Your reaction was a bit like that of a rabbit caught in car headlights when you are driving on a country road, it just 'freezes' and you think 'for God's sake, just get out of the way'. Our responses to threat are built in, one response is flight, the second is to do battle with what is coming at you, 'fight', and the third is to just 'freeze' and hope that you are not noticed. But they are all instant emergency reactions, occurring before your brain is plugged in and switched on. With hindsight, one reaction might have been better than another, but at the time you have to react.

Paul: I suppose it is like watching a slow-motion action replay of a part of a football match in which the player clearly should have passed the ball to another player who could have easily scored but instead he has shot for goal from a difficult angle and missed.

Th: Yes. In reality, you don't have the space to sit back as we are doing now, consider all the options and choose the best bet. What we call hindsight bias is the pretence that you had sufficient information available at the time, that it was perfectly possible to choose a course of action that would have resulted in a better outcome.

Paul: The crane driver made it worse by coming over as I lay on the ground screaming 'you shouldn't have been in the way', it makes me think I should have done something and I keep going over what I might have done.

Th: Apart from the crane driver what did your other colleagues say?

Paul: They were furious with Management for letting an untrained guy loose.

Th: Have any of your colleagues blamed you?

Paul: No.

Th: What do you make of it that they have not criticised you at all?

Paul: They probably think it could just have easily been them on the receiving end.

Th: Why then do you keep going over and over the incident trying to find what you could have done differently?

Paul: Beats me, now everything has to be spot on, if my Mum leaves the fridge door open and it starts beeping I go ballistic on her and its' not fair to her, she is getting on.

The above exchange involves psychoeducation about trauma responses, but this is best delivered by utilising the client's experiences rather than as an abstract lecture. The focus is not on the trauma itself but on his post-trauma musings on what he should have done, albeit that this touches tangentially on the trauma itself. In the following dialogue, the role of emotional avoidance is explored:

Th: So since the incident, everything has to be just so?

Paul: Yes.Th: What is so bad about things not being 'just so'?

Paul: Nothing really, I just can't stand it.

Th: It is almost like you believe that if you could get everyone doing things 'just so' then calamities could be avoided.

Paul: Yes, if the crane driver operated it properly, I would not be sitting here now!

Th: Could he operate it properly with virtually no training?

Paul: Well, no.

Th: It seems like you have a magical belief that people can do things 'just so', and if they did everything would be ok.

Paul: Sort of, but my Mum is getting old and a bit forgetful so I shouldn't be expecting her to get things just right.

Th: But it is not just you expecting others to get things just right, you also do the same for yourself.

Paul: Yes, I should be in work, earning to support my daughter.

Th: But how could you with your back pain?

Paul: Well, I can't can I?

Th: But, it sounds like you believe you can do anything if you tried?

Paul: It is a bit daft really, a footballer can't play with a bad back.

Th: But you even apply it to the incident, colleagues saw it happen and none of them said you could have done anything differently.

Paul: Apart from the crane driver, but he was just trying to avoid being blamed.

Th: As the bucket came towards you, you said that you felt helpless?

Paul: The worst moment of my life.

Th: Maybe you would rather find some fault in what you did on the day, avoid that fault in the future so you could 'guarantee' that you would never again experience that feeling of helplessness.

Paul: I spend my time going on an impossible search, instead of just accepting **** happens.

Th: Yes.

Paul: But that makes me feel worse, so stupid.

Th: I don't think that you deliberately choose to do it, anymore than your daughter might choose to jump over the cracks in the pavement on the way to school so the teacher won't shout at her. Adults can do the same magical thinking as kids after an extreme trauma. You have devoted all your energies since to trying to avoid the same intense feelings of helplessness, even though the situations have little or no threat in them. It is what we call emotional avoidance.

Paul: So, when I'm getting angry in a situation it's not really to do with the situation but me wanting to avoid any chance of being like a totally helpless kid.

Th: Yes.

Paul: It is weird, like one of the people on the Pain Management Course having a pain in his thigh, but the Specialists had told him his thigh is fine but he has a trapped nerve in his back.

Th: Yes. We could see how you get on monitoring your anger, standing back from the situation and considering that there is a good chance the problem is somewhere different to where I'm looking. For both flashbacks/nightmares and alterations in mood, you could use Table 7.1 to track your actions and trace were the real problems lay. It will help you to be more aware of how emotional avoidance can creep in and sabotage situations, like a poisonous gas without a smell, at the first signs you can come at things another way, at least with a bit of practice.

At the following session, the client's use of the MOOD chart Table 7.1 was reviewed and the therapist noted that many of the dips in the client's mood were associated with pain. The therapist drew this to the client's attention:

Paul: Yes, the pain reminds me of the incident, and it can wake me at night and then I start thinking of the incident and can't get back to sleep. I thought the Pain Management Group would help.

Th: What happened there?

Paul: I just got so angry with people leaving their walking sticks at the side of the room then walking to sit in a circle, complaining of pain and they had not been through what I had been through. The therapists knew I had PTSD but didn't have the space for individual sessions, hence I'm seeing you.

Th: So you dropped out after two sessions?

Paul: The orthopaedic surgeon put me onto it, I wasn't keen, but I thought I would give it a go.

Th: If you had had the MOOD chart then and noted in the first column that you got angry about people leaving their walking sticks at the side of the room, what would you have written for your thoughts at the time in the second column?

Paul: They haven't got a real problem, they need to get their act together, I'm out of here.

Th: What might you have put in the third column that would have been more helpful?

Paul: It can't be any fun for anyone to have to come here, stop being a little kid and saying 'my pain is worse than yours' and pulling a face.

Th: Is there a problem putting yourself in other people's shoes since the incident?

Paul: Yes, I saw a girlfriend from when I was at school and I think, but I'm not sure, she wanted to start a relationship again, but I know I haven't got the space and would just get ratty, I just made excuses that I was very busy getting my Mum's house sorted after returning to live with her after the incident. This is sort of true but not the whole story.

The above exchange highlights the extensive interpersonal issues that arise in post-traumatic stress disorder. They may have long-term consequences often beyond the period of impairment that comes with disturbing intrusions but are rarely a focus in trauma-focussed CBT. During the sessions, this client mentioned two friends who continued to be supportive, and the following dialogue illustrates how these 'assets' were capitalised upon:

Paul: My friend Dean still visits, my Mum makes a fuss of him because she knew his mum who has now passed away. He had a bad accident on the Motorway in which he hit the central reservation.

Th: Does he still drive?

Paul: Yes, he is one of these 'if you fall off a horse you've got to get straight back on'.

Th: If we could wave a magic wand over your back and make it better, do you think you would go back to a building site?

Paul: I'm really not sure.

Th: What do you make of Dean getting back driving after the Motorway crash?

Paul: He is a good lad.

Th: What if he said to you 'I can't, it might all go pear-shaped again'.

Paul: I'd tell him not to be stupid, it was just a one off.

Th: What stops you saying your incident on the building site was a one off?

Paul: There was a similar incident in the newspaper the other day, I couldn't get it out of my mind and it brought back my own accident.

Th: Was it at the same site?

Paul: No.

Th: How long have you worked on building sites?

Paul: 14 years.

Th: Has anything ever gone very badly pear-shaped in the sites you have been at?

Paul: No.

Th: So, in the thousands of days, you have been on site there has been only one extreme trauma.

Paul: Yes, but you do hear of others.

Th: If Dean said he had heard of other very serious road traffic accidents, would you have said it should put him off?

Paul: No, news is only about bad things, most of life is 'same old, same old, boring'.

Th: It seems that the 'glasses' you use to look at life have a 'war zone tint', Dean's are a normal pair, like the one's you would have used before the incident. When you get frightened take off the 'war zone glasses' and replace them by the 'specs' you would have worn before the incident, dare to do what you would have done before.

Paul: I should have done that when I was in the hardware Superstore, I jumped out of my skin when an assistant was showing a customer how a chain saw operates, I wanted to look for some new paintbrushes to go with the paint I bought for my Mum's house, but I left without them.

The dialogue above is premised on the idea that in order for a client to regain their sense of identity the client has to begin to do what they did before their trauma. However, such efforts can be easily sabotaged by the sense of 'terrified surprise'. The swapping of the 'war zone glasses' for the 'pre-trauma specs' is a graphic way of marginalising the sense of 'terrified surprise' and of refocusing such that the extreme trauma is not seen as central. But the utility of the 'war zone glasses' often needs elaboration in the therapy sessions, as the following transcript exemplifies:

Paul: I thought I was doing ok, and I was watching a film with my Mum and in it, there was an incident on a construction site, and everyone gathering around just like in mine, I had to leave the room and make a cup of tea, my Mum wanted to know what was wrong and I felt stupid because it was only a detective story and someone was murdered but it was made to look like an accident.

Th: The problem with the 'war zone glasses' is that sometimes they are perched on your head and they slip down without realising it and it feels like you are in the middle of the battlefield, and you just run. The secret is to stay put, while you get your pre-incident specs out and just do and think what you would do before in this particular situation.

Paul: I'll try that, maybe I can use the specs my Dad used to wear, not used them since he died a few years ago.

Th: Yes, going by how he would respond, rather than the incident taking over and dictating your actions.

Paul: I was still in a state when my Dad's friend, John arrived to see how I was, it was good talking to him and we agreed to do a little cycle ride along a converted rail path. Felt too dangerous on the road but also not sure how my back will hold up.

Th: Did you cycle on roads before the incident?

Paul: Yes, no problem cycled to work.

Th: Interesting how the 'war zone glasses' slip down.

Paul: Oh yes, never realised.

The above transcript indicates how the state of 'terrified surprise' permeates almost every context in PTSD and not just those that obviously relate to the extreme trauma. So that, treatment becomes 'how to navigate in a fog'.

References

American Psychiatric Association. (2000). *Diagnostic and statistical manual of mental disorders* (4th ed., Text Revision). Washington, D.C.: APA.

American Psychiatric Association. (2013). *Diagnostic and statistical manual of mental disorders* (5th ed.). Washington, D.C.: APA.

Chapter 11

A Marked Target?

Many trauma victims harbour a belief that they are especially vulnerable. This leads to safety behaviours that others in the same cultural context would see as excessive. In turn, this means that they live life in a 'bunker' with a resulting deterioration of mood because of a loss of stimuli. They become a prisoner of their own imaginings. In this chapter, the reader is introduced to a witness of an armed robbery and the steps taken to release her from her 'prison'.

Tanya

Tanya had driven to her local supermarket for her weekly Friday, shop. It was late morning, as she walked towards the Store she could see a commotion. As she crossed the roadway outside the Store she heard men in black balaclava's, and guns scream 'get down', the robbers ran towards her, she had fleeting eye contact with one of the robbers a moment before he knocked her over, stumbled and cursed. Tanya had a severe panic attack and was attended to by a paramedic at the scene. The police wanted to question her but she told them that she could not speak now and gave them her address. A member of the Store staff took her phone and rang her friend Cordelia to collect her. Since the robbery, she had been getting her friend to do the shopping.

Diagnostic Interview

Tanya was assessed using the QuickSCID-5 (First & Williams, 2021). Given her panic attack at the time of the incident, an enquiry was made using the 'current panic disorder' module. The gateway questions to this module ask about whether the person has had a panic attack in the past six months and whether at least two of her attacks were uncued. Tanya answered that her attacks were initially daily but now once or twice a week. She said that the attacks happened whenever she tried to go places. But it took the therapist a little time to be clear whether at least some of her attacks occurred 'out of

DOI: 10.4324/9781003178132-13

the blue', a requirement for a panic disorder diagnosis. Further, when the therapist asked her about particular symptoms her reply was often 'sometimes'. Glancing at the QuickSCID-5 (First & Williams, 2021), the therapist was reminded to focus on the worst attack during the past six months and assess all symptoms with respect to that particular attack. Thus, the therapist ensured that there was a focus on the simultaneous presence of symptoms in making a diagnosis. However, when she was asked whether she was worried about these attacks between occurrences or worried about the consequences of an attack she said that she did not. Thus, though she had panic attacks she was not suffering from panic disorder and the QuickSSCID-5 directed the therapist to a consideration of the 'current agoraphobia' module'. Tanya reported that she had lost her confidence to go out alone and to stores. Her rationale was that she might be recognised by the robber. She now rarely went out alone and always avoided stores. Tanya, therefore, met the criteria for agoraphobia. The trauma was extreme enough to warrant detailed enquiry about the possibility of PTSD and she reported being disturbed by the image of the robber's eyes, this in turn affected her ability to get to sleep. To the therapist's surprise when enquiring about possible avoidance symptoms, Tanya gave an affirmative response to the question of using alcohol to 'numb' yourself or to try to forget what happened. In turn, this led to examining the possibility of substance use disorder. It emerged that from about a month post-trauma she had been drinking alcohol 'to help get asleep', but the next day she could not be bothered cleaning up and it would be midday before she got dressed. She met the criteria for substance use disorder. Tanya had many of the symptoms of PTSD including excessive security precautions, she had had two mortice locks put on her front door and felt compelled to investigate the source of any disturbance outside her flat. But she had insufficient symptoms of negative alterations in cognition and mood to merit a diagnosis of PTSD but would be regarded as having a sub-syndromal level of the disorder.

A study by Pietrzak et al. (2021) suggested that of those with subsyndromal PTSD a third (34.3%) go onto developed full PTSD over a 7 year period, compared to less than a tenth (7.6%) of those without subthreshold PTSD. Care has to be taken in interpreting these findings as they were based on self-report measures and the sample were veterans, but the differential is nevertheless stark. Further subthreshold PTSD is also linked to higher rates of suicidal ideation above and beyond the effect of major depressive disorder Marshall et al. (2001).

Tanya met the criteria for depression. Her response to one of the questions relating to suicidal behaviour 'Have you thought about taking your own life?' was 'if I carry on like this, there will be no point in being here'. Whilst there were no other indicators of suicidal behaviour, the therapist thought Tanya's response was on the border between passive suicidal ideation and active planning, and that it would need monitoring.

Treatment

Tanya was disturbed by images of the 'eyes' of the robber who knocked her over when making his escape. She said that she wanted to focus on getting rid of the eyes, in the first treatment session the exchange went:

Tanya: He was staring right through me.
Therapist: And you were staring at him?
Tanya: Yes.
Therapist: What colour were his eyes?
Tanya: I don't know, it all happened so quickly.
Therapist: Could you then have been staring at each other?
Tanya: It seemed to go on forever, but it must have been seconds. In my dreams, I meet those eyes again, I'm afraid to go to sleep because I know what I'll meet and if I am woken from a bad dream about them I can't get back to sleep because I will go into them again.
Therapist: You look at life now literally through those 'eyes' and life has become a warzone and you hide in your bunker.
Tanya: Yes.
Th: What makes you take those eyes seriously now?
Tanya: He might know me and be out to get me.
Th: If you can't remember the colour of his eyes, why would he be able to remember yours?
Tanya: He probably wouldn't.
Th: Putting yourself in the robber's shoes, what do you think would have been uppermost in his mind at the time?
Tanya: He was probably just thinking about escaping. I know one of them had hit a security guard over the head and he was rushed to Hospital. Maybe, he was wondering whether they had killed him.
Th: Did he think that you were so significant that he stopped in his tracks and took a photo of you?
Tanya: No, it sounds stupid when you put it like that.

In this dialogue, the therapist has challenged her idea that she is central to the robber's concerns, without denying that the robbery was an upsetting event. For homework, Tanya was asked to remind herself that eye contact with the robber was momentary and not relevant to today in that, her increased security measures were probably unnecessary. The next therapy session began:

Tanya: I began thinking that the eye contact, wasn't like the eye contact with a potential lover where you remember every detail and know where this may all go.

Th: It sounds as if you have come up with a quite different story of the incident.

Tanya: Yes, I'm not drinking until later in the day and I don't binge as much.

Th: Binge?

Tanya: Yes, I have been eating like a pig since the incident, put on 1.5 stone I look disgusting.

The therapist then proceeded to ask the questions contained in the current binge eating disorder' module of the QuckScID-5 (First & Williams, 2021) and found that she met the diagnostic criteria. This exemplifies how assessment is rarely a one-off procedure conducted at the inception of contact. In turn, this leads to a modification of treatment. It was suggested to Tanya that she should only eat at the dining room table with a knife and fork and this gave her a sense of control over the eating. This was akin to the emerging sense of control she had by postponing the beginning of her drinking for an hour. With both disorders, there was an implicit challenge to her belief that some people had 'will power' and some do not and that she was one of the unfortunates. Just as she was encouraged to 'nudge' herself forward in relation to both disorders she was encouraged to engage in 'baby step dares' with regards to going out alone and to Stores. This was a challenge to her 'all or nothing thinking' that she either did what she was supposed to do or do nothing at all. The whole approach to Tanya's difficulties was incremental, but because of the possibility of the sub-syndromal PTSD becoming full PTSD, she was monitored every three months for 18 months post-treatment with advice to return if symptoms escalated. At the follow-ups, the therapist emphasised the importance of her re-connecting with those in her social network and forging additional relationships as an important protective factor with regard to suicide and PTSD.

References

First, M. B., & Williams, J. B. W. (2021). *Quick structured clinical interview for DSM-5 disorders.* Washington, D.C.: APA.

Marshall, R. D., Olfson, M., Hellman, F., Blanco, C., Guardino, M., & Struening, E. L. (2001). Comorbidity, impairment, and suicidality in subthreshold PTSD. *The American Journal of Psychiatry, 158*(9), 1467–1473. 10.1176/appi.ajp.158.9.1467

Pietrzak, R. G., Javier, F. G., Krystal, J. H., & Southwick, S. M. (2021). Subthreshold post-traumatic stress disorder as a risk factor for post-traumatic stress disorder: Results from a sample of USA veterans. *British Journal of Psychiatry.* 10.1192/bjp.2021.17

Chapter 12

The Amplification of Vulnerability

Clients may present after an obviously extreme trauma but may have pre-existing non-trauma-related problems and unrelated post-trauma stressors.

Overview

In this chapter, the case of Mariam, a refugee from Syria, is considered, she had undergone displacement from many friends and relatives there, but accompanied by her mother she came to the UK with the help of her uncle, a UK resident. At home in Syria, she had problems with bedwetting and being separated from her mother, but both Mariam and her mother saw these as understandable responses to their fragile existence as Christians in Syria and the disappearance of her father. At the age of 16, she was subjected to a racist attack and left with a scar on her face. Unfortunately, Mariam's mum developed COVID and was hospitalised and suffered long-term COVID. Up to the time that Mariam was attacked she had been doing well in the two years that she had been at school in the UK.

Diagnostic Interview

The standardised semi-structured interviews have only been validated for adults with the exception of the CAPS for Children and Adolescents (Pynoos et al. 2015), and this was therefore used to examine Mariam, and confirmed that she was suffering from PTSD. She was very fearful of groups of young white males. But care had to be taken using the CAPS (Pynoos et al., 2015) as Mariam's English though good was not perfect. Mariam was very determined to study law in the sixth Form and become a lawyer. Mariam considered herself a 'bad person' because her mother needed her support but she had become very irritable with her since the attack. The QuickSCID-5 (First & Williams, 2021) contains screening questions, inter alia, for separation anxiety disorder 'have you been especially anxious about being separated from people you're attached to?', body dysmorphic disorder, 'have you been very concerned that there is something wrong with

DOI: 10.4324/9781003178132-14

your physical appearance or the way one or more parts of your body look?' and excoriation disorder 'have you been repeatedly picking at your skin?' Detailed exploration of her responses to these questions revealed that her separation anxiety had been re-ignited by the assault as had her bedwetting. In addition, she was suffering from body dysmorphic disorder and excoriation disorder. Having had to care for her mother post-COVID and having seen its devastating impact, she did spend a lot of time thinking that she might contract it, and the therapist did wonder whether this would constitute DSM-5 (American Psychiatric Association, 2013) defined Illness Anxiety Disorder but decided to leave this matter in abeyance until there was a real-world improvement in the other conditions, by which time its significance may have faded. However, though she had some symptoms of depression, she was not clinically depressed.

Treatment

The therapist's intent was to address all the identified disorders and to re-examine for Illness Anxiety Disorder when Mariam had made significant gains. But the first treatment session took an unexpected turn in that she said that she did not want her mum present, the session began:

Th: The therapist handed her a tissue as she began gently sobbing and enquired is it your mum? [Mum was sitting in the waiting room].
Mariam: No, its not her, I don't like to upset her, she has been through enough.
Th: What was triggering the tears?
Mariam: It's my Dad's birthday, it's 10 years since I last saw him, we just don't know what has happened to him, he went to work one day and never returned.
Th: Were you close to him?
Mariam: Yes, I was a proper Daddies girl, probably spoilt, he would sit and read me stories over and over and I'd cuddle in.

The above dialogue underlines the importance of giving the client the space to express what is troubling them rather than steam-rollering in the therapist's agenda. In this way, the fabric of the treatment protocols can be made germane to the client's experiences. This personalisation of treatment is the only way to bring about lasting change. In the next dialogue, the therapist could have switched tacks to something more obviously aligned to the identified disorders but chose instead to validate the client's experience:

Th: What did your Dad read to you?
Mariam: *Brightening* he read Winnie The Pooh over and over, I've still got Tigger, he's very battered but he's been through everything with me.

Th: Maybe give him a makeover?
Mariam: He could certainly do with a wash, but I better do him by hand and see how that goes. I keep meaning to get him the eye that he lost coming from Syria.
Th: Maybe you would feel nearer to your Dad if you did that.
Mariam: Yes, I could see him smiling looking down at the restored Tigger.
Th: Yes, in many ways what we are trying to do in therapy is restore you to what you were like before the assault.
Mariam: But my face isn't the same.
Th: But you are still Mariam.

The above transcript highlights a smooth transition from open-ended questions that elicit the panorama of a client's difficulties, to zoom in on sections of that vista. It is a matter of maintaining a dual focus on the foreground and the background. The next session began thus:

Th: How did you get on with Tigger?
Mariam: Good, but I think he needs restuffing.
Th: Last time we talked a little about restoring your life, did you have any further thoughts on that?
Mariam: I want to just move on but keep on getting dragged back.
Th: How do you mean?
Mariam: Mum was trying to fill in the form for the Criminal Injuries Compensation Authority and she starts asking me for details of the assault, but I got ratty with her, I don't want to talk about it. Then, my Uncle joins in telling me off for talking to Mum, like that and then asking me questions about it.
Th: Do you think it is right to put in a Claim?
Mariam: Yes, it is part of justice.
Th: But there might be a price for getting justice.
Mariam: Well, these things have got to be sorted, like what was happening to Christians in Syria.
Th: You are right, there is no point in going over horrible things for the sake of it, but you still have to ask what does the horror mean about today if anything. You don't have to say that the horror means everything about today but inspect it enough to see any implications for today. That is why the horror comes back in a flashback or dream it is just asking you is this relevant in any way for today, so long as you calmly answer the question there is no problem, but if you try and shoot the question or the carrier of the question, like your Mum that becomes a problem.
Mariam: I suppose, it is like seeing an exam question, I just have to keep my cool about it and answer the best way I can, it would be stupid to complain about the examiner.

In this dialogue, the therapist has used the client's own experience, to provide psycho-education on the function of intrusions and the appropriate response. Underlining that it is the centrality accorded to the trauma that can become a problem, not the trauma itself. But that is not to say that the memory of a trauma may not have implications for today, the session continued:

Th: Did you feel that justice was done to the lads that assaulted you?

Mariam: Well there were four lads, but really only two of them were mouthing off, one said 'you really fancy me don't you Paki'. I said his geography was crap, then the lad next to him said 'smart ****' and pushed me and I fell hitting my forehead on the corner of a park bench, there was blood everywhere, I thought I was going to be raped. But one of the lads, with red hair from my school who hadn't spoken, said 'let's go', just then an old man walking his dog came over to us. The police went to school then to the red-haired lad's home, he told them who the other lads were. But school and the police said that this lad has lots of personal and family problems, so he wasn't suspended and was very apologetic when I saw him in the Head's office. He just puts his head down whenever he sees me. Not sure what happened to other lads, I didn't recognise them. But they should pay for this scar, *she said this moving the fringe of her hair to reveal it.*

Th: Now that you have pointed it out I can notice it, but I don't think anyone would spot it if they weren't looking for it.

Mariam: You're just being nice.

Th: You could have your fringe down Monday, Wednesday and Friday and your hair brushed back other days and see if there are any differences in people's reactions on the different days.

Mariam: Like an experiment?

Th: Yes, go by the results and not how you feel.

Mariam: hmmm

In the above dialogue, the therapist has not curtailed the client's discussion of the trauma but signalled that it need not have the last word on any particular day and that the weighting given to it will depend on the context for that day. Historically, the diagnosis of body dysmorphic disorder (BDD) has been largely reserved to those with an imagined defect in appearance that they are pre-occupied with, but DSM-5 adds that BDD is also possible in response to 'a minor physical anomaly' but does not specify what 'minor' is. The therapist went on to suggest that just as the trauma did not have to be the window through which she viewed her personal world so to the scar did not have to be the window through which she viewed her interactions with others or defined her worth. But when the therapist put this to her she responded:

Mariam: Look at me I'm having to wear a long-sleeved blouse to cover my arms on a sweltering hot day. Mum had to get up in the middle of the night because I had wet the bed, I sleep with her since the assault. It is not fair to her she is still getting over COVID, she was in the High Dependency Unit (HDU) for a month in the first lockdown, lying on her stomach hearing the groans of the other patients. That was six months ago she still gets exhausted walking just to the local shops and she doesn't cook like she used to because her taste and smell aren't quite right.

Th: That must have been an awful time when she was in HDU?

Mariam: Yes, the good thing was that she never had to go to Intensive Care and a ventilator.

Th: How did she cope?

Mariam: Weirdly, she decided it was a good time to practice the meditation/prayer she had been trying to do for years but always got distracted, so she wasn't as disturbed by the sounds she heard or her worries about how things were going to turn out.

Th: I suppose she was making other things more central?

Mariam: Yes, but a bit of a weirdo?

Th: But it worked?

Mariam: I guess.

In the above dialogue, the therapist is following the client's concerns and not rigidly adhering to a treatment protocol. This contrasts sharply with the findings of Drew et al. (2021) who examined the transcripts of early Improving Access to Psychological Therapies (IAPT) sessions and found an almost total absence of the personalisation of treatment. The therapist was also capitalising on the opportunity to use a significant other to act as a role model for looking through a different window even in the direst of circumstances. In such lies part of the creativity of therapy. The next session continued:

Th: Last time you mentioned a host of problems bed wetting, separation anxiety and the picking of skin on your left forearm, I'd like to come with a game plan for each of these by the end of the session. The danger is we mix all the problems up together and it all feels too much.

Mariam: Just doing a bit on each, sounds good. It's like doing revising for my Mock GCSE's, if I think of all of it I just want to give up.

Th: Yes, it is like putting all the subjects in a queue outside a turnstile, letting a little bit of one subject thru at a time, then have a break then the next. See it as a waste of timekeeping on looking at the length of the queue. Where would you like to start?

Mariam:	Well, I've decided not to fuss over my scar, when I look at some of the other Asylum Seekers from Syria my scar doesn't begin to compare and they just get on with it. I have been telling myself 'get a life'.
Th:	So, what could you tackle next?
Mariam:	I need to go and sleep in my own room, so at least I won't disturb Mum with the bedwetting. I would take Tigger with me.
Th:	What has stopped you doing that so far?
Mariam:	It is stupid, but when I tried to after the assault, as I was trying to get to sleep I imagined the lads coming for me.
Th:	How could you handle that if it came to mind tonight if you tried sleeping in your own bed?
Mariam:	I need to tell myself it is nothing like the chances of being bombed when we were in Syria.
Th:	Sounds good, even if you can only stay in your own bed for 30 minutes it is a start and you can gradually build up.

In the above extract, the therapist is inoculating the client against possible failures. The therapist is also capitalising on her resilience in having coped with war-torn Syria, albeit that it had resulted in bedwetting and separation anxiety at the time. But she had had a period post-Syria when she was free of these problems. The therapist went on to suggest discussing the use of a 'bell and pad' (bedwetting alarm) with her Mum and a Health Visitor, as her bedwetting appeared secondary to the assault but it would be important to exclude a physical trigger i.e. that there was a primary enuresis problem. This method consists of a device worn at night that has a sensor, making a noise when it becomes wet and ideally waking up the child in time for her to stop the stream and go to the bathroom. But it can take several months to be effective. It was suggested that the excoriation disorder, be addressed by developing a sense of control over it by postponing skin picking with a competing behaviour, by manipulating modelling clay or making figures with it and gradually extending the periods of postponement. Then, as the appearance of her forearm improved not covering it up. But care had to be taken at this stage so that the locus of her body dysmorphic disorder was not extended to her forearm.

Importantly the therapist also suggested that the threat levels were nothing like Syria, which were so bad that she had to escape. But that if she stayed at home rather than ventured out she was donning war zone glasses, which were poor fashion accessories. She was encouraged to leave home in a graded fashion but some reminders would make her want to run for cover – rather like hearing fireworks go off in the UK initially created a state of terrified surprise, which abated as she moved from fireworks at home to going to a public display. Her concerns about possibly contracting COVID had largely evaporated by the end of treatment, and they were not made a direct focus. But as part of the follow-up, the therapist asked her whether she was pre-occupied with the possibility of getting COVID and her response was negative.

References

American Psychiatric Association. (2013). *Diagnostic and statistical manual of mental disorders* (5th ed.). Washington, D.C.: APA.

Drew, P., Irvine, A., Barkham M., Faija, C., Gellatly, J., Ardern, K., Armitage, J. C., Brooks, H., Rushton, K., Welsh, C., Bower, P., & Bee, P. (2021). Telephone delivery of psychological interventions: Balancing protocol with patient-centred care. *Social Science and Medicine*, 277. 10.1016/j.socscimed.2021.113818

First, M. B., & Williams, J. B. W. (2021). *Quick structured clinical interview for DSM-5 disorders*. Washington, D.C: American Psychiatric Association.

Pynoos, R. S., Weathers, F. W., Steinberg, A. M., Marx, B. P., Layne, C. M., Kaloupek, D. G., Schnurr, P. P., Keane, T. M., Blake, D. D., Newman, E., Nader, K. O., & Kriegler, J. A. (2015). *Clinician-Administered PTSD Scale for DSM-5 - Child/Adolescent Version*. Scale available from the National Center for PTSD at www.ptsd.va.gov.

Part III

Managing the Crises That Can Derail Trauma Treatment

Introduction

For many trauma victims, their experience of life consists of one or more extreme traumas combined with lesser traumas that may be protracted. The lesser traumas do not easily fit into the prescribed protocols for the treatment of trauma-related disorders. However, in the following three chapters, brief vignettes are described regarding the management of such cases. Consistent with the theme of centrality evinced throughout this volume, these clients are encouraged not to let the lesser traumas become the window through which they view their sense of self and the safety of their personal world.

Not only extreme traumas but also negative life events can produce debility. If the negative life events are protracted as in the case of prolonged bullying or being the main carer for a relative with a progressive neurological disorder this may lead to what Scott and Stradling (1994) have termed prolonged duress stress disorder (PDSD). This is reminiscent of PTSD in that there are similar symptoms of intrusion and avoidance but without the sense of terrified surprise. Further, the gateway to PDSD is not an extreme trauma. However, PDSD is not a recognised disorder in any official classificatory system, but the author has found that it has a clinical utility. PDSD can also occur alongside other officially recognised disorders making for a slightly different slant on treatment.

The next chapter, Chapter 13, considers the treatment of a client, Barney, with what might be considered PDSD, as a result of bullying at work. Additionally, he was struggling to cope with the added stress of an Industrial Tribunal, which in turn impacted his depression.

The pandemic has created its own cloud of uncertainty both with regard to health and employment. In Chapter 14, the focus is on a Healthcare Assistant, Bernice, who had to contend with the effects of the pandemic whilst her own depression is addressed. Her long-term prejudice against herself served as a vulnerability factor.

War can be profoundly damaging both mentally and physically, the person's resilience can be gravely tested if it occurs in the wake of apparent

DOI: 10.4324/9781003178132-15

recovery from a possible fatal illness. Angela is the focus of Chapter 15, she was a soldier who suffered from non-Hodgkins lymphoma, recovered sufficiently to return to active service then lost her dominant hand when an improvised explosive device was triggered. She had flashbacks not only of the explosion but also was troubled by memories of being told that she had cancer, of the hospital visits then and more recently over her hand and the possibilities of a prosthesis. After discharge from the Army, the family home that was bequeathed to her was subject to periodic flooding, because it was on a flood plain and she felt overwhelmed.

Reference

Scott, M. J., & Stradling, S. G. (1994). Post-traumatic stress disorder without the trauma. *British Journal of Clinical Psychology*, 33, 71–74.

Chapter 13

Prolonged Duress Stress Disorder

The advent of the Vietnam war played a pivotal role in the codification of the stress response to extreme trauma, resulting in the diagnosis of PTSD entering the diagnostic nomenclature. But this may have obscured that lesser and sometimes prolonged trauma e.g. witnessing a partner die of cancer over 12 months, may also produce flashbacks of worst moments, and avoidance e.g. of hospitals/funerals. It seems likely that there is at least some degree of overlap between response to lesser traumas and PTSD that strategies applied to the latter may also have relevance to the former. However, in the authors experience the lesser traumas rarely lead to a sense of 'terrified surprise'. A case example of what Scott and Stradling (1994) have termed prolonged duress stress disorder (PDSD) follows.

Overview

Barney had worked in Nursing Homes catering for the elderly for 30 years, he had enjoyed the work until conflicts with his Manager began 3 years before. After 12 months of working with this manager, he found it so intolerable that he sought a move to another Nursing Home run by the same Care group, but unfortunately, 6 months later his former Manager moved to the same Home and became his boss. Within 6 months, he was given written warnings and finally sacked. Barney was repeatedly humiliated in front of other staff because of his poor report writing and fault was found with his not dressing/feeding residents appropriately. He was taking his employer to an Industrial Tribunal but told that this would take one to two years. The lack of income strained further his relationship with his wife and he felt that he was letting down his sons, who were in their late teens.

Diagnostic Interview

Using the QuickScid (First & Williams, 2021), it was established that Barney was suffering from depression. Although he did not meet the gateway stressor criteria for PTSD, he met the symptom criteria. However, he was

DOI: 10.4324/9781003178132-16

neither hyper-vigilant nor did he have an exaggerated startle response, and thus he would not be regarded as being in a state of terrified surprise. He met the criteria for PDSD. Barney ruminated constantly about his Manager's behaviour in the past 6 months of his employment. He did this to the extent that he rarely walked his dog or went for a bike ride. Barney had flashback's of his Manager angrily throwing down a report he had written and saying 'you write and spell like a 6-year-old' and a young colleague shuffling away in embarrassment. Barney had always struggled with literacy and recent testing had revealed that he was dyslexic.

Treatment

For Barney, his job performance was the litmus test of his worth. The loss of this overvalued role triggered his depression. Treatment was therefore focussed on decoupling his sense of worth from his job performance. The therapist noted that only one of his two teenage sons was in employment. Barney was asked whether the employed son was more worthwhile than the unemployed son. He was aghast at the suggestion. Barney readily accepted the idea that he should be as compassionate to himself as he is to his unemployed son, but nevertheless thought that there would remain a pervading sense of worthlessness. The therapist agreed that this might be the case, but he had a choice about whether to attach significance to the felt sense of worthlessness.

Barney needed to prepare for the Industrial Tribunal, but there was a danger of this legitimising a rumination on his last months in work. To counteract this, it was agreed that he would, three times a week dictate to his cousin the material that would be necessary for the Tribunal, but he was not allowed to 'pick' at these materials at other times. This strategy also helped with his dyslexia. It was agreed however that he could make phone calls in relation to his work-related matters.

Barney dismissed the idea of working because he would need a reference from his last employer and he was certain this would be very negative. The therapist suggested that he might utilise the extensive network of contacts he had developed in the social care sector over the years, to possibly engage in some voluntary work. Barney thought that this might be a different route back into employment. In reviewing this exchange, the therapist highlighted how 'all or nothing thinking' contributed to his difficulties i.e. he was either in the employment situation he wanted or he was unemployed. This led to a discussion of his interactions with his partner and the dichotomous way in which he viewed the relationship, either she was the perfect partner as earlier in their relationship or she was without any merit. He conceded that she had particular difficulties over financial matters because of problems with her family of origin and he needed to make allowances for this. Barney said that she often asked him how he was feeling, but he got annoyed about this as he thought she should just know, the therapist suggested that this was an example of 'mind reading'. He acknowledged that he would not know how a resident was feeling without asking them and it was, therefore, inappropriate to expect his partner to mind read. It was also suggested that perhaps he was mind reading in assuming that his sons felt let down by his unemployment, Barney conceded that he had no actual evidence that they were critical of him in this respect.

This example illustrates how it is possible to engage in restorative cognitive behavioural therapy with a person who has literacy problems if careful attention is paid to their social context and the data that it furnishes, but this latter requires careful listening to the client's story. Nevertheless, though Barney verbally conceded the need for investments in life beyond work, he took no active steps. The therapist realised that Barney's problem with mental time travel was not confined to retrieving 'toxic' material from the past and seeing it as especially relevant to today, but in travelling forward in time he was not able to graphically envisage a typical day in which he engaged in a variety of work alternative behaviours such as working as a volunteer in a Charity shop, embarking on a fitness regime etc. As a homework, he was encouraged to 'colour in' what a typical day might be. This then acted as a prompt for activity scheduling and the addressing of his depression. Barney's case illustrates that with regards to trauma the focus tends to be on what is retrieved from the past but the problem can be as much to do with the construction of the future.

References

First, M. B., & Williams, J. B. W. (2021). *Quick structured clinical interview for DSM-5 disorders.* Washington, D.C.: APA.

Scott, M. J., & Stradling, S. G. (1994). Post-traumatic stress disorder without the trauma. *British Journal of Clinical Psychology, 33,* 71–74.

Chapter 14

Weathering the Pandemic

The focus of cognitive behaviour therapy is primarily on the treatment of specific disorders, but clients do not exist in a vacuum, psychosocial stressors may necessitate considerable adaptation to treatment. Just as post trauma, the treatment focus is on not giving the trauma itself an exalted status, so the unexpected negative life events need to be prevented from becoming the sole window through which life is viewed. The primary issue to be addressed with regards to both the trauma and negative life events is one of centrality.

Overview

In this chapter, a Healthcare Assistant in a Nursing Home was subjected to bullying by a Manager and felt unable to return to her much-loved work. This in turn resulted in financial problems and persistent low mood. The pandemic struck and she felt she was letting her colleagues down by not returning to work. However, her nine-year-old daughter was very upset at the prospect of her returning to work because of the dangers of contracting COVID. Matters were further complicated by her husband, a delivery driver, who contracted COVID. Within weeks, she too contracted COVID and was bedridden for two weeks, her GP was so concerned about the pain in her lungs that he sent her to the hospital. At the hospital, she was alarmed that there appeared to be no clear separation of COVID patients from others. She saw many distressed unaccompanied elderly people, felt very concerned for them but wanted to escape, fortunately, she was seen to recover fairly quickly and returned home after a few days. But on her return home found that an elderly neighbour living opposite to her had died and another neighbour was hospitalised and was on oxygen.

Diagnostic Interview

Bernice attended her initial assessment face-to-face interview and said she began to feel 'snappy' about nine months ago. She said that Management

DOI: 10.4324/9781003178132-17

was very unsympathetic to her juggling between her shifts to fit in with those of her husband, a delivery worker. Bernice felt outraged at this as she had given 14 years of good service. In particular, she felt betrayed by her Line Manager whom hitherto she regarded as a friend. Bernice felt the 'last straw' was when her Line Manager complained about the sick note for three months from her GP. The therapist conducted the DIAMOND (Tolin et al., 2018) diagnostic interview and established that she was suffering from depression. She had had a few panic attacks in the previous months but was not concerned about them and they did not interfere with her functioning. The therapist noted however that when Bernice was about the age of nine when her parents separated, they were both upset and she felt she could not upset them, by expressing her upset. From age 15, she had lived with her grandmother, who was very caring and more stable than mum, but she felt she missed out on the family life her siblings had had with her father.

Bernice was not regarded as meeting the DSM-5 gateway stressor criteria for PTSD because her visit to the triage ward was not regarded as an extreme trauma. Asmundson and Taylor (2021) have observed that rates of PTSD amongst those affected by COVID-19 range from as low as 5% to more than 50%, because of (a) a failure to specify the COVID-19 stressor and whether it would meet the DSM-5 gateway criteria e.g working in a COVID ward vs. being placed on a ventilator and (b) differences in the reliability of the measure used to diagnose PTSD. But a study by Janiri et al. (2021) using the CAPS (Weathers et al., 2015) interview with COVID-19 patients suggested a prevalence of 30%.

Treatment

By the time of the third scheduled treatment session, the pandemic had set in and whilst it was agreed that the treatment sessions could take place via a video link, Bernice was fearful of using the technology. The therapist was led to understand that Bernice's phone was an Android device and attempted to contact her on WhatsApp but found this was not possible because she had not downloaded the App and did not know how to. Unfortunately, Bernice took this as yet further evidence of her stupidity. In work situations, she had always declined opportunities of promotion because of perceived inadequacies. However, with the help of her husband she was able to communicate via Facetime on his i-pad. Bernice dated her sense of inadequacy back to her early teens, and found that she would ruminate over any 'failings', felt uncomfortable with praise and had a habit of twisting neutral comments, from others – much to the annoyance of her partner.

A case formulation of Bernice's difficulties suggested that in keeping with Beck's (1976) conceptualisation, her depression arose from the matching of a vulnerability factor and a triggering event. Bernice had low self-esteem from childhood but attempted to compensate for this by seeking approval. She admitted that she always needed her 'fix' of approval, in Beck's (1976) terminology, she was a sociotrope. Unfortunately, in her conflict with her manager/friend, praise was not forthcoming and this ushered her into depression. The depression was maintained initially by financial problems and missing friends and residents in the Care Home in which she worked. Latterly, the effects of the pandemic also served to maintain the depression.

Bernice was introduced to the use of the MOOD Chart, Table 9.1 to track her mood, critically appraise her first thoughts and distil more helpful second thoughts. In her case, it was very important that she ceased ruminating on the content of the last encounter with her Line Manager. Thus, the final element MOOD the 'D decide what to do and do it' had a particular salience.

Because her husband was helping with the technology initially, he was present at the early sessions and able to give specific examples of how her information processing biases contributed to miscommunication, in particular, Bernice's penchant for 'mind reading' and 'all or nothing thinking'. The technology unwittingly facilitated the engagement of her husband in the treatment which was greatly valued by Bernice as she felt he understood 'where I am coming from'.

Since the conflicts at work, she had given up her beauty therapy and seeing two or three clients on her days off, with home visits. Unfortunately, the pandemic provided a further reason for not making the home visits. As part of a strategy of widening her investment portfolio, she decided to take some online courses on 'nails'. She found that she enjoyed this more than expected and began to consider that after the pandemic she might open a beauty/nails shop. This positive flashforward helped her to lift her mood and she felt slightly less dependent on her current employment working out when she returned. When she returned to work her Manager largely ignored her and Bernice was able to focus on her relationship with residents and other staff.

But difficulties with her daughter continued after she returned to work. Her daughter regularly reminded Bernice of 'all the deaths in Nursing Homes'. Bernice tried to counter by saying that nobody had died of COVID in her particular Nursing Home, but her daughter's reaction was 'you've been lucky so far'. Matters were compounded because twice her daughter had to self-isolate following track and trace in school. Bernice wondered whether her daughter needed a professional mental health referral. The therapist suggested that her daughter had understandable concerns rather than disorder and that it might not be easy for her daughter to shake off whatever 'sticky label' any therapist might put on her. It was agreed that Bernice would introduce her daughter to calculated risk-taking by using the analogy of driving. Her partner worked making home deliveries for a leading supermarket. So, Bernice began her discussion with her daughter about what would happen to the 'housebound' people if her Dad did not make the deliveries in the pandemic. Her daughter was able to see that Dad was taking a calculated risk of both driving and contracting COVID and agreed that he should do so. In moving the discussion away from herself and her own experiences of having to self-isolate she was able to see her father's approach as a credible template for approaching risk.

References

Asmundson, G. J. G., & Taylor, S. (2021). Gabage in, garbage out: The tenuous state of research on PTSD in the context of COVID-19 pandemic and infodemic. *Journal of Anxiety Disorders, 78.* 10.1016/j.janxdis.2021.102368

Beck, A. T. (1976). *Cognitive therapy and the emotional disorders.* New York: New American Library.

Janiri, D., Carfi, A., Kotzalidis. G.D., Bernabei, R., Landi, F., & Sani, G. (2021). *Post-traumatic stress disorder in patients after severe COVID-19 infections JAMA Psychiatry Published online February 18th 2021.*

Tolin, D. F., Gilliam, C., Wootton, B. M., Bowe, W., Bragdon, L. B., Davis, E., Hannan, S. E., Steinman, S. A., Worden, B., & Hallion, L. S. (2018). Psychometric properties of a structured diagnostic interview for DSM-5 anxiety, mood, and obsessive-compulsive and related disorders. *Assessment, 25*(1), 3–13. 10.1177/1 073191116638410

Weathers, F. W., Blake, D. D., Schnurr, P. P., Kaloupek, D. G., Marx, B. P., & Keane, T. M. (2015). *The Clinician-Administered PTSD Scale for DSM-5 (CAPS-5) – Past Month / Worst Month* [Measurement instrument]. Available from https://www. ptsd.va.gov/ https://www.ptsd.va.gov/professional/assessment/adult-int/caps.asp

Chapter 15

From One War Zone to Another?

In the wake of extreme trauma, it can be extremely difficult to concentrate on the now. Indeed, one of the diagnostic symptoms of PTSD is experiencing the trauma as if it is happening now. In extreme cases and very rarely, this may involve a total loss of awareness of the surroundings but more commonly clients report a sense of 'nowness' about the trauma. There is a sense that they are not just remembering the trauma but re-experiencing it. This degree of dissociation interferes with the adaptive functioning.

The mnemonic TIC/TOC is an aid to switching from task-interfering cognitions (TICs), e.g. 'I'm going to make a mess of this exam, I'm not up to it' to task-orientated cognitions (TOCs), e.g. 'I'll just make a start on the first question and see how it goes'. But cognition refers not only to thoughts but also to images. An unbidden image of receiving notification of a previous examination failure might equally sabotage the performance. This might be offset by calling to mind an image of receiving notification of a past success in an examination. The more graphic the imagery the more powerful it is likely to be. For example, recalling the taste of the drink that you had when you celebrated your exam success is likely to be more potent than simply recalling the scene when you received a positive notification. The TICs and TOCs can be regarded as two parallel streams of thought competing for attention, the former can be regarded as background noise and the latter as the main signal. Thus, the therapeutic task is to focus on the main signal and to ignore the inevitable background noise. Implicitly, there is an acceptance of the 'back-ground noise'. This has particular salience for those who have been traumatised and may understandably wish to rid themselves of the traumatic memory. Just as it is impossible to rid an electrical signal of background noise, so to adaptive functioning today involves some budgeting for interference, with a gradual better tuning in, with practice. This metaphor provides an antidote to cognitive avoidance.

Debility post-trauma almost always involves unbidden images of the trauma. In restorative CBT, the goal is to make current functioning replicate pre-trauma functioning as far as possible. Thus, the graphic recall of functioning well pre-trauma, in a not too dissimilar context to the trauma, is at a

DOI: 10.4324/9781003178132-18

premium. This image then competes for attention with the traumatic memory. Task orientation involves selecting this memory as more relevant to today.

But once traumatised, there can be a multiplicity of intrusive images, stemming from a variety of traumas, of varying severity. The case of Angela described in this chapter reflects this complex history.

Angela

Angela had been a soldier in the Army for seven years when she was sent to Afghanistan. She was badly injured by an improvised explosive device and lost her left hand. Angela remembered trying to assist an injured colleague, but then had no memory of events until she regained consciousness in a Field Hospital. She had only returned to duty six months earlier after a year's absence fighting non-Hodgkin's lymphoma. After the explosion, she was troubled by not only intrusive images of the latter, but also of being told that she had cancer and of waiting for the results after the different rounds of chemotherapy. Back in the UK, she had inherited a family home from her grandparents but unfortunately, it was located on a flood plain and two years previously her aged grandparents had to vacate the property for a year whilst it was restored. Angela was pleased that flood defences in the area were being strengthened but was fearful that they may prove insufficient. She would have liked to move to be nearer to some former colleagues but in the circumstances her home was not marketable. Angela reflected that in any case she could not visit her friends because of the pandemic. Her psychological therapy was conducted via video link but it had not been possible to refine her prosthesis for her left hand because of the pandemic.

Diagnostic Interview

Angela was assessed using the MINI interview (Sheehan et al., 1998) and found to be suffering from PTSD with associated trauma-related guilt. She said that she lost consciousness as she was trying to apply a tourniquet to the leg of a colleague who, subsequently died. Angela met up with her colleague's partner and her little girl at the Memorial service and though she very much enjoyed the encounter, and left with promises to keep in touch, afterwards she felt terribly guilty about the child growing up without a father. Unfortunately, keeping in touch was made more difficult because of the ensueing pandemic, but her colleague's partner had herself been a soldier in the first year of Angela's military service, leaving to have her child. Angela felt trapped by her physical and mental state, which she regarded as 'imprisonment'.

Treatment

Careful listening to Angela's story was a springboard for treatment, in particular what might release her from a sense of 'imprisonment'. Angela noted that since the pandemic she had noticed a great increase in the number of people walking a dog, and thought that it would give her a reason to get up of a morning and go out. She recalled how she enjoyed the family dog as a child but realised they take a great deal of care and might limit her mobility. The therapist informed her of the development of service dogs being used with US military personnel with PTSD. Whilst these dogs were not intended as pets but trained to e.g., to wake veterans from nightmares it was possible that a pet may serve a not too dissimilar function. Angela decided to offer her parents a 'respite' from caring for their dog, Moss, and to see how that worked out. She was already familiar with Moss and noted that when she was on walks with him and particularly sullen he would go around in front of her, turn to face her and bark. The therapist suggested that it was in just a circumstance that she could apply the Mood Chart (see Table 9.1) and she was able to find better second thoughts than the usually exaggeratedly negative first thoughts. She also found that the presence of Moss served as a reminder to be in the present moment when she had intrusive flashbacks, by stroking her dog. The dog also reminded her of happy times in childhood walking the family dog. Angela was introduced to the TIC/TOC procedure in which the traumas were seen as inevitable background noise that had the potential to sabotage the construction of life now, 'the main signal'.

However, there were ongoing issues about her trauma-related guilt (TRG) and the possibility that her cancer may return. With regard to the TRG, the therapist asked Angela whether she blamed her colleague who died for not attending to her injuries in the aftermath of the explosion and she replied, 'of course not'. The therapist then asked whether she was any more able to care for the wounded than he was and she agreed that she was not. Angela was then encouraged to treat the TRG like a mental cold, a nuisance, but not be taken seriously. Her uncertainty about the return of cancer was addressed in the same manner as her fearfulness about getting flooded, whilst the chances were not non-existent it was important that these events were not made central to her day-to-day functioning. Angela agreed to make a special time of the day when she could address these fears on paper if she felt she needed to, but was not be allowed to pick at them at other times. In this way avoiding depressive rumination.

Angela found that when she was with her dog she felt less need for hypervigilance and found e.g. that if there was an unexpected noise outside of her home, she did not feel compelled to go and find the source of the disturbance. She also found that when she was startled, she could calm herself quickly by stroking the dog. Thus, Moss helped her address her state of 'terrified surprise' and management of intrusions. Unfortunately, because of the pandemic, it was not possible to modify her prosthesis to the extent that she could make fine movements with it and she experienced phantom limb pain at times. However, with a mild-to-moderate level of phantom limb pain, she was able to switch her attention to music or stroking her dog to make the pain more manageable.

Angela was encouraged to initiate contact with former soldier colleagues including the partner of the deceased soldier and her child but had to be content with doing this via video link. She was told to resist the temptation of resorting to her 'bunker', a metaphor that had great resonance for her.

Reference

Sheehan, D. V., Lecrubier, Y., Sheehan, K. H., Amorim, P., Janavs, J., Weiller, E., Hergueta, T., Baker, R., & Dunbar, G. C. (1998). The Mini-International Neuropsychiatric Interview (M.I.N.I.): The development and validation of a structured diagnostic psychiatric interview for DSM-IV and ICD-10. *The Journal of Clinical Psychiatry, 59 Suppl 20*, 22–57.

Part IV

Disseminating Trauma Treatment

Introduction

The cognitive behaviour therapies were developed by academic clinicians who endorsed the view that psychological therapists were scientist-practitioners (Hofmann, 2013). Notwithstanding that the latter rarely had the resources to read the research publications or conduct independent research. Further, the reward structure for academic/clinicians is totally different to that for psychological therapists, the former is dependent on successful grant applications, publications in peer-reviewed journals, the latter is judged largely on organisational commitment. More realistically, psychological practitioners are more akin to engineers who are concerned with the application of the sciences to everyday life. The development and dissemination of the personal computer were made possible by engineers who translated the functioning of room-sized computers, that were developed by physicists/mathematicians during and after the Second World War, into something that was portable. The dialogue between engineers and scientists is so fluid that in Research and Development teams an individual's precise background would often be unclear. But between academic/clinicians and psychological therapists, the traffic is largely one way with the former proscribing the functioning of the latter in routine practice in primary care. The higher managerial posts are held by academic/clinicians who like almost all senior managers believe 'my door is always open', but this makes for conflicts of interest when evaluating the effectiveness of service provision.

Groups are an attractive option for any manager (Scott, 2011), but whilst there is reliable evidence for their effectiveness with depression and some anxiety disorders, it is lacking for trauma-related disorders. These considerations are the focus of Chapter 16. Given that academic/clinicians have developed the protocols for the treatment of trauma-related disorders, that are effective to a degree, they have a vested interest in their promotion. This makes it likely that they would define therapeutic competence in such a way as to legitimate their approach, 'effort justification'. But if a mathematician were asked what is the correct way to add two, two-digit numbers say, 43

DOI: 10.4324/9781003178132-19

and 29, he would likely say there is not a 'correct way' so long as you conclude the answer is 72. Just as there are many pathways to successful addition, the literature reviewed in this volume suggests that there are likely many effective routes to trauma treatment. What matters is whether the treatment can be shown to make a 'real world difference'. Those claiming a monopoly on the determination of competence, whether they be cognitive behavioural therapy lead organisations or academic clinicians, are appealing to their eminence rather than the evidence, such are the considerations of the final chapter, Chapter 17, of this volume.

References

Hofmann S. G. (2013). Bridging the theory-practice gap by getting even bolder with the Boulder model. *Behavior Therapy*, 44(4), 603–608. 10.1016/j.beth.2013.04.006

Scott, M. J. (2011). *Simply effective group cognitive behaviour therapy: A Practitioners guide*. London: Routledge.

Chapter 16

Groups Post-trauma

Groups are an attractive option for service providers, offering the prospect of reduced waiting lists and greater access to therapy. But comparisons of group interventions show them to be inferior to individual therapy post-trauma and to offer no added benefit to treatment as usual.

Kearney et al. (2021) compared the effectiveness of group cognitive processing therapy (CPT) for the treatment of PTSD with group loving-kindness meditation (LKM) which involved the silent repetition of phrases intended to elicit feelings of kindness for oneself and others. The proportion of veterans who lost their diagnostic status i.e. who no longer suffered from PTSD did not differ at the end of treatment (CPT – 29%, LKM – 27.5%). Each intervention consisted of 12 weekly 90-minute group sessions but the mean number sessions completed was only six in CPT and seven in LKM. Resick et al. (2017) found that in a population of veterans group CPT was inferior to individual CPT.

Preparatory group treatment for CPT or prolonged exposure does not enhance outcome. Dedert et al. (2020) examined whether a preparatory group with a focus on psychoeducation, coping skills, sleep hygiene and an introduction to PTSD treatment options added benefit to the trauma-focussed interventions, it did not. Further, those who went through a preparatory group did less well than those who did not in whatever trauma-focussed CBT they went onto in terms of PTSD symptom reduction. There is no evidence that initial Stabilisation Groups contribute to treatment effectiveness. However, the aforementioned studies were all on veterans, so care has to be taken in generalising from the results. But a study by Mahoney et al. (2020) of women prisoners who reported a history of interpersonal violence and trauma found that a ten-session group psychoeducational programme, Survive and Thrive, conferred no benefit over treatment as usual. There appears to be no benefit to a phase-based approach, in which the first phase has as its goal safety and stabilisation, despite the inherent attractiveness of this option.

DOI: 10.4324/9781003178132-20

References

Dedert, E. A., LoSavio, S. T., Wells, S. Y., Steel, A. L., Reinhardt, K., Deming, C. A.,... Clancy, C. P. (2020). Clinical effectiveness study of a treatment to prepare for trauma- focused evidence-based psychotherapies at a Veterans Afairs specialty posttraumatic stress disorder clinic. *Psychological Services*. Advance online publication. PTSDpubs ID: 1557789. 10.1037/ser0000425

Kearney, D. J., Malte, C. A., Storms, M., & Simpson, T. L. (2021). Loving-kindness meditation vs cognitive processing therapy for posttraumatic stress disorder among Veterans: A randomized clinical trial. *JAMA Network Open, 4*(4), e216604. 10.1001/jamanetworkopen.2021.6604

Mahoney, A., Karatzias, T., Halliday, K., & Dougal, N. (2020). How important are Phase 1 interventions for complex interpersonal trauma? A pilot randomized control trial of a group psychoeducational intervention. *Clinical Psychology & Psychotherapy, 27*(4), 597. 10. 10.1002/cpp.2447

Resick, P. A., Wachen, J. S., Dondanville, K. A., et al. the STRONG STAR Consortium (2017). Effect of group vs individual cognitive processing therapy in active-duty military seeking treatment for posttraumatic stress disorder: A randomized clinical trial. *JAMA Psychiatry, 74*(1), 28–36. 10.1001/jamapsychiatry.2016.2729

Chapter 17

Therapeutic Competence

What would therapeutic competence, with a trauma victim, look like? The main thrust of this volume has been on personalising treatment, and thus a necessary condition for the demonstration of competence would be listening to the client's story. This sounds like a statement of the obvious, but a study of transcripts of low-intensity telephone-based guided self-help in routine practice by Drew et al. (2021) revealed 'We show the ways in which the lack of flexibility in adhering to a system-driven structure can displace, defer or disrupt the emergence of the patient's story, thereby compromising the personalisation and responsiveness of the service. Our study contributes new insights to our understanding of the association between personalisation, engagement and patient experience within a high volume, low-intensity psychological treatment services. Our research on the telephone delivery of IAPT is particularly timely in view of the current global COVID-19 health crisis, as a result of which face-to-face delivery of IAPT has had to be (temporarily) suspended'.

In this context, it is not surprising that it has not been possible to demonstrate a robust relationship between therapeutic competence and outcome whether in relation to low-intensity interventions (Branson et al., 2018) or high-intensity interventions (Branson et al., 2015; Liness et al., 2019). The failure to find a relationship between therapeutic competence in IAPT and outcome applies whether the yardstick for competence is a standardised role-play or the CTRS (Young & Beck, 1980). It could be the case that there are deficiencies in the measurement of outcome, reliance on self-report measures as opposed to an independently conducted diagnostic interview. However, it could also be the case that there is a deficiency in the metric for an outcome – the CTRS (Young & Beck, 1980) was designed originally as a measure of competence in the treatment of depression, but it has been pressed into service as a measure of competence across depression and anxiety disorders.

In a study of the CTRS by Shaw et al. (1999) of diagnosed depressed clients, it was found that the extent to which sessions are structured, i.e where the therapist sets an agenda, paces the focus on the different items on

DOI: 10.4324/9781003178132-21

the agenda and sets and reviews homework, is the biggest single predictor of outcome in the CBT treatment of depression. But the effect was modest, accounting for just 19% of the variance in the outcome on a clinician-administered measure and with no relation with self-report outcome measures. However, given the high levels of comorbidity between PTSD and depression, this finding may nevertheless be pertinent to the treatment of trauma victims. Further, the aspect of competence that was most associated with outcome was structured (this referred to setting an agenda, assigning relevant homework and pacing the session appropriately). By contrast, general therapeutic skills or specific CBT skills did not predict outcome. A revised version of the CTRS (CTS-R; Blackburn et al., 2001) has been pressed into service in routine practice for disorders other than depression and in contexts in which there have been no reliable diagnoses. But there is no indication that CTS-R score relates to the outcome. The validation study of the CTS-R did not include any clients with PTSD or a specific phobia, nor was a diagnosis made with a standardised diagnostic interview. Though the CTS-R claims to be a measure of both adherence and competence (Blackburn et al., 2001), it is difficult to see how the former can be achieved without a reliable diagnosis. The CTS-R is of doubtful validity, e.g. it does not refer to 'exposure' as a treatment strategy, yet it is the common metric used to evaluate a therapist's performance, encouraged by CBT training courses with little regard to the validity issue.

The treatment protocols for the different disorders are so varied that it is scarcely credible that a single measure of competence will suffice. Further consideration of competence apart from adherence, is like a fish out of water, e.g. a therapist's performance might be rated using the CTS-R (Blackburn et al., 2001) but if the client was suffering from a trauma-induced specific phobia, illness anxiety disorder and generalised anxiety disorder, it would say little about whether the appropriate disorders were identified and being treated i.e. whether there was appropriate adherence. The admonition in the CTS-R (Blackburn et al., 2001) to focus on 'key cognitions' is meaningless unless the particular set of cognitions is flagged up by an identified disorder. Consider a surgeon with demonstrated competence say in keyhole surgery, if you were his patient you would wish to know that not only he/she is competent in this skill but also knows which problems it is or is not appropriate for. From a client's/patient's perspective, this is absolutely crucial.

The treatment of trauma victims in routine practice suffers from the same deficiencies as the treatment of non-trauma-related disorders (a) a failure to specify the disorders from which they are suffering (b) a failure to specify and implement appropriate treatment targets and a matching treatment strategy and (c) a failure to specify whether the treatment has made an enduring real-world difference. However, trauma victims are additionally disadvantaged with regards to treatment in routine practice because (a) their inherent reluctance to talk about their trauma may itself be seen as an indicator of psychopathology and treatment prematurely terminated or continued with a fractured therapeutic alliance and (b) the inappropriate grouping of trauma victims either for preparatory trauma-focussed interventions or for group treatment that is not evidence-based. These latter considerations were addressed in detail in the previous chapter.

But lead organisations stress the importance of competence, were they not to do so they would not be deemed accountable. The very survival of lead organisations depends on their inculcating in powerholders that their membership, demonstrate, at least on the whole, this attribute. The danger is that lead organisations insist on their definition of competence, typically a score of over 36 on the CTS-R and for the outcome a reduction in psychometric test scores of 50%, but this is eminence-based, not evidence-based. The therapist is not allowed to challenge the metrics, protest may be seen as confirmation of inadequacy. In a similar vein, if the IAPT therapist has a client who has committed suicide they personally are hung out to dry, with no acknowledgement that there are structural problems within the IAPT organisation for not conducting appropriate suicide screening. Once again, the spectre of not listening rears its head. The danger for lead organisations with regards to psychological therapies is that they say more than they know, impose their definition of competence and unwittingly prevent the therapist from listening to the client's story and accompanying them along the therapeutic road. Hopefully, in this volume, the reader will be encouraged to an enhanced sense of the importance of listening, accompanying and structuring the treatment of trauma victims. The central focus ought to be on making a 'real-world' difference to clients' lives, not living in fear of the organisation's vagaries on competence. Restorative CBT is not about returning the traumatised to the 'real world' but about helping them to calibrate the extent to which they see their experience as relevant to their functioning today and tomorrow.

References

Blackburn, I. M., James, I. A., Milne, D. L., Baker, C., Standart, S., Garland, A., & Reichelt, F. K. (2001). The Revised Cognitive Therapy Scale (CTS-R): Psychometric properties. *Behavioural and Cognitive Psychotherapy, 29*(04), 431–446.

Branson, A., Shafran, R., & Myles, P. (2015). Investigating the relationship between competence and patient outcome with CBT. *Behaviour Research and Therapy, 68*, 19– 26. 10.1016/j.brat.2015.03.002

Branson, A., Myles, P., Mahdi, M., & Shafran, R. (2018). The relationship between competence and patient outcome with low-intensity cognitive behavioural interventions. *Behavioural and Cognitive Psychotherapy, 46*(1), 101–114. 10.1017/S1352465817000522

Drew, P., Irvine, A., Barkham, M., Faija, C., Gellatly, J., Ardern, K., Armitage, J. C., Brooks, H., Rushton, K., Welsh, C., Bower, P., & Bee, P. (2021). Telephone delivery of psychological interventions: Balancing protocol with patient-centred care. *Social Science & Medicine (1982)*, *277*, 113818. 10.1016/j.socscimed.2021.113818

Liness, L., Beale, S., Lea, S., Byrne, S., Hirsch, C.R., & Clark, D. M. (2019). The sustained effects of CBT training on therapist competence and patient outcomes. *Cognitive Therapy and Research*, 46, 631–641.

Shaw, B. F., Elkin, I., Yamaguchi, J., Olmsted, M., Vallis, T. M., Dobson, K. S., Lowery, A., Sotsky, S. M., Watkins, J. T., & Imber, S. D. (1999). Therapist competence ratings in relation to clinical outcome in cognitive therapy of depression. *Journal of Consulting and Clinical Psychology*, *67*(6), 837–846. 10.1037// 0022-006x.67.6.837

Young, J., & Beck, A. T. (1980). Cognitive therapy scale: Rating manual. *Unpublished manuscript, Center for Cognitive Therapy*. Philadelphia, PA: University of Pennsylvania.

Appendix

DSM-5 Criteria Interview Questions

The questions discussed later, cover all the symptoms related to enquiry about the common disorders that may be triggered or exacerbated by a trauma. However, the questions are <u>not</u> intended to be used as a checklist, in which monosyllabic 'yes' or 'no' answers are required from the client. Usage as a checklist will result in many false positives. Rather, when there is an affirmative response to a question, the assessor should ask for examples, with additional questions such as 'how did that show itself? The assessor then makes a judgement, on the basis of the client's response and on any other information that might be available e.g. partner, records, whether the symptom has impaired functioning or simply made the person uncomfortable.

The focus of the questions is on current functioning. However, if the client has experienced traumas prior to the one that has been pivotal for their recent attendance, the client might also be asked 'after trauma X, was there a period when you experienced....how long did that go on for or does it still affect you now?

Depression

During the past two weeks:

1. Have you been sad, down or depressed most of the day nearly every day?
2. Have you lost interest or do you get less pleasure from the things you used to enjoy?
3. Have you been eating much less or much more?
4. Have you been having problems falling asleep, staying asleep or waking up too early in the morning?
5. Have you been fidgety, restless, unable to sit still or talking or moving more slowly than is normal for you?

DOI: 10.4324/9781003178132-22

6. Have you been tired all the time nearly every day?
7. Have you been bothered by feelings of worthlessness or guilt?
8. Have you had problems taking in what you are reading, watching/ listening to or making decisions about everyday things?
9. Have you been hurting or making plans for hurting yourself?

If the client answered 'yes' to five or more questions (at least one of which has to be question 1 or 2), then it is likely that the client is suffering from depression.

Post-traumatic Stress Disorder

A. Trauma

    a. Have you been in a situation in which you thought you were going to die as a result of what happened?
    b. Have you been in a situation in which you thought others were going to die as a result of what happened?
    c. Have you been in a situation in which you thought yourself or others were going to have a serious injury as a result of what happened?
    d. Have you been in a situation in which you were or thought that you were going to be sexually violated?

A positive response to at least one of the questions is required.

B. Intrusions

    1. Do memories of a traumatic incident play on your mind?
    2. Do you get upset by them?
    3. Do you have distressing dreams of the traumatic incident?
    4. Do you lose awareness of your surroundings when you get pictures/ thoughts of the traumatic incident coming into your mind?
    5. When something reminds you of the traumatic incident, do you get distressed?
    6. Do you get any particularly strong bodily reactions when you come across reminders of the traumatic incident?

A positive response to at least one of the questions is required.

C. Avoidance

    1. Do you block out thoughts or pictures of the incident(s) that pop into your mind?
    2. Do you avoid conversations or people or places that bring back memories of the incident(s)?

A positive response to at least one of the questions is required.

D. Negative Alterations in Cognition and Emotion

1. Is there an important gap in your memory of the incident?
2. Since the incident(s), do you feel very negative about yourself, others or the world, or more negative than you used to?
3. Do you blame yourself or others for the incident(s) more than you really need to?
4. Since the incident(s), do you feel negative emotions such as fear, anger, horror, guilt or shame most of the time?
5. Since the incident(s), have you stopped doing activities that used to be important to you or lost interest in them?
6. Since the incident(s), do you feel cut off from others?
7. Since the incident(s), are you almost always unable to feel good?

A positive response to at least two of the questions is required.

E. Hyperarousal

1. Since the incident(s), are you more snappy or having more outbursts of anger?
2. Since the incident(s), do you do dangerous or destructive things?
3. Since the incident(s), are you on guard, checking things?
4. Since the incident(s), do you jump at unexpected noises or sudden movements?
5. Since the incident(s), have you had problems with concentration?
6. Since the incident(s), do you have problems either getting to sleep or staying asleep?

A positive response to at least two of the questions is required.

Alcohol/Substance Dependence

1. Have you felt that you should cut down on your alcohol/drug taking?
2. Have people got annoyed with you about your drinking/drug taking?
3. Have you felt guilty about your drinking/drug taking?
4. What is the longest period that you have gone without alcohol/substance since the incident? Did you get withdrawal symptoms such as shaking and sweating when you stopped?

A positive response to the first three questions, and either no withdrawal period or withdrawal symptoms during abstinence would indicate likely dependence.

Specific Phobia

1. Since the incident, do you avoid any particular situation, that is related to it? Is that avoidance all of the time, some of the time or a little of the time?

2.   If you are around a particular situation that is linked to the incident, are you uncomfortable or is your distress more than that?
3.   Does being fearful of situations that resemble the incident cause any significant problems for you?

A positive response to all the three questions indicates a likely specific phobia.

Obsessive-Compulsive Disorder

Obsessions

1.   Are you bothered by thoughts, images or impulses that keep going over in your mind?
2.   Do you try to block these thoughts, images or impulses by thinking or doing something?

Provided the client's concerns are not simply excessive worries about everyday problems and provided the client sees these thoughts/images as a product of their own mind, then 'yes' responses to questions 1 and 2 indicate a likely obsession.
    Compulsions

1.   Do you feel driven to repeat some behaviour e.g. checking, washing, counting, or to repeat something in your mind over and over again to try to feel less uncomfortable?
2.   If you do not do your special thing, do you get very anxious?

'Yes' responses to these last two questions indicate a probable compulsion. Note: the client has to be aware that their obsession and compulsion are excessive or irrational and they must also significantly interfere with functioning or cause significant distress.

Panic Disorder and Agoraphobia

1.   Do you have times when you feel a sudden rush of intense fear that comes on, from out of the blue, for no reason at all?
2.   Does it take less than ten minutes for the panic attack to reach its worst?
3.   During your last bad panic attack, did you have four or more of the following:

    i. Heart racing
    ii. Sweating

   iii. Trembling or shaking
   iv. Shortness of breath or smothering
    v. Feeling of choking
   vi. Chest pain
  vii. Nausea
 viii. Dizzy, light-headed, unsteady or faint
   ix. Things around seemed unreal
    x. Fear of losing control
   xi. Afraid you might die
  xii. Numbness or tingling sensations
 xiii. Chills or hot flushes

If the client answered 'yes' to each of the first two questions and endorsed the presence of four or more symptoms, it is likely that they are suffering from panic disorder.

Some people with panic disorder avoid certain situations for the fear of having a panic attack e.g. going places alone and crowded shops. If this is the case, then it is necessary to establish whether this avoidance interferes with their daily routine, job or social activities. If the answer to this is also 'yes' then they are probably suffering from panic disorder with agoraphobic avoidance. The agoraphobic avoidance would be regarded as severe if they are totally unable to go out by themselves, mild if they just can't go great distances by themselves and moderate if how far they can go by themselves is in between. But in the DSM-5, it is also possible to meet the criteria for agoraphobia without meeting the criteria for panic disorder.

Social Anxiety Disorder

1.   When you are or might be in the spotlight, say in a group of people or eating/writing in front of others, do you immediately get anxious or nervous?
2.   Do you think you are much more anxious than other people when the focus is on you?
3.   Do you think that you are more afraid of social situations than you should be?
4.   Do you avoid social situations out of a fear of embarrassing or humiliating yourself?
5.   Do these social anxieties bother you?

If the client answered 'yes' to each of the five questions, then it is likely that they are suffering from social phobia.

Generalised Anxiety Disorder

Ask the client if they would regard themselves as a 'worrier', in the sense that they always find something to worry about and if they are not worrying, they worry that they are not worrying? If the worry has been excessive or uncontrollable (more days than not) for at least six months and they have three or more of the following symptoms (more days than not):

1. Tiring very easily
2. Restlessness, keyed up or on edge
3. Difficulty concentrating or mind going blank
4. Irritability
5. Muscle tension
6. Difficulty falling or staying asleep

Then, it is probable that they are suffering from a generalised anxiety disorder.

Adjustment Disorder

Since the incident happened, have you been different? For the better or worse? In what ways worse? Has it caused problems with your close relationships or with working or studying? Has it lowered your mood or made you anxious?

The adjustment disorder diagnosis is only made if (a) the person does not meet diagnostic criteria for another disorder (b) the symptoms begin within three months of the trauma.

Further, this diagnostic label cannot be used if impairment persists for more than six months after the occurrence of their trauma, albeit that a chronic adjustment disorder diagnosis can be made for symptoms in relation to say ongoing pain triggered by the trauma.

Index

Page numbers in *italics* refer to figures. Page numbers in **bold** refer to tables.

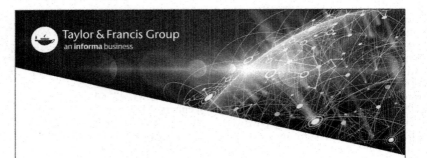